KU-768-933

A CONCISE HISTORY OF WESTERN MUSIC

Engaging, clear and informative, this is the story of western music –
of its great composers and also of its performers and listeners, of
changing ideas of what music is and what it is for. Paul Griffiths
shows how music has evolved through the centuries, and suggests
how its evolution has mirrored developments in the human notion
of time, from the eternity of heaven to the computer's microsecond.
The book provides an enticing introduction for students and begin-
ners, using the minimum of technical terms, all straightforwardly
defined in the glossary. Its perspective and its insights will also make
it illuminating for teachers, musicians and music lovers. Suggestions
for further reading and recommended recordings are given for each
of the twenty-four short chapters.

Born in Wales, **Paul Griffiths** has written books on music, novels
and librettos. Among the first are *The Penguin Companion to Classical Music* and *The Substance of Things Heard*, a selection from the
reviews and essays he produced during more than thirty years as a
music critic in London and New York. Composers with whom he
has collaborated include Ludwig van Beethoven, Elliott Carter,
W. A. Mozart and Frances-Marie Uitti.

A CONCISE HISTORY OF WESTERN MUSIC

PAUL GRIFFITHS

CAMBRIDGE
UNIVERSITY PRESS

CAMBRIDGE UNIVERSITY PRESS
Cambridge, New York, Melbourne, Madrid, Cape Town, Singapore, São Paulo,
Delhi, Mexico City

Cambridge University Press
The Edinburgh Building, Cambridge CB2 8RU, UK

Published in the United States of America by Cambridge University Press, New York

www.cambridge.org
Information on this title: www.cambridge.org/9780521133661

© Paul Griffiths 2006

This publication is in copyright. Subject to statutory exception
and to the provisions of relevant collective licensing agreements,
no reproduction of any part may take place without
the written permission of Cambridge University Press.

First published 2006
First paperback edition 2009
Reprinted 2012

Printed at MPG Books Group, UK

A catalogue record for this publication is available from the British Library

Library of Congress Cataloguing in Publication data
Griffiths, Paul, 1947 Nov. 24–
A concise history of western music/Paul Griffiths. – 1st ed.
p. cm.
Includes bibliographical references and index.
ISBN-13: 978-0-521-84294-5 (hardback)
ISBN-10: 0-521-84294-8 (hardback)
1. Music – History and criticism. I. Title.
ML 160.G823 2006
780.9 – dc22 2005029842

ISBN 978-0-521-84294-5 Hardback
ISBN 978-0-521-13366-1 Paperback

Cambridge University Press has no responsibility for the persistence or
accuracy of URLs for external or third-party internet websites referred to
in this publication, and does not guarantee that any content on such
websites is, or will remain, accurate or appropriate.

for Anne

Contents

Acknowledgements

Penny Souster asked for this book; Lucy Carolan saved it from many errors. They have my lasting thanks.

P.G.
Manorbier, November 2005

Prehistory

Someone, sitting in a cave, punctures holes in a bone drained of marrow, raises it mouthwards, and blows – into a flute. Breath becomes sound, and time, through that sound, is given a shape. Being sound and shaped time, music begins.

It must have begun many times. Almost certainly it began at Geissenklösterle in southwest Germany and Divje Babe in Slovenia – two places where fragments of hollow bone with otherwise inexplicable holes have been found from 45,000–40,000 years ago, close to when our species arrived. No sooner were we here than, in all probability, we were making music. We must have done so on other instruments, which have disintegrated or gone unrecognized, perhaps including reed flutes, log drums, ringing stones and shakers made from seedpods, not to mention stamping feet, slapping or clapping hands, and voices.

A thousand generations later (17,000–11,000 years ago), other broken bone flutes represent the music of the Magdalenian, cave-painting people of southern France and Spain, whose contemporaries on the eastern Mediterranean coast were producing bullroarers (objects whirled on strings) and rattles. Whole flutes made from crane wingbones survive from the neolithic village at Jiahu in central China dated to 9,000–8,000 years ago – one in good enough condition to be played, and to suggest its maker knew how to place the holes for a scale of six notes to the octave, though beyond that we cannot know what music once came from these flutes.

We can listen, though, to the archaeology in our own bodies, for we are living fossils of the musicians of the Stone Age, with the same lungs, hearts, limbs and rhythms. The actions of singing or flute playing would require periodic pauses for breath, and so suggest phrases lasting no longer than ten seconds or so. Pulse – especially if music went with movement, as it often does in modern cultures – would likely have been in paired beats at around one pair per second (corresponding to the left-right swing of walking pace) or two (for a run or energetic dance). Fast speeds, of two up to three iterations per second, would come near a simple instrument's limits, and suggest the pumping of the heart in excitement – the excitement of hunting, combat or sex, all abiding musical themes. Playing a flute, a musician must also have pondered how to end, and so been faced with questions of finding the properly conclusive note, therefore of harmony, and of accomplishing the transition back to silence, therefore of completion and extinction. These too are matters – formal, structural, expressive, existential – that attached themselves to music permanently.

There is further constancy in the psychology of hearing. The experience of sound is produced by variation in air pressure at the ear. If that variation is irregular, what we hear is a noise: the slam of a car door, the scrunching-up of a piece of paper. But if the pressure variations reach the ear as regular vibrations, the effect is a sound with a distinct pitch, higher or lower depending on the frequency of vibration: a note. The lowest notes (from large drums, for example) correspond to frequencies of about thirty cycles of vibration per second, the highest (whines and whistlings) to several thousand, the range of human voices being in the hundreds. Music is made from notes in combination. All the evidence, whether from laboratory tests or from musical cultures around the globe, shows that the brain is specially responsive to combinations of notes whose frequencies are in simple ratios, the simplest possible being 2:1, which corresponds to the octave. The same broad evidence indicates that combinations of two notes are heard as less pleasant if the gap goes below a sixth of an octave. So the Jiahu flutes represent, right at the start, universals in human music.

Of course, these fixed points of human biology have not prevented abundant change. Cultures through history and around the globe have differed not only in music's sound but in its purpose. Even the definition of music has changed. The term, with equivalents in most European languages, derives from the generic name of the ancient Greek muses, and originally it embraced the full range of poetic and performing arts under their aegis. In many other cultures, too, there is no word for an art of sound divorced from dance, ritual or theatre. Yet equally there is no human culture that has failed to develop what would, in modern western terms, be recognized as music: the chants of the African bush and the European cathedral, the sounds of plucked strings on an Indian sitar or an electric guitar, the tuned breath of Andean panpipes, orchestral flutes or, indeed, the bones of Jiahu. Here is a rainbow of variety, but with a sameness that comes from our physical selves.

Music, so intimately engaged with perception, lights up the mind. Music, being immaterial, touches on the immaterial – on the drift of thought and feeling, on divinity and death. Music, as sound, can represent the auditory world: the moan of wind, the repeated whispers of calm waves, the calls of birds. Music, as idealized voice (even in the almost super-human range of the Jiahu flutes), can sing or sigh, laugh or weep. Music, as rhythm, can keep pace with our contemplative rest and our racing activity. Music, in proceeding through time, can resemble our lives.

PART I

Time whole

Music, being made of time, can travel through it. A performance of, say, a Beethoven symphony will bring a whole structure of time forward from two hundred years ago, so that we may experience it now. And because we cannot see or touch music but only hear it, it reaches us out of its past with an unusual immediacy. Things we see or touch are necessarily outside of us: music, though, seems to be happening inside our heads, imposing itself directly on our minds and feelings. It is right here with us, and yet simultaneously back there in the past in which it was made. It may thereby take us into its past, give us a sense of being in a different era, experiencing time as it was then. Or it may tell us of continuities through time, constancies of thought and feeling.

For all this to happen we need to inherit not only music's instruments but also its instructions, which may come down to us orally, through generations of direct transmission, or else in written form, as musical notation. All musical cultures depend on handing information on from generation to generation, no doubt with changes; that is how traditions are made. What sets the tradition of western music apart is its great dependence also on notation, which has several important consequences.

In the first place, notation opens a distinction between composers (who create music that will last) and performers (who recreate that music for the moment). This distinction exists in some other cultures, such as the traditional Chinese, but there is no parallel elsewhere for the western concept of a musical work, such as a Beethoven symphony, which is set out in detail, which can therefore give rise to performances that will be instantly recognized as versions of the same thing, and which may be used in discussions of its composer's style, of the orchestra or, indeed, of the history of music. In music, as in most things, there are no stable certainties, and this idea of the changeless work needs to be modified, to take account of how the meaning of notation may be altered over time or even lost, or of how the difference between performances may seem more important than their sameness. Nevertheless, western classical music is largely defined by its composers and its works. These have given it not only a tradition, changing through time like a weathering landscape, but a history — the possibility, through notation, of glimpsing parts of that landscape in earlier states, even if imperfectly.

We should recognize also how this history itself changes. For instance, a hundred years ago the history of music began, for all practical purposes, with Johann Sebastian Bach (1685–1750), the earliest composer whose music was performed with any regularity. Now, with compact discs offering the chance of listening repeatedly to almost anything, compositions from several centuries before Bach are generally available, and music has so much longer a history. That history is also wider, in that the recorded repertory includes a great deal more music of any particular age: virtually all of Bach's output, for example, rather than the tiny fraction by which he was once known, and the works of dozens of his contemporaries. The existence of record-ings has also made music's recent history thicker, for not only can we perform music that was notated in, for exam-ple, the 1930s, we can also hear music that was recorded then – whether music of the time (Stravinsky, Cole Porter) or earlier (Beethoven as conducted by Wilhelm Furtwängler or Arturo Toscanini). A recording may thus present us with three times at once: the now in which we hear it, the then in which it was made, and the further then of when the piece was composed.

Before recording, and before notation, there was only the now. Music could not be fixed. It was like the forest and the sea, always being renewed and always remaining the same. It could last only as long as memory, for memory was the only means of holding onto past time.

For people familiar with memory, and uniquely depen-dent on it, the past is not strange: it is present, in the mind. Time is whole. Its measures are all in natural observation: the cycles of the day and year, the ageing of people, animals, plants and things, the flowing of water or the burning down of candles.

Music for such people – the music of the most ancient traditions we know, including in western Europe the chant in which church services were delivered – is made to the measure of memory and moves without anxiety through its medium of time. It is not going anywhere. It is there.

CHAPTER I

From Babylonians to Franks

Notation was invented in several ancient cultures – Babylonian, Greek, Indian, Chinese – but only for very occasional purposes (in theoretical works, or more rarely to set down a melody), and only after a great change in social structure. The new urban civilizations of the fourth and third millennia BC introduced new instruments, especially instruments with plucked strings: harps, lyres and lutes first in Mesopotamia, then in the eastern Mediterranean and north Africa, zithers in China. With these arrived élite music, the music of temples and courts, represented by such spectacular finds as the metre-high gold-covered lyre from a royal tomb of around 2500 BC at Ur. Though Sumerian weavers and builders must have sung, the music most prized (the gold suggests) was that of a new profession – the musician – whose distinction was intensified by a gathering lore of tuning, interval and instrumental practice. Then came composers, of whom the earliest known, around two centuries after the great lyre, was Enheduanna, high priestess of the moon god at Ur.

In tuning and playing their new instruments the Mesopotamians and Chinese discovered the relationship between the length of a string and the note produced by plucking it – a relationship holding because a string's length determines its frequency of vibration (all other things being equal), the shorter the faster. If a string is stopped at half its length, it will vibrate twice as fast and so give a note an octave higher, and so on. This gave musicians a way of prescribing notes and therefore scales, of which there are examples given on a Mesopotamian tablet of around 1800 BC — seven-note scales that much later were adopted in Greece.

Another tablet, from the ancient city of Ugarit (modern Ras Shamra, in Syria, near the Mediterranean coast) and about four centuries more recent, is inscribed with the earliest notated music so far discovered: a hymn to the moon goddess. However, since the notation is rudimentary, and the all-important tradition of interpreting it long lost, this prototypical score can offer no more than a faint echo. Other echoes, from around the same time, come from the bronze and silver trumpets laid in the tomb of the boy pharaoh Tutankhamen (c. 1325 BC), from the praise of music in the earliest hymns of India and from the bells of Shang dynasty China.

In the next millennium, as instruments and theory developed in tandem, philosophers tried to guide them. Confucius (551–479 BC) distinguished wholesome from unwholesome music, the former productive of harmony within the individual and order within the state. His views were seconded by Plato (c. 429–347 BC), one of the earliest Greeks to write about music; Aristoxenus, two generations younger, concerned himself with the theory of intervals, scales and melodic composition. Melodies were being notated in Greece by this time, with letters representing notes, though nothing survives before some fragments of the third century BC, and nothing complete before two hymns inscribed at Delphi in the late second century BC. Melodic notation was simultaneously evolving in China, though again little has come down to us.

Written evidence shows that the singing of psalms was well established in Christian lands by the fourth century AD. One witness, St John Chrysostom (c. 345–407), followed Plato in distinguishing between good and harmful music: 'Lest demons introducing lascivious songs should overthrow everything, God established the psalms, in order that they might provide both pleasure and profit.' Other theologians of the time, such as St Jerome (c. 340–420), found Biblical support for Plato's doctrine in the story of David at his lyre calming Saul, while the Roman philosopher Boethius (c. 480 – c. 524) concurred with Plato in his statements not only of music's power – 'Nothing is more characteristic of human nature than to be soothed by sweet modes and disturbed by their opposites' – but also of its essence, writing that 'the soul of the universe is united by musical concord' and describing three levels of music: that of heavenly bodies in rotation (the music of the spheres, which, according to later theorists, we cannot hear because it is always there), that of the human being (the concord of body and soul) and that of instruments. These ideas, and a detailed account of Greek musical theory, made Boethius's treatise *De institutione musica* (Fundamentals of Music) the principal authority for medieval musicians.

By his time, across Eurasia from France to Japan, people were finding better ways to write music down. Once more the region around Mesopotamia led the way: Christians there applied signs to Bible texts to show how they should be chanted. These signs can no longer be interpreted, but in their time they spread westwards to Jews, Byzantines and the Latin church, and perhaps eastwards to Tibet. Meanwhile, an entirely different system of notation – tablature, which provides instrumentalists with diagrammatic instructions – was developing in China and Japan. Where the music notated in the Judaeo-Christian world right to the end of the thirteenth century was all sung, being sacred chant, in east Asia what laid strongest claim to memorializing was instrumental music – which in the west was virtually ignored until the sixteenth century. Rare tablatures for the noblest Chinese instruments, the qin (zither) and pipa (lute), are found from the Tang dynasty (618–907), while the court instrumental music of Japan, gagaku, has rich archives going back to the eighth century, including works inherited from Tang China and from Korea.

A musical world tour in the eighth century would have found traditions of chant throughout the Christian world, refined solo instrumental playing in China, variegated court ensembles there and in Japan, and a great richness of instrumental and theatre music in India (now known only from treatises and representations of music-making) – not to mention the largely unrecorded musical cultures of Java, Burma, Central America and many parts of Africa, and the totally forgotten music of other regions. Yet even where the evidence is strongest, this is all still silent music – music whose notation cannot be accurately deciphered or was never meant to be more than skeletal. Writing not for the future but for themselves and their pupils, musicians in these diverse locations were as one in seeing no need to give more than a mnemonic device. Who could be listening 1,300 years later?

Then came change, arising most vigorously in western Europe from a need to communicate music – specifically chant – around the region. Having that music in written form, as notation, helped in this, and became a necessity when, as soon happened, more and more new chants were composed as part of a larger cultural rebirth, taking the body of hymns and services beyond what a church's religious personnel could be expected to remember.

Charlemagne's coronation as emperor in 800, at the hands of the pope in Rome, confirmed both his place as protector of the Church and his authority to continue the work of his father, Pippin III, in reforming the liturgy of their Frankish domain (by his time covering much of western Europe, from central Italy to the edge of Denmark and from the Pyrenees to the Danube) according to the practice of Rome. One result was a new repertory of chants for the principal ceremonies (mass and the 'hours', or services for different times of day), chants in which the Roman models were simplified. Transmitted orally, these chants were adopted by the great churches and monasteries of Charlemagne's empire, and gradually, during the next three centuries, conveyed to other parts of western Europe, back to Rome, and to newly Christianized areas to the east and north. Meanwhile, the myth grew that this increasingly universal music had come not from Frankish musicians in the eighth and ninth centuries but from the Holy Ghost, singing into the ear of Pope Gregory the Great (reigned 590–604): hence the term 'Gregorian chant'.

Modern notation seems to have begun in the first half of the ninth century in the form of 'neumes': graphic symbols inscribed over the words to stand for single notes and short groups. Thus although Charlemagne's successors had nothing to compare with the instrumental ensembles of the Tang emperors ruling contemporaneously, their cantors and churchmen did possess a tool of huge consequence for the future: a rudimentary musical storage routine, and therefore the base for the vast corpus of written compositions that would set western musical traditions apart.

More important to them, though, was to connect with the honoured past – with the musical knowledge of the ancient Greeks. Chant they codified in terms of eight modes, each based on a scale of seven notes to the octave (represented by the white notes on a modern keyboard, leaving aside questions of tuning). This classification was directly inherited from the Byzantine world, but it had roots in Boethius and thereby in ancient Greek theory. Indeed, it went back further, for ninth-century theorists were, albeit unaware, adding just one mode to those of the Babylonians nearly three thousand years before.

However, none of the neumes of the ninth and tenth centuries can be read unambiguously today, for what was still missing was a consistent grid to measure melodic rises and falls. That was provided by a set of parallel horizontal lines (the staff), with a key to which notes these lines represent (the clef) – still now the essentials of musical notation. Once this system was in place, as happened when the innovations Guido of Arezzo put forward in his *Micrologus* (c. 1026) were generally adopted, chant melodies could be written down in a form readable and singable by those acquainted with the notation wherever they might be – and indeed whenever, down to the present. It is this legible notation that has given western music a history quite unlike that of other musical cultures, and this is the story that now will be followed alone.

As is often the way, a technical innovation – in this case staff notation, backed by the modes – simultaneously pruned existing luxuriance and promoted new growth. Much was lost. Chants had been composed under widely differing circumstances of place and time, and in the two centuries since Charlemagne many distinct local traditions had developed, in notation and surely also in performance.

Not all of this varied music could have settled comfortably into a uniform notational language and a homogeneous modal system derived at a very distant second hand from classical Athens. Also, several liturgical traditions had been marginalized by Charlemagne's reforms – among them the Ambrosian chant peculiar to Milan, the Mozarabic chant of Spain and the Old Roman chant of the papal city – and these were notated only in part or not at all.

On the positive side, staff notation encouraged the wider distribution of chant and created a supranational culture within which composers could, in the fourteenth century and later, travel from England to France, or from France and the Low Countries (modern Belgium and the Netherlands, with adjoining areas) to Italy, finding everywhere the same music. More immediately this notation seems to have promoted musical composition, for pieces of music could now be communicated on paper, just like literary works. Melodies, through the great age of chant composition that in western Europe was drawing to a close by Guido's time, could be learned from their singers. But it was not so easy to pick up music that had two or more distinct melodies being sung at the same time – polyphony – whose development notation crucially abetted.

Accurate notation also enabled the chant of Guido's age to go on resounding, if in changing styles of interpretation, through the thousand years to the present.

But what are we hearing from back then? One of the great recording successes of 1994 was 'Chant', an anthology from the Benedictine monastery of Santo Domingo de Silos, near Burgos in Spain. The selection opened with *Puer natus est nobis* (Unto us a boy is born), a piece which, though written as a mass introit (introductory salutation) to be sung and heard only in monastic churches on Christmas Day, was now available anywhere at any time under any circumstances. Moreover, the melody was taken not from some medieval source but from an edition dependent on the great renewal of chant headed by the abbey of Solesmes, in northwest France, in the late nineteenth and early twentieth centuries. Similarly the performance style – calm in speed and volume level, and with generally even durations modified to create a smoothly flowing rhythm – stemmed from Solesmes, and so from a tradition that began no earlier than the 1850s, when the monks there began transcribing forgotten medieval sources, and that can be securely traced only as far back as 1904, when those monks' successors made the first chant recordings.

This might seem disappointing, that Gregorian chant as we hear it is only as old as the aeroplane, or at best the umbrella. We want more from it. We want it, as the oldest music in staff notation, to stand at the head of a thousand-year continuous history, through which elements have been maintained, developed or abandoned. *Puer natus est nobis,* with its melody of narrow range, shaped to the text's phrases, belongs in what Guido and his predecessors classified as the seventh mode, also known as 'Mixolydian' to medieval and later writers – the 'white-note' mode on G: G–A–B–C–D–E–F–G. Appropriately, this Christmas introit starts with a burst of light in a rise to the fifth note of the mode (G–D), the fifth being one of the most harmonious intervals on account of the simple frequency ratio it represents (3:2). Significant, too, is the ending. A melody in a mode has to return to that mode's basic note, or 'final' – in this case G, which is confirmed in a little up–down motif, G–A–G. We know such melodic features to be old. When they return in later music – as sometimes they do in that of a composer who came from the same culture as the Solesmes palaeographers: Debussy – we take them as tokens of the medieval.

Yet if chant melodies speak of the past, we cannot be sure they do so with the past's voice: the original traditions of singing chant, which were evidently diverging as fast as Charlemagne and his ministers could standardize them, are irrecoverable. One ninth-century treatise illustrates the possibility of 'organum', whereby the singers were to split, some singing the chant while others took a line in harmony with it, largely in fifths. Moreover, an 'organum' of a different sort, the church organ with pipes and keyboard, had arrived in western Europe from Byzantium and Islam by the tenth century, and could have accompanied chanting with a drone (sustained tone) or even a separate melodic voice. What else was it there for?

If such possibilities are rarely explored in modern performances, that may be because we want to hear chant as coming from a uniform choir, providing a single experience of time and a unitary vehicle for the listener's own interior voice. Also relevant here is the fact that the modern chant revival is essentially a recording phenomenon, with no parallel in concert performances. Through the medium of recording – through invisible sound – the listener may seem to make immediate contact, across the centuries, with the monks or nuns of some great abbey in the high middle ages. That impression ignores error, gaps in the evidence and wishful thinking, but it is compelling and may not be wholly unjust. A chant is like a ninth-century round-arched window in the wall of a church. It may have been restored in the nineteenth century, and perhaps shows signs of more recent care, but if we stare hard enough we may see through it all the light there is.

The recovery of early music — beginning sporadically in the nineteenth century, gaining strength in the mid-twentieth and entering maturity in the 1980s — has taught us the importance not only of scholarship in the handling of sources but also of imagination where sources are deficient. Imaginative restitution can powerfully evoke even worlds that are totally lost, such as that of ancient Icelandic myth-telling, and has a place in more familiar contexts. Any musical performance — any musical listening — is a heroic exercise against time's depredations, an attempt not only to learn from the past but to make it, again, real.

PART II

Time measured 1100–1400

Notation gave western music a means of written record, but at first only for a kind of music, chant, that was believed to have originated half a millennium and more in the past – to be, effectively, ageless. Early medieval chants sprang from the whole time of eternal sameness, which they so readily convey, and similarly there was no measure of the time within them – the rhythm. Then measure came. And with it came the first identifiable composers and precisely datable works.

Where chant was of a piece with other musical traditions in being self-sufficient melody, working within a modal system, belonging to no creator (but to God) and designed for worship, the new music of the twelfth century opened a distinctively western path. The measuring of time was the beginning not only of rhythmic notation – known, far beyond Europe, to the Indian theorist Śārngadeva in the first half of the thirteenth century – but also of music involving coordination among singers carrying different melodies, of polyphony. This, too, was by no means confined to the wedge of land between the Mediterranean and the Atlantic: the gamelan music of Bali, a tradition independent of Europe, is comparable with early western polyphony in its superposition of different time streams, fast and slow, while the music of many sub-Saharan African peoples often piles up dissimilar rhythmic layers in ways foreign to Europe outside certain special repertories (fourteenth-century song and some music since 1950). But, from the twelfth century to the fifteenth, polyphony in the west gradually moved away from the repetitive structures that were retained on Bali or in central Africa as Europeans discovered how harmony could result in continuous flow.

The source, as of so much in western culture, was a misunderstanding of classical Greek knowledge, again acquired through Boethius. He had nothing to say about harmony in the sense of chords, but he conveyed a Greek satisfaction in the primacy of the octave and the fifth, which medieval musicians took as models of consonance (the euphonious combining of notes). Just as essential were dissonant combinations, lacking euphony, for these would intensify the need for consonance. A dissonance placed immediately before a final consonance would produce a firmly conclusive ending – a cadence, such as became an essential of western music. Extending back from the cadence, the forces of harmony, marshalled through relationships between each chord and the next, could amplify the directional sense already present in the melody – the sense of movement towards a resting point on the last note. Thus time measured became time decisively having a goal, and music could emulate the progress in every human soul towards eternity.

Music mirrored, too, how time generally was being told. Guido's staff notation came roughly when water clocks were reintroduced from Byzantium and Islam, enabling monks to know when a service was due from the level reached by water slowly filling a vessel. Thus reading, whether of a chantbook or a water gauge, substituted for memory and intuition. Exact synchrony between music and time was lost a little when clockwork mechanisms appeared in the mid-thirteenth century, half a century later than the gear-driven music produced at Notre Dame in Paris. However, the perfection of clockwork with hour-chiming capabilities, in the astronomical clock made by Richard of Wallingford for St Albans Abbey (1327–36), strikingly coincided with the perfection of rhythmic notation that spread from Paris and gave music its own machinery of time lengths.

CHAPTER 2

Troubadours and organists

Chant's power is strengthened by anonymity: chantbooks do not identify authors, and only a few of the writers and even fewer of the composers are recorded in chronicles. Chant may therefore seem the voice, if not of the Holy Spirit informing a pope, at least of a suprapersonal entity.

But there is also chant that comes to us with a robust individuality, that of the German abbess, preacher and seer Hildegard of Bingen (1098–1179). She is a striking figure, not least in having so recently burst into the seeming fixity of history. Her compositions, mostly chants, appear never to have reached beyond the small area on the Rhine where she spent her life, and were soon forgotten. Then near the end of the twentieth century, with a reawakening of Christian mysticism and a new openness to the female vision, her music gained enormous attention, thanks to the release of several books and numerous recordings, both scholarly and speculative. Indeed, she exploded so far out of her context that her true importance became hard to discern. Features of her melodies that seem remarkable and personal – wide intervals, a wide range – may have been common in her age and environment. She was not the only composing abbess of her time, and by no means the only chant writer. The hymns of Adam of St Victor, attached to the royal

Augustinian abbey outside Paris, were admired far more widely and lastingly, for they included features that were fundamentally changing both poetry and music: accentual metre and rhyme. In that respect Adam marched with contemporaries in southern France who were discovering a new language (Provençal) and new subjects: love, longing, lament and the creation of song itself. These troubadours – *trobadors*, as they called themselves in their own language: finders – were poet-composers attached to princely courts. Some of them were princes themselves, including Guilhem IX, Duke of Aquitaine and Count of Poitiers (1071–1129), the first whose poems survive, together with an incomplete strand of music. Others depended for their living on their art, including three active at the height of troubadour culture in the second half of the twelfth century: Giraut de Bornelh, Arnaut Daniel and Bernart de Ventadorn. They and other colleagues were creative artists, whose songs, with the same melody for every stanza, would be performed by musicians known later as *joglars* in Provençal or *jongleurs* in northern French. The troubadours' roamings may well be apocryphal (crusading was a popular venture reported in their biographies, and Richard Coeur-de-Lion a popular lord), but certainly their songs travelled, and stimulated parallel efforts, especially from the trouvères of northern France (where French was the language of their poems and their name) and the Minnesinger of Germany, so called from their literary advocacy of *Minne*, or chivalric love, devotion to an unattainable lady.

This art of love was a direct inheritance from the troubadours, whose own sources may have included, besides folksong and Islamic love song, chant. On the poetic level, desire infused the liturgy as a spiritual metaphor: desire for fulfilment in heaven, for protection meanwhile by an adored lady (the Virgin). Musically, too, there were connections between troubadour song and chant. Legible notation had been restricted to liturgical music for fully a quarter-millennium before the songs of the troubadours, trouvères and Minnesinger began to be written down, around 1300, so it is not surprising that those songs should have been recorded in the same system of eight modes. They could well have been composed that way, from within an increasingly versatile musical order.

Giraut de Bornelh's superb *Reis glorios* (Glorious king) opens exactly like *Puer natus est nobis*, with a rising fifth. It proceeds, though, in a very different manner, in phrases that move in measure with the metrical lines, and that balance one another according to the rhyme pairings, to make, indeed, a song rather than a manner of recitation. This was more than a change of form, for phrase structure provided music with definable ideas and ways to vary them — with the means, therefore, to model patterns of feeling. When the refrain of *Reis glorios*, 'Et ades sera l'alba' (And soon will come dawn), sinks back into the final, it not only completes an action begun in the opening lift but does so with a sense of release; music becomes expressive — of the words, of an emotion and of its own nature. Though troubadour songs have been in performance again for an even shorter time than Solesmes-style chant (the earliest edition came out in 1960, even if before that, indeed from the 1930s, recordings were made sporadically for historical anthologies), and though we cannot know how they were originally sung (in particular, whether with instruments or not, for fiddles, lutes and harps were all known in western Europe by this time), their language of lyric utterance, inscribed in notation, seems to connect us directly with the musician-poets of eight centuries and more ago.

The troubadours' arrival coincided with another, as church musicians developed the technique of organum to produce, at the cathedral of Notre Dame in Paris, compositions of unprecedented length and elaboration. Earlier organum had always been in two vocal parts, the chant melody carried by one part (the tenor, literally 'holder') while the other moved around it (generally above), favouring the Boethius-sanctioned intervals of fifth, fourth, unison and octave. Examples survive from the great pilgrimage centre of Compostela and from the abbey of St Martial in Limoges, on the way to Compostela, the manuscripts from both (of c. 1100–60) apparently documenting improvised practices. (The purpose of notation, right into the fifteenth century, may well have been to record rather than to prescribe, though modern performers have had to understand it in the latter sense.) The added voice could proceed with the chant note by note, in what was known as 'discant' style, or it could unfold florid decoration over each note, in a style for which the multivalent term 'organum' was used. In pieces from St Martial and Compostela these styles were alternated, with each other and with pure chant, as they were in what appear to be the earlier pieces from the Notre Dame repertory, compiled in a 'great book' (*Magnus liber*) of which three copies have come down to us. But around the end of the twelfth century the repertory was overhauled, from a new enthusiasm for discant – discant propelled, as sometimes it had been before, by rhythm. With rhythm, which was not notated in chantbooks and troubadour songs, time could be measured out in similar blocks. With rhythm the Notre Dame composers could build, as the masons around them were building the immense cathedral.

This rhythm came, it seems clear, from song, and so from poetry. Rhythms would be given by one of six rhythmic modes, each a recurrent pattern of short beats, long beats or both, after the fashion of a poetic metre – e.g. the iambic short–long, short–long (second mode). From these patterns phrases could be created – most often phrases of four such units, comparable in size and shape with the lines of many troubadour songs and Latin hymns. Elements of similar size form the basic pieces of human languages and of such remote – from medieval Paris – musical cultures as that of central African pygmies, strongly suggesting they conform to what the brain can digest as an item. No wonder that the four-bar phrase would continue to resound in western music for centuries. At Notre Dame phrases would most often be conceived in pairs, corresponding to the rhyming lines of a couplet; and this paired phrasing was also to remain a constant of western music. Meanwhile, much more slowly, the chant would proceed, each note continuing through several bouncing phrases and pairs of phrases – the bounce, at the start of each little phrase, being off from a consonance, most usually a fifth or, in the case of settings in three or four parts, a fifth plus an octave.

To modern ears this harmony is stark, like white flame, and it gives Notre Dame organum a fierce intensity as well as a decisive sense of antiquity. At the time, though, the former may have been as inaudible as the latter. Much of our knowledge concerning this music comes from the theorist known to scholarship as Anonymous IV, whose treatise probably dates from the 1270s, long after the event. This treatise is largely concerned with the rhythmic modes and the notation of rhythm, but it also considers consonance, and reveals that thirds – highly mellifluous in later music, not least the love duets of Italian operas – were regarded as dissonant, except in England (whose music of this period is almost all lost, like so much from the middle ages), while the sixth was a 'vile and loathsome discord'.

Anonymous IV also says a little about the composers at Notre Dame, notably Leonin and his successor Perotin, ascribing to the latter the two earliest examples of four-part organum, which are also the earliest instances of the four-part texture that was to become another norm in western music. Both pieces are graduals (sections of the mass coming between the readings of epistle and gospel) for the Christmas season, datable to the last years of the twelfth century: *Viderunt omnes* (All saw) and *Sederunt principes* (Princes sat). They are immense compositions, taking about a quarter of an hour to sing right through, and their effect must have been astonishing in a world that knew nothing like them. Suddenly would come this blaze of sound from soloists trained in the new skills of holding a part against others, the three added parts moving closely together in lively measured step around the drone of the original note, creating an effect like painted initials in the text of the surrounding chant.

All the evidence (including that of Anonymous IV) suggests that organum was composed additively, in two dimensions. To the original chant a first organal line would be written, and this could be followed by a second and a third. Similarly, from the viewpoint of progress through time, the piece would be considered a succession of segments, with a separate *clausula* of polyphony for each word, each *clausula* made up of subsections, one for each note of the basic chant. Formally, then, the piece would be a concatenation on several levels, from rhythmic unit through phrase, subsection and *clausula* to the complete gradual.

This structure, piecemeal and repetitive, becomes vigorously forward-moving under harmonic forces, acting within

phrases (through the similar chord progressions in each of a
pair, and through the perpetual swinging away from and
back to the bare fifth), and at the ends of *clausulae*, which
are dramatized by a powerful arrival on the last chant note
of the word. Despite having been created bit by bit and line
by line, as Anonymous IV partly confirms, the music nevertheless suggests a composer aware of the whole texture and
shape, and therefore able to engineer a play of repeat and
variation in chord progressions, or of reiteration and change
in melodic patterns, as well as to manipulate such delightful
incidents as the exchanging of material between voices.

The outstanding qualities of Perotin's two four-part
organa have been recognized since the discovery of medieval music in the mid-nineteenth century, but the music
rejoined the life of performance only in the twentieth.
In 1930 the German scholar Rudolf von Ficker published
an arrangement of *Sederunt principes* for symphony orchestra, and numerous recordings – closer to the original
resources – have been made since the 1970s. Shortcircuiting
many centuries, Perotin became completely comprehensible
as a colleague of Stravinsky's, or as a master of the jubilant
repetition, grand harmonic shift and momentary clash
found also in the music of Steve Reich.

Perotin's works also have a place in the larger sweep
of western musical history, and not only in pioneering
symmetrical phrasing and four-part counterpoint (music
in which four lines proceed simultaneously, their notes
related as point against point). They show, like most music
in the west, a distinction between the composer, working on
paper, and the performers, who must also be readers. Moreover, notation was not just a neutral medium but immediately left its mark on what was written, so initiating another
great theme of western music, the dialogue of ear and pen,

between writing what may be heard (in reality or in imagination) and hearing what may be written. Where the notation of chant, troubadour song and early organum could easily have been no more than an aid in teaching, recording and transmitting music that existed essentially in people's memories, Perotin's structures could never have been created except on paper, and one has to suppose they were learned — and probably also performed — by singers having the written material before them. These structures also have a sense of the written in how they sound — in the regular returns to octave–fifth consonance, or in such details as the voice exchanges, where a visual pattern becomes audible.

Their splendour, or perhaps their difficulty, seems to have silenced imitation. Collections of pieces, and also treatises such as that of Anonymous IV, prove that Notre Dame organum remained current well into the second half of the thirteenth century, and that both the original Parisian repertory and its compositional principles were known over a wide area of western Europe. But nothing on the scale of *Sederunt principes* and *Viderunt omnes* was written again (unless to be lost), and by the end of the thirteenth century the great wave of organum seems to have passed. As it went, so its rhythmic modes were replaced by a new system — advocated by Franco of Cologne, a theorist contemporary with Anonymous IV — by which neumes gave way to notes, and a greater variety of rhythmic patterns could be notated, by means of signs indicating the 'mensuration', i.e. whether long notes were divided into two smaller units or three, and whether those were further subdivided into two parts or three. Threefold divisions were regarded as perfect, for their association with the Trinity, but imperfect divisions could be introduced for contrast. Meanwhile, throughout the thirteenth century, composition in three melodic parts was the norm, allowing a great variety of chords and cadences leading always to what continued as the omnipresent consonance of octave plus fifth.

During this century organum was superseded as the commonest polyphonic form by the motet, its direct descendant. Organum had required singers to maintain the same vowel sound through long roulades or ricochets of notes, and it was perhaps in order to make such music more interesting, or more memorable, that people began adding words: hence conductus, a twelfth-century genre in which up to four discant-style vocal lines with the same words were composed independently of a tenor, and hence the motet, in which, as it were, a segment of discant took on a separate existence, with lines other than the tenor carrying new text (which gave the genre its name, from the Latin *motetus*, word-bearing). This was the basis of 'cantus firmus' technique, in which the tenor was regarded as a 'fixed song', to be joined by others composed to it in accord with developing rules of counterpoint – the technique that remained fundamental into the fifteenth century.

Franco's rhythmic notation, developed by the motet composer Petrus de Cruce, enabled composers in the late thirteenth century to create motets in which the very slow tenor would be joined by two fast, flexible voices, all three still in much the same vocal range. Though most thirteenth-century motets have texts in Latin (French entering more and more towards the end of the century), and though they arose in ecclesiastical circles (to which musical literacy was confined), they were not devised for liturgical use: the texts may be secular as well as sacred, and their meanings are often ambiguous and involuted, playing on the connections and abrasions between two different texts and on the ironies of their relationship to the tenor. We know almost nothing of how, or under what circumstances, these intricate compositions were performed and appreciated: the tendency now is to regard them, like organum, as purely vocal and as works of art. As with most music, the original context has been replaced by those of the concert hall, the specialist performing group and the record collection.

Other songs of the period were, like the troubadours', lone melodies for which an improvised instrumental accompaniment is plausible. Many of these songs – in this respect quite unlike the troubadours' cultivated productions of individual sensibility – reflect popular enthusiasm, both religious and of other kinds. Examples include the more than four hundred *Cantigas de Santa Maria* (Songs of the Virgin Mary) collected at the behest of the Spanish monarch Alfonso the Wise (1221–84), the chants of the lively Play of Daniel from early thirteenth-century Beauvais (important to the twentieth-century revival of medieval music), the collection of rumbustious Latin songs held by the Bavarian abbey of Benediktbeuern and called by their nineteenth-century editor *Carmina burana* (Songs of Beuern), the *laude* (devotional songs) of Italian cities and the precious few examples of English song, the most remarkable of which, like *Man mai longe lives weene* (Man may expect long life), grieve over the worthlessness of the world. Closer to the troubadours, Adam de la Halle, active in the 1270s and 1280s, and one of the last trouvères, wrote a play with songs, *Le jeu de Robin et de Marion* (The play of Robin and Marion), while the Minnesinger tradition continued a little later, up to Frauenlob (d. 1318). By that time, though, revolution was close again in Paris.

CHAPTER 3

Ars nova and Narcissus's clock

Philippe de Vitry (1291–1361), one of the foremost intellectuals of his time and later an adviser to the French king Jean II, wrote a musical treatise boldly titled *Ars nova*: new practice. What was most new in it, and most lasting, was its change to rhythmic notation. But it came into a world that was discovering an altogether new spirit in music – a new alignment both with mathematics and with mirroring feeling (by no means opposed directions of musical endeavour). Music was gaining a new tunefulness and a greater formal reach: where thirteenth-century motets are over in a minute or two, those of Vitry and his successors are twice or three times as long. The name of Vitry's treatise has duly been applied to a whole wave of musical history, lasting to around the end of the fourteenth century and even beyond.

On the purely rhythmic level, Vitry, while keeping the mensuration system, clarified the notation of individual durations, by means of signs that are the direct ancestors of those in use today, the basic units being minim, semibreve, breve and long, which today would be notated as quaver (eighth-note), crotchet (quarter-note), minim (half-note) and semibreve (whole note). With these in place, changes to the pattern of beats were instantly apparent and a greater variety of rhythmic detail could be notated.

Liveliness in this dimension features in Vitry's few certain works, motets suggesting his brilliance of mind. Often the topic is satire, as it is in a lengthy musical-poetic allegory of the period, the *Roman de Fauvel* (Romance of Fauvel), some of whose motets may be his as well. We have very much more music by his junior contemporary Guillaume de Machaut (c. 1300–77), who also had connections with the French royal house, but who kept away from Paris and retired around the age of forty to the life of a canon at Rheims. There he supervised the compiling of luxury copies of his complete musical works, an effort to which we owe the survival of almost a hundred lyrical songs by him, twenty-three motets, nineteen lais, or long narrative songs, and a mass, making him by far the most fully known composer before Du Fay in the next century. His works had, accordingly, a leading place in the revival of medieval music. His mass was quoted in histories of music from the beginning of the nineteenth century, was recorded in part in 1936, and was joined by the rest of his output as the subject of monographs, editions and recordings from the 1950s onwards. As his music became known, so it began influencing the composers of six centuries on, including Stravinsky (in his own mass), Olivier Messiaen and Jean Barraqué. Soon others, notably Harrison Birtwistle and György Kurtág, were making arrangements of pieces by him.

What intrigued all these distant colleagues was, at least in part, the resolute way he handled rhythm as a component interlocking with harmonic structure but not smoothly integrated, involved rather in its own patterns. This was something he inherited from thirteenth-century motets, many of which repeated the chant melodies of their tenors to give the other voices time to say what they must – but repeated them to rhythmic patterns recurring at a different rate. For example, in his motet *De bon espoir – Puisque la douce rose* (In firm hope – For the sweet rose: two titles for the texts of the two added voices) the chant melody, also known as the *color*, is heard four times, but attached to a rhythmic sequence, or *talea*, that repeats six times, the second three times at double the speed of the first three. The *color* thus starts again half way through the second *talea*, and the two coincide only at the beginning of the third repeat of the *color* and fourth of the *talea* – the point where the speed of the tenor (but not of the other two voices) increases. This technique of 'isorhythm', repeating rhythmic patterns independently of the melodic notes, could affect all the parts, as for example in the Amen that concludes the Credo of Machaut's mass.

That mass, the *Messe de Nostre Dame* (Mass of Our Lady) as the composer called it, is a setting of parts of the service that are always present, voicing corporate acts of prayer, praise and affirmation: the Kyrie, Gloria, Credo, Sanctus and Benedictus (treated as a pair), Agnus Dei and, finally, the response to the dismissal 'Ite missa est'. Leaving out this last item, the five-movement cycle was to become the most substantial form available to composers from the mid-fifteenth century to the end of the sixteenth, but Machaut's example is by far the earliest (setting aside a couple of masses assembled in Barcelona and Tournai from unrelated movements). It is also a robust and dazzling composition. Like Perotin a century and a half before, Machaut wrote for four men's voices, but now in two distinct registers (tenor and bass, or possibly countertenor and baritone, since we cannot be sure what his pitch standard was), allowing fuller chords, yet still with the octave plus fifth as primary consonance. Instead of moving in more or less similar small circles, though, the harmony exerts a strong yet subtle power over larger spans, proceeding towards strident cadences from neighbour notes contained in what would later be called a minor chord (thus resolving, for example, from C♯–E–G♯–C♯ to D–A–D). This omni-present cadence articulates both the short segments of the Gloria and Credo, where the four voices chant the text mostly together, phrase by phrase, and the longer sections where a minimal text – just 'Amen' at the end of the Gloria as well as the Credo – is the opportunity for ingenuity of isorhythm and counterpoint.

Machaut's motets are similar in style, most of them having isorhythm at least in their tenors. But the mass's long melismas (flows of notes for each syllable), are replaced in the motets by streams of words in the added parts, whose diverging texts resemble those of motets from the previous century. As before, too, the motet is not a liturgical genre, even in the few Machaut examples that address sacred topics in Latin. The more usual French texts concern what had been the chief subject of vernacular song since the troubadours: love, the promise of constancy, the anguish of separation, the pain of ingratitude. In Machaut's motets, though, the lover's resolve and suffering become peculiarly intense, as the cadence is delayed through a long stretch of polyphony negotiating bitter dissonances. Also, the multiple voices of each motet (most often two in roughly the same range over a tenor below) chart dis-putes within a single persona. For example, in *Dame, je suis cilz – Fins cuers doulz* (Lady, I am of those – Sweet noble heart) – a song of particular harmonic plaintiveness, if unusual in its straightforward three-beat patterns and lack of isorhythm – both voices are close to despair at the prospect of having to stay away from a lady who wishes it so, and both can find satisfaction only in obedience to the point of death, but only one ventures hope for a change of heart on the lady's part. Nor are such differences only to be found in the words, the composer's own. The slightly more optimistic voice is also the musically livelier, and the setting makes its own commentary on the texts in how it aligns the voices, makes one answer the other, or has one continue the other's thought. Poetic structure, as conveyed by rhyme and metre, matters to the music much less than this dialogue it creates.

In other songs Machaut followed the way of his troubadour and trouvère predecessors in composing musical phrases that do not ignore but rather conform to poetic lines – especially in three types that became the *formes fixes* (fixed forms) of the next century: the ballade, rondeau and virelai. Like his motets, Machaut's ballades and rondeaux are mostly for three voices; they differ in their regular phrasing, which places his tunefulness more in relief, and in being generally more melismatic. Here the virelais differ, for they are largely syllabic (having one note per syllable). Also, as naked melodies, with no added parts, most of them cast back directly to older traditions, and some have a folksong tone, sprightly (*Quant je suis mis au retour*: When I turned back) or wistful (*Comment qu'a moy lointeinne soies*: However far from me you may be).

Versatile, and surely proud of his achievement (hence his care over presentation), Machaut enjoyed appreciation in his time. Like no composer before him (but many since), he received the posthumous honour of a memorial in his own art: a ballade by the greatest French poet of the next generation, Eustace Deschamps, set by the otherwise unknown composer Andrieu. One of his own poems was set by an Italian composer, Antonello da Caserta, confirming the evidence of far-flung manuscripts that his music was widely valued, and his influence was felt by a leading successor, Solage (again known only by a last name), who may have been his pupil, and who developed his style to a point of ravishing harmonic refinement. Many others in the later fourteenth century were, if not carrying on from him directly, at least extending the possibilities of the ars nova he had brought to its classic perfection, the main centres now being in southern France, in bordering territories in Italy and Spain, and on the island of Cyprus, where knowledge of his music had reached the furthest limit of western European civilisation.

Among composers of this period, the Florentine Francesco Landini (c. 1325–97) stands out for the size of his surviving output and the variety, even though he concentrated almost exclusively on Italian songs in two or three parts: some are dance-like, set to a lively pulse; many more have the irregular yet fluid rhythm he may have inherited from the French ars nova by way of Italian contemporaries of Machaut, such as Jacopo da Bologna and Lorenzo da Firenze. What partly distinguishes all these Italians is how details of melody and harmony may be directly expressive of the words, in a way that looks forward to the madrigals of two centuries later. For example, in Landini's song *Quanto piu caro faj* (The dearer you make), the image of growing fire is reflected in motifs that trill like flickering flames, and the word 'never' is given a long elaboration, as if the music wants never to end.

Similarly suggestive of the emergent Renaissance is the increasing use, in both Italian and French songs of the later fourteenth century, of full triads (chords with the third as well as the fifth, e.g. D–F–A or F–A–C – chords that would become fundamental to the major-minor system of the seventeenth century and later) and of places where one polyphonic voice imitates what another has just sung. Neither of these elements was entirely new. There are triads intermittently in Perotin, and imitative counterpoint in a very straightforward form — as a round, where several voices sing the same thing one after another — dates back at least to the mid-thirteenth-century English song *Sumer is icumen in*. Now, though, composers were starting to use both harmony and counterpoint to create a smooth unfolding, in which musical events have audible causes and consequences — a parallel, in the art of time, to the perspective that was beginning to guide painting.

Landini's presence in art-loving Florence is significant here. He was the son of a painter, Jacopo da Casentino, and might have followed his father had he not, as a child, contracted smallpox and lost his sight. Presumably he created his compositions at the organ, on which he was an acknowledged master, and had them written down by an assistant — which raises the question of the range of musical literacy. Though a training for the church (such as most composers before the sixteenth century underwent) would have included instruction in reading plainsong, the ability to construe the rhythmic niceties of Machaut or Landini is unlikely to have been often required or widely developed. Singers must have been rare virtuosos — instrumentalists too, where they took part in polyphonic music and were not confined to the boisterous dances of which a few survive from this century.

Competent performers were surely even scarcer for the highly involved music created in southern France and northern Italy around 1400, the music for which the modern label 'ars subtilior' (subtler practice) was invented. When this repertory was first revived, in the 1970s, what excited particular interest was the rhythmic strangeness that invited

comparison with the newest music of the time: an extreme
example is Matteo da Perugia's ballade *Le greygnour bien*
(The Greatest Good), close to the music of Pierre Boulez
in its highly nuanced values or to Conlon Nancarrow's in
the independence of its parts. Here was a voice from the
past that sounded, like Machaut's a little earlier, remarkably
contemporary. And so it has remained, in changing ways.
As more ensembles have specialized in medieval song,
the importance of performers' choices, backgrounds and
assumptions has become ever more manifest, exactly as with
ensembles for new music. For all the notational precisions
of a Matteo da Perugia — or, in our own time, a Brian
Ferneyhough — the music takes its life from how it is presented. Indeed, music that is over-prescribed — telling us
more than we can take in, more than musicians can give
utterance to — may be more pliable in performance, not less.
And music that has to communicate in diverse voices
through complex machinery, even if from a time long gone,
speaks directly to our present.

Matteo's bizarre piece is exceptional even within the ars
subtilior repertory, and is only one extraordinary element in
the variegated musical world of the early fifteenth century.
Music was moving towards Renaissance ideals in other
respects than consistently consonant harmony and imitation
between lines: melodic lines were becoming more continuous and uniform in flow, polyphonic parts more alike in
speed and rhythmic detail, musical images more responsive
to the rhythm, sound and meaning of the words. But
different composers were moving at different speeds along
these parallel directions, as if the whole course of the art
were a piece of late ars nova polyphony. The songs of Paolo
da Firenze (c. 1355–?1436), coming out of the Landini
tradition and similarly ranging from dance numbers to

suavely expressive pieces, have melodies that move effort-
lessly and with purpose: they run over one another in fluent
imitation and bring the words to life, yet within a harmonic
world from around the time of the composer's birth — that
is, of Machaut's heyday. Conversely, the English composer
Pycard — known only as the author of two mass sections in
the Old Hall Manuscript (c. 1415–21), a rich collection of
sacred music probably compiled for Henry V's brother
Thomas, Duke of Clarence — was a master of sonorous,
consonant harmony, made up largely of triads, with exciting effects of imitation between voices, and yet his
strongly pulsed rhythm and clear separation of functions
(some voices fast, some slow) looked back to the thirteenth
century, or even the twelfth.

Another pattern in the music of these two composers is
that of national traditions, for Paolo's way of bringing
voice, word and melody into a mutual caress sounds thoroughly Italian, while Pycard has an English solidity and
humour. Such distinctions maintained themselves partly by
outbreeding. Music had long been spread in written form:
that was how chant, Notre Dame polyphony and the ars
nova style had all been distributed. Now composers themselves were starting to travel — and where Machaut had
done so merely as secretary to Jean de Luxembourg, King
of Bohemia, his successors were invited abroad for their
musical prowess. Johannes Ciconia, who was born in Liège
around 1370, spent most of his adult life in Rome (through
the 1390s) and then Padua, where he died in 1411. He thus
beat the path from the Low Countries to Italy that was
taken by several composers over the next two centuries,
including Du Fay, Josquin and Lassus, and like all of them
he was polyglot, setting words in more than one language
(Italian and French in his case) and combining different

musical traditions (with him the French ars nova and an Italian sense of tune and expressivity). His music circulated as far as Poland, and the charm of his song *O rosa bella* (O fair rose) was recognized up to half a century after his death, for the piece was repeatedly arranged by later composers, one of whom based a mass on it. If this song represents him as a crypto-Florentine, in his motets for Padua and Venice he foreshadows the Venetian state music that was to flower two hundred years later in Giovanni Gabrieli and Claudio Monteverdi.

Perhaps Paolo da Firenze looks forward further still. Like Ciconia he was a priest; he was also a Benedictine, and rose to the rank of abbot. But his music consists almost exclusively of secular songs, among which *Non più 'nfelic* (No longer unhappy) fixes on the image of Narcissus's gaze, and does so with such constant intensity – the phrases moving slowly between fast scalewise ripples, the harmony motionless – that the music itself becomes a pool of reflection. Melodic figures are reflected as one line imitates another; the cherishing of vocal sound, whether sustained or quietly voluble, brings the human body into the image, as surely as Narcissus's body is presented in the mirror of the water surface; and in all – the fixity, the eroticism, the quietness – we can make out an Italian composer of six centuries later, Salvatore Sciarrino. Of course, it may just be that performers of Paolo's music now are living in the world from which Sciarrino speaks: indeed, they may sometimes be performing his music as well. That does not change the fact that here in the twenty-first century the middle ages are not over.

Though a monk, Paolo had things to leave in his will. They included a table clock. Time was being domesticated.

PART III

Time sensed 1400–1630

The term 'Renaissance' was not introduced until 1855 (by the French historian Jules Michelet), but people in the fifteenth century were certainly aware of living through a period of rebirth. As the theorist Johannes Tinctoris (c. 1435–?1511) put it in a treatise of the 1470s: 'The possibilities of our music have been so marvellously increased that there appears to be a new art, if I may so call it, whose fount and origin is held to be among the English.' This was already an old theme. Thirty years earlier Martin Le Franc (c. 1410–61) had sounded it, in a poem referring to two composers he would have known as a follower of the artistically rich courts of Burgundy and Savoy, Guillaume Du Fay (?1397–1474) and Gilles de Bins, known as Binchois (c. 1400–60): 'For they have found a new way of making lively concord . . . and have adopted the English manner [*la contenance angloise*].' Moreover, both Tinctoris and Le Franc singled out John Dunstable (c. 1390–1453) as the head of the English school.

Le Franc's few lines here, from a poem of 24,000, have been endlessly scrutinized, for not only are they vague, they refer to a period from which very few compositions can be dated with any precision. Three things, though, seem clear: there was a general shift around 1430 in music in the Low

Countries, France and Italy; English music – perhaps introduced by the presence of English prelates with their singers at the Council of Constance (1414–18) – was remembered as having had a catalytic effect; and the agent responsible was the triad. Tinctoris, in another treatise, from 1477, positioned the change quite accurately: 'Although it seems beyond belief, there is not a single piece of music not composed in the last forty years that is regarded by the learned as worth hearing.' Like the other arts and sciences, music was running with new ideas, not the least of which was that music was to be judged not according to criteria drawn from ancient philosophy but by how it sounded.

What principally marked the Renaissance was this respect for nature as humanly perceived. Paintings came to have natural colours, with shading to indicate volume, with consistency of scale and, above all, with perspective, so that the image would have the look of the real world. Architects based their designs on simple shapes and proportions, which the eye could immediately and intuitively grasp, and which would therefore seem natural. Tinctoris's dating situates the musical Renaissance at almost exactly the same time as Masaccio's paintings and Brunelleschi's epoch-making building plans. And again the impulse came from a wish to mirror reality as perceived by the senses: the reality of time (newly experienced as smoothly continuous and orderly in the early fifteenth century, when the first accurate clocks were made) and the reality of hearing.

Just as Renaissance painting welcomes the eye into what looks like a real scene, so Renaissance music invites the ear into expanses of time that are lucid, where harmony and rhythm recognize the nature of hearing. Of course, no piece of music can resemble heard reality in the way that a painting can imitate what is seen, and because that is so, we may, in music, accept as natural what is merely familiar. The naturalness of the triad, in particular, is a contentious matter: do we experience triads as full and smooth, by comparison with the 'bare' fifths of Perotin, because of how we hear or because of what we have heard — because of how our ears work or because of how they have adapted to the omnipresent triadic music of western traditions, classical and popular? Perhaps the question itself contains an answer, for it may be that the triad could not have gained this dominance without latching into aural processing.

Such latching has sometimes been attributed to the simple frequency ratios represented within the triad, but what may matter as much, or more, is how the triad works as a signpost — its quality not as sound but in time. Having three notes, triads are much more strongly interconnected than are simple two-note intervals. A Renaissance piece in the Mixolydian mode, for example, will have the chord G–B–D as its resting place and ultimate goal, with an array of other triads that can be heard as standing at different degrees of closeness to that chord (e.g. the alternative stackings of those same notes as B–D–G and D–G–B) and distance. Melody will have the power to lead a congruent line through this harmonic labyrinth, and rhythm can support that melodic journey by providing a sense of regular steps — regular at the levels of the beat, the metrical unit and the phrase, as was the case in Perotin but had ceased to be so in the subtle music of the fourteenth century. Hence the increased prominence in Renaissance polyphony of the top line as the guiding melody, the growing function at the same time of the bottom line as a bass to the harmony, the move from the three-part textures of the thirteenth and fourteenth centuries to a norm of four parts, allowing full triads with the main note at top and bottom (e.g.

G–B–D–G), and the pruning of rhythmic variety in favour of cycles as regular as breathing.

Time was not made by this music so much as discovered. Where Machaut's mass, for instance, robustly stakes out its positions in empty time, the masses of composers of the fifteenth and sixteenth centuries move through temporal spaces that seem already to be in existence, because these spaces are created and sustained by harmonic relationships. In this most essential respect Renaissance music indeed accords with what and how we observe, for it offers us models of how we sense the passing of time.

CHAPTER 4

Harmony, the light of time

The Renaissance did not happen overnight. Not only did the essence of its music – triadic harmony, with melody going in company with a calm, even rhythm of chord change – develop gradually through several decades in the late fourteenth century and early fifteenth, but medieval features stayed in place sporadically through the fifteenth century, and in some cases into the sixteenth. Most long-lasting was the technique of creating polyphony over or around a cantus firmus (still most commonly a piece of chant), though it seems unlikely that composers in the fifteenth century were still putting their music together voice by voice: the flow of their music suggests a change of view from the horizontal, writing one voice part after another, to the vertical, conceiving the whole texture together, the new voices incorporating the given cantus firmus in a continuous harmonic unfolding.

Also surviving somewhat from the middle ages was a more angular kind of melody, whose contours were not smoothly integrated with the harmony but would stick out, and similarly a more complicated sort of rhythm, again working against the sense of the one continuity in all voices. Such complexity might involve flurries of small values or moments in which simultaneous voices proceed in different metres, for medieval mensuration, continuing unchanged, made it easy to switch between three-part and two-part divisions on two levels, so that one voice might suddenly move to a nine-beat pattern in the context of four-beat rhythm. Also, isorhythm, involving rhythmic patterns more easily seen on paper than heard, was still favoured for motets by Du Fay in his full maturity.

Remarkably, the musical Renaissance came with no essential change to the notational system, which lent itself to rhythmic complications, as spectacularly in the hands of Matteo de Perugia and others. Music was also, until the mid-sixteenth century, laid out in partbooks, with all the vocal parts for a composition or section written separately on one opening. Modern performers have often taken this to imply a group of singers small enough to have clustered around the book, though choirs could have been larger, their members copying out their parts or learning them. Equally unclear is how widely polyphony, whether in church music or song, was performed with instrumentalists or with boy choristers. Fifteenth-century songs sound well when the lower parts are played on lute, harp or the wind instruments of the period, whose tones are as exotic as their names: kortholt, crumhorn, sackbut. The existence of the Buxheim Organ Book (c. 1470) proves that songs could be understood as contrapuntal inventions at the keyboard, their words omitted. But they can sound good, too, when performed by wholly vocal ensembles. As for church music, instrumentalists were sometimes noted at important ceremonies, but perhaps more generally the music was the responsibility solely of the choir. The common four-part texture of the fifteenth century (found too in the fourteenth) has two tenor lines with a baritone below and, above, a part that could have been taken by countertenors or by boys.

Certainly composers often began as boy choristers, Du Fay's career being exemplary in this as in other respects. He was taken into the cathedral choir at Cambrai (in present-day France close to the Belgian border) probably when he was eleven or twelve, and remained a singing boy there until he was about sixteen. Cambrai Cathedral was an important place, a vast edifice of great wealth and prestige, in close contact with Rome and visited by kings on account of possessing a portrait of the Virgin Mary that St Luke was believed to have painted. Accordingly its musical establishment included several composers — though to identify someone as a composer in this period is probably anachronistic: these were people (all men, inevitably, at a male church) who served in various capacities as teachers and choirmasters, and who were all also priests. The young Du Fay, like any boy with talent but lacking noble birth, would have been led to make his life in the church, which by the time of his youth had begun to find wider use for the polyphony confined largely to secular song through most of the preceding century. Typical of the new age, too, was the speed with which a young man's renown could travel, so that Du Fay in his mid-twenties was serving the Malatesta family of Rimini. He spent much of his thirties in the retinue of the pope, Eugenius IV, and later accepted invitations to the court of Louis I of Savoy (an alpine-Mediterranean region now partitioned among Switzerland, France and Italy), but maintained his positions in Cambrai, and died there in his seventies.

Throughout most of Du Fay's adult life his home city of Cambrai belonged to the realm of the duke of Burgundy, Philip the Good, a great patron of the arts. Binchois, who came from the same area, was in longstanding service to the duke, and the two composers were probably in regular contact. Unlike their predecessors, they may also have had some sense of themselves as composers, since this was how, as Martin Le Franc attests, they were widely known. Together with such contemporaries as Donatello and Jan van Eyck, they had the evidence of their reputations that the world valued them for their creative work, and so perhaps possessed an artistic self-confidence that only Machaut among previous musicians could have known. Du Fay, in particular, was called on for occasions of great moment, including the dedication by the pope of Florence Cathedral in 1436, for which ceremony he wrote a motet, *Nuper rosarum flores* (Recently garlands of roses).

The isorhythmic foundation of this piece is, unusually, a pair of lines, both appropriately quoting a chant from the liturgy for the dedication of a church, and heard four times over, at speeds in the proportions 2 : 3 : 6 : 4 — proportions seemingly based on those of the building for which the work was written. Just as that cathedral, begun in 1294, placed Renaissance features on a medieval plan, so Du Fay's motet has its medieval substructure support an upper pair of lines moving with Renaissance limpidity and ease. These higher voices — one above the other, carrying identical words — provide the music's harmonious continuity, completing or implying triads over the isorhythmic parts that recurrently chime in, and that perhaps originally did so on instruments. Hearing all this for the first time must have been not only the pope, wearing the tiara he had commissioned from the Florentine master Lorenzo Ghiberti, but also those who had contributed to the cathedral's completion: Brunelleschi, designer of its dome, and Donatello, who had carved statues for it. Here Du Fay could feel himself in a community of artists.

But now we are at the limits of what may be imagined. There was nobody to collect anecdotes about the great composers, as Giorgio Vasari did for the painters, sculptors and architects. The single surviving letter by Du Fay, a business document addressed to the Medici princes of Florence, reveals nothing of his personality, nor can we glean much from his music, beyond the evident clarity, agility and inventiveness of his mind — though justifiable pride, too, comes across here and there. He seemingly initiated the practice of writing a mass on a tenor not from chant but from a polyphonic song — and did so by choosing his own *Se la face ay pale* (If my face be pale). He composed for himself a Requiem, or funeral mass (now lost), and asked in his will for his setting of the *Ave regina celorum* (Hail, queen of the heavens) to be sung as he lay dying by three men and the choirboys, proving that, at least by 1474, boys were singing in polyphony. He also signed this piece. Twice the text includes his name in prayers for mercy, the second time with the word 'miserere' (have mercy) touchingly emphasized.

The esteem he enjoyed is equally clear. His music was appreciated by the foremost patrons, including — besides the pope and the Burgundian and Savoyard dukes — Lorenzo de' Medici, 'the Magnificent', who as a youth of eighteen had a poem sent to the composer for setting (though the music, if it was ever written, is lost). Very possibly he was associated with the Feast of the Pheasant, which Philip the Good mounted in 1454 in the vain hope of encouraging a crusade against the Turks following the capture of Constantinople the year before: his letter to the Medici family calls attention to four laments he had written on the city's fall (of which only one survives). Further testimony to his standing comes from how much of his music escaped the fate of the three lost laments – far more than for any other composer of his time, and covering a much broader range of forms and styles. We have over a hundred small pieces of church music, including not only the ambitious and superb isorhythmic motets but also simple chant harmonizations; a similar number of songs, mostly to words in French, whether ebullient or melancholy; and perhaps nine masses, the attribution being uncertain in some cases.

Without discounting the splendour of the motets, or the charms of the songs and of other church pieces, the masses are his most remarkable achievements, by virtue of their incidental features as well as their scale. How he profited from the latter is easy to hear. The 'cyclic mass', with sections musically connected, was one of his inheritances from English music, for both Dunstable and Leonel Power (c. 1375–1445) had written such works for three voices, possibly in the 1440s, reinstituting the tradition broken since Machaut. Du Fay's masses, though, are all in four parts, and they show his skills at a supreme level. Several of them are comparatively late works, including one whose tenor is the anonymous song *L'homme armé* (The armed man).

This tune was used again and again in the later fifteenth century and beyond, its appeal based perhaps on the mysterious alarm-call of its words, perhaps on esoteric meanings having to do with the labyrinth, but certainly on the abrupt leaps of its melody. In the Du Fay example, as in any cantus firmus mass, the tenor normally proceeds slowly in the medium-low part of the contrapuntal fabric, but it can be changed in speed and melodically ornamented. There are also passages from which it was absent – notably the duets which, as in *Nuper rosarum flores*, contrast with sections of full texture, the technique being common throughout the fifteenth century and beyond. The tenor could be highlighted or hidden; Du Fay often hides his in this mass, whose overt integrity comes, rather, from the fluency of the melody through the characteristically regular chord changes, from the expertise with which resolutions (on the triad over the mode's final) become points of departure, so that the entire long Credo presents itself in two great spans, and from the starting of each section with a new version of the same airy duet, as if to re-establish the narrative after the intervening parts of the service. Extending with perfect equanimity, this music offers us time as if under natural illumination.

By the time Du Fay was at work on his late masses he was well over fifty, and the centre of compositional activity was back where it had been in his boyhood: in the Low Countries, northern France and England. Also, a new generation had arrived, its members including the Netherlander Jean de Ockeghem (c. 1410–97), the Frenchman Antoine Busnois (c. 1430–92) and the Englishmen Robert Morton (c. 1430–97) and Walter Frye (of uncertain dates). Busnois and Morton were both associated with the Burgundian court, where they followed Binchois in concentrating on French songs. Though Ockeghem was older – perhaps not much more than a decade younger than Du Fay – he seems to have been a late starter, his surviving music all dating from the period after 1450, the long period of his service to the French royal chapel (not a building but a body of clerics and musicians travelling with the king). During this time he visited Du Fay in Cambrai at least twice; he surely also knew Binchois (who may indeed have been his teacher), for not only did he create one of his finest masses on Binchois's song *De plus en plus* (More and more) but he composed an imposing ballade in Binchois's memory, *Mort tu as navré* (Death, you have wounded).

Like all composers of the fourteenth and fifteenth centuries Ockeghem also wrote polyphonic love songs, but the bulk of his output is in masses — sonorous works quite different from those of Du Fay at roughly the same time. When fifteenth-century music was first rediscovered, in the mid-twentieth century, Ockeghem was seen as a master of the arcane — of complex rhythmic relationships and artful manipulations of the cantus firmus. And indeed there is that aspect to his work, as more widely there is a strain of the hermetic to Renaissance thought, along with the clarity, rationalism and humanism: the influential theorist Franchino Gafori (1451–1522), for example, wrote on correspondences between the modes and the planets, and many Renaissance pieces were precisely calculated to represent, by how many rhythmic units they contained, a significant number, such as forty for the name 'Maria' (counting letters according to their alphabetical positions).

But exposure to Ockeghem's music as sound — greatly facilitated since the late 1980s by a new sureness in performances and recordings of fifteenth-century polyphony — has revealed a rather different composer, still enigmatic, perhaps, but movingly private. Where Du Fay's melody and harmony create a sense of proceeding continuously through light-filled space, Ockeghem's music is at once clear and obscure: moves are made with immediate logic, but the longer goal is not in sight. The difference is that between a sacred picture of saints in a landscape, where perspective opens on the imaginary distance in broad daylight, and an interior scene, where the viewing eye is held in a narrow space. Perhaps the reason is that Ockeghem's world was the north, not Italy, which he never visited. His music evokes comparison with the Flemish painters of his time, notably Petrus Christus, in its sombre restraint and dark colouring; his single Italian song — *O rosa bella*, to the poem Ciconia had set decades before — is a striking essay for two voices in his flowing but involuted counterpoint, where often the voices seem to be thinking their own thoughts, one perhaps rotating an idea while the other forges on, as if the two were strangers in the same room. The image of Ockeghem passed on by contemporary records — that of a wise, saintly man quietly devoted to his art — fits well with the inward character of that art.

His English contemporaries Morton and Frye make a contrasted pair, except in that biographical details for both are lacking. Morton appears to have become fully Burgundian; Frye stayed more English. He worked in the third quarter of the fifteenth century, the period of Ockeghem's central maturity and Du Fay's late masses, but his music is different again, its harmony swinging back and forth, bell-like, between resting consonances, the interims enlivened by jostling rhythms through recurrent patterns of notes in the upper parts. This is a style that seems to have been particularly English, traceable to the previous generation of Dunstable and Power, and conveyed to composers working at the century's close — though Frye is unusual in his harmonic expressiveness. Like Morton, he may have welcomed opportunities abroad when England had become the dynastic battleground of the Wars of the Roses. His works, and their wide dispersal, remind us that polyphonic music was cherished across Europe, from Portugal to Prague, and also that its rules, formalized by Tinctoris, were no bar to national tradition and even individuality.

Ockeghem's style, too, is highly individual, even if it was imitated by younger composers, and yet he was thoroughly at one with his contemporaries in his sacred subject matter. Aside from the *L'homme armé* tradition (to which he and

Busnois both contributed), most masses of this period are based on chants to the Virgin Mary or on songs which, like *Se la face ay pale* and *De plus en plus*, are voiced by one dying for love of a distant or unyielding lady. That lady, in the new religious context, is to be identified with the Virgin, whose image shines through the masses of this period as much as through so many painted Madonnas. She is there, too, in many of the age's other most imposing sacred pieces, such as Du Fay's *Ave regina celorum*. Through the topic of the pure adored, composers were commingling sacred and profane love as surely as had the troubadours and hymn writers of the twelfth century, and turning the universal memorial of the mass into a prayer for personal salvation.

Death and salvation are seldom on young minds, but the experience of hearing such music – or even singing it – must have impressed the choirboys of the 1450s and 1460s, which might be why many of them became composers themselves. One, Loyset Compère (c. 1445–1518), wrote a splendid piece in which fifteen other composers are mentioned; it appropriately starts with the words 'Omnium bonorum plena' (Full of all good things). Just possibly it was written for an occasion when the Burgundian and French courts gathered at Cambrai in 1468, and perhaps all these composers were there: youngsters like Compère himself, the middle generation of Ockeghem, Busnois and Tinctoris, and at the head Du Fay, saluted as 'moon of all music and light of singers'. More than thirty years after the great day in Florence Cathedral, Du Fay was now surrounded by another community, of musicians beginning to feel themselves fellow members of a guild, with their own responsibilities, traditions and techniques. Possibly the youngest named among them was the man who would be music's next moon: Josquin des Prez.

CHAPTER 5

The radiance of the High Renaissance

Some stability was maintained through the century from Du Fay's youth to the later years of Josquin (c. 1450–1521). Four-part polyphony remained the norm, in sacred music and songs. Masses and other church music, still often addressed to the Virgin Mary, would apply cantus firmus technique to a tenor from chant or song. The mensuration system survived well into its third century, and the primary consonance of octave plus fifth, on which pieces would end, was inherited all the way back from organum, being responsible for what today sounds most medieval in the music of Josquin's generation. And all the while the Low Countries, France and England continued to produce many of the most prized composers.

Even so, a mature work by Josquin – such as his late mass on the hymn *Pange lingua* – reveals a new world of sound. Everywhere the music is guided by imitation and, since there has to be something to imitate, by a succession of motifs, each leading a passage in which the voices wind round one another. Moreover, the motifs are often related to the tenor, which is no longer an almost secret presence, as it was in much of Du Fay's *L'homme armé* mass, but is floridly exposed in how the voices behave. The motive principle is placed on display, and music is disclosed to the listening ear, given a lucidity in accord with Renaissance humanism. A perspective through time is not just serenely there, as in Du Fay, but audibly in process of creation in the voices' interlocking. Meanwhile, a straight path opens to the triumph of criss-crossing imitation in the fugues of Bach and Handel.

Josquin's music is not only more frankly comprehensible but also brighter in sound, thanks to a change to the previously common four-part layout of alto, two tenors and baritone, opening the texture to give each voice its own centre and produce a new norm of soprano, alto, tenor and bass, which is still the standard for choral composition half a millennium later. Happening at the same time as the arrival of imitation, this might have been a linked development, for voices entering with the same melodic line will sound most effective if they do so in different registers. A connection with choral personnel is also implied, since the widened pitch range now definitely indicates a group including boys. And there could be further richness and brilliance from the addition of more voices to the basic four. Where Du Fay wrote nothing in more than four parts, five or six were quite usual for motets by Josquin and his contemporaries, and the Easter mass *Et ecce terrae motus* by the Frenchman Antoine Brumel (c. 1460 – c. 1515) has twelve.

Also, music responds more to the words – to the sorrow and harshness of the Crucifixion or to the elation of promised glory. This again was in agreement with a Renaissance principle, as propounded, for example, by the Florentine philosopher Marsilio Ficino (1433–99) in the last of his *Three Books on Life*: 'Song is a most powerful imitator of all things. It imitates the intentions and passions of the soul as well as words; it represents also people's physical gestures, motions and actions.' Ficino goes on here to note that music, though existing only in the air, has qualities of motion like a living body and can carry meanings like a mind, 'so that it can be said to be a kind of airy and rational animal'.

Josquin, whose music this description so well fits, might have come into contact with such ideas during the periods he spent in Italy from the later 1480s to the early years of the new century, serving in turn three powerful patrons: Cardinal Ascanio Sforza, Pope Alexander VI and Ercole d'Este, duke of Ferrara. Other details of his biography are sparse. He came from what are now the borderlands between France and Belgium, and that was the region to which he retired, so that his life began and ended after the pattern of Du Fay's. Possibly he had some training from this great compatriot and musical grandfather; there is also a tradition that he studied with Ockeghem, for whom he wrote an elegy, *Nymphes des bois* (Nymphs of the woods).

But the frank appeal he made to his listeners' comprehension, structural and expressive, is that of a new generation, and again connects with other elements in the maturing Renaissance. It implies a view of musical ability — at least in listening — as a common human attribute, at a time when music was becoming universal also in practice (at least among the well placed), moving out of the clerical-professional circles to which knowledge of notation had hitherto been confined. Baldassare Castiglione's *Book of the Courtier* reveals that singing to the lute and playing the viol (a string instrument with frets, like the lute or guitar, but played with a bow) were well established as aristocratic pursuits by Josquin's later years. And what Castiglione described as courtly behaviour was surely what his readers among the emerging urban bourgeoisie wanted to take into their own lives.

Both the lute and the viol seem to have spread rapidly around Europe at the very start of the sixteenth century from Spain, and thereby from Islamic culture (the former's name is derived from the Arabic *al 'ūd*). Both could be used in performances of vocal polyphony, as could the keyboard instruments imported or invented earlier but now coming into their own, notably the organ and the harpsichord. Even when some composers began writing specifically for instruments, imitative polyphony was often the model, and perhaps its success as a compositional style was partly due to how easily it could be adapted to instrumental performance, having a logic independent of sung words. Hence the ready supply of pieces for a solo keyboard or lute player – or a consort (group) of viols or wind instruments such as recorders – under various names: fantasia, fancy, sonata ('sounded' piece), ricercare (piece based on a theme treated in imitative polyphony). Together with these the early sixteenth century also invented variation form, taking a song or chant theme, or a favourite chord progression, and repeating it with diverse alterations. The other possibility for instrumental music – a niche so much enlarged by the availability of leisure time to the new bourgeoisie – was to accompany dancing.

Castiglione is also among those bearing witness to Josquin's contemporary fame, if in his case wrily, when he remarks that a new piece performed for the Duchess of Urbino 'never delighted nor was reckoned good, until it was known to be the doing of Josquin'. This brand-conscious duchess may have been receiving her Josquin by the new means of printed music, for in 1501, in Venice, Ottaviano Petrucci (1466–1539) published the first volume of music printed from movable type (rather than engraved blocks), followed soon by several more, of songs, lute music, masses and motets (the term now covering any sort of shorter setting for the Latin liturgy). Petrucci – evidently sharing the duchess's taste, or perhaps merely aware of market values – strongly favoured Josquin, providing further testimony to the composer's reputation. We also have the view of one of Ercole d'Este's agents, in a comparison with another composer of the period, Henricus Isaac (c. 1450–1517): 'Josquin composes better, but he composes when he wants to and not when he is wanted.' Ercole must have preferred quality to pliability, for Isaac remained with the court of the Austrian emperor Maximilian.

Yet another of Josquin's referees was the church reformer Martin Luther (1483–1546), who averred that 'Josquin is the master of the notes, which must do as he wishes, while other composers must follow what the notes dictate.' Even long after his death the name of Josquin retained the allure the duchess had recognized. His name heads a list of musicians drawn up in 1560 by the French poet Pierre de Ronsard (1524–85) in a preface for a book of songs, and he was the great model praised by the Swiss theorist Heinrich Glarean (1488–1563) in an important treatise on the modes published in 1547, this Josquin who 'brought forth nothing that was not delightful to the ear and approved as ingenious by the learned'.

Josquin's colossal reputation – together with, and partly explaining, the large amount of his music that survives – has left his contemporaries in danger of sounding secondary and irregular. Yet this was a charmed generation, including many other masters of the new imitative polyphony, just as it included many leading painters, such as Leonardo, Botticelli, Perugino and Bosch – though the artist nearest

Josquin in terms of prestige, then and later, was a generation younger: Raphael. Like Raphael, Josquin gave the style of his time a model of clarity and grace. There were other composers, though, who held positions of importance and had their works widely distributed in manuscript and printed forms, among these contemporaries being Isaac in Austria, Compère and Jean Mouton (c. 1455–1522) with the French court, the widely travelled Brumel and similarly peripatetic Alexander Agricola (c. 1450–1506), and one who, like Brumel and Josquin, spent a short while at the court of Ferrara: Jacob Obrecht (1457/8–1505).

In common with his contemporaries, always excepting Josquin, Obrecht was forgotten soon after his death, and his music was little known until scholars and performers began bringing it back into circulation in the 1990s. One result was to demonstrate that Obrecht had a style quite distinct from Josquin's. Leaving aside some early works written under Ockeghem's influence, his music belongs with Josquin's in proceeding as imitative polyphony; it has even been suggested he was the forerunner of this technique in the 1480s. However that may be, he used it in his own way. Both composers work through their texts phrase by phrase, often repeating each phrase in different voices imitatively, but where Josquin's melodies are shaped by the rhythm and meaning of the words, Obrecht's are impelled by a purely musical energy, which tends to push through a piece or section from beginning to end, without the regular restarts Josquin makes as new phrases arrive to be set. In Obrecht the words are not so much expressed as irradiated.

Textural splendour abounds, too, in the English music of the late fifteenth century, growing now in relative isolation. Unlike their predecessors from Dunstable and Power to Morton and Frye, English composers of the Josquin generation did not travel, nor was their music widely copied: indeed, the greatest of them, John Browne (b.c. 1453), is known from just the one source, the great choirbook of Eton College, into which works by him were inscribed around 1490. Similarly, continental musicians did not cross the English Channel, and foreign music after Du Fay's does not seem to have circulated in Britain. Browne, like other composers represented in the Eton Choirbook, may nonetheless have been aware of continental techniques of imitation and expressing the text: his six-part setting of the Crucifixion poem *Stabat mater* (The mother stood), for instance, has downward trickles of notes to suggest sorrow, such touching details being thoroughly integrated into music of majestic sweep and thrilling sound. But, like his colleagues, he maintained mid-century elements, notably pairings and other groupings of long lines that are quite separate in their melodic turnings and rhythmic embellishments, yet in perfect fit. These composers also delighted in wide textures and high voices, generally writing two parts for boys, in soprano and mezzo-soprano registers; that same *Stabat mater*, covering a range of three octaves, is exceptional only in its quality. It belongs with many of the choirbook's other items not only in style and range but also in its appellant address to the Virgin Mary, whose image the college choir had to honour every evening with the singing of a motet. Similar practices must have been widespread, to judge from the quantity of Marian motets by British and continental musicians of this period. Nowhere, though, can the effect have been as glorious as at Eton and in other English chapels where the music of Browne and his contemporaries was sung. The comparison is often and aptly drawn with the Perpendicular architecture that was similarly an English speciality of the time, and that was represented at Eton by the chapel for which the choirbook was put together, a building then under construction. In the soaring of both sound and stone, Renaissance symmetry and light joined with medieval pattern and ornateness.

While the chapel and choirbook at Eton were both being assembled, in the years around 1500, music was on the ascent also in Spain and Portugal, thanks in part to contact with musicians of the Franco-Netherlandish school. Spain was visited by both La Rue and Agricola, Josquin was (as everywhere) revered, and imitative polyphony was absorbed by the leading local composers, among them the Spaniard Francisco de Peñalosa (c. 1470–1528) and the Portuguese Pedro de Escobar (c. 1465 – c. 1540). Cultural progress in Spain was further spurred by the unification of the country and the overthrow of the last Moorish enclave in 1492. Soon, though, Spaniards came into contact with new alien kinds of music through the conquests of Mexico (1521) and Peru (1533) – as indeed did Mexicans and Peruvians. The first Spanish observers interpreted what they heard of Aztec and Inca music either as fundamentally familiar or else, in fully Renaissance fashion, as exemplifying the naturalness presumed of music in ancient Greece. Their reports are all we have, for the only music written down was for the religion of the conquerors.

Almost too neatly, the first teacher of European music in the New World, arriving in Mexico in 1523, was a man from the Low Countries, Pedro de Gante (i.e. Ghent, ?1486–1572), who therefore came from the same area and time as two composers who carried Franco-Netherlandish polyphony towards its final phase of international triumph: Nicolas Gombert (c. 1495 – c. 1560) and Adrian Willaert (c. 1490–1562). Each of these latter attained a leading position when Pedro was fresh in Mexico City. In 1526 Gombert, who may have studied with Josquin, joined the chapel of the emperor Charles V, ruler not only of the Austrian empire but also of Spain, the Low Countries and, indeed, Mexico. The next year Willaert, a pupil of Mouton, took charge of music at the state basilica of St Mark's in Venice, where the republic was staging its religious ceremonies with increasing pomp. Both composers pursued the imitative polyphony of their predecessors but made it more fully and smoothly consonant, less inclined towards modes other than the major (e.g. C–D–E–F–G–A–B–C) and natural minor (e.g. A–B–C–D–E–F–G–A), and destined to reach rest on a complete triad rather than a bare fifth. These were the basic features, too, of the music of such younger composers as Cristóbal Morales (c. 1500–53), a Spaniard who was with the papal chapel in mid-career, and the Netherlander Jacob Clement (c. 1512–55/6), posthumously given the humorous nickname Clemens non Papa (Clement not the Pope, i.e. not Pope Clement VII, who was his contemporary). The latter's extraordinary productivity may reflect both a facility in the new musical language and an awareness that the need for Catholic church music was now global.

A secular song would have a more local appeal, on account of its language, but here, too, there was voluminous activity during the working lives of Gombert, Willaert, Morales and Clemens, all of whom wrote in this form, while other composers of the time were song specialists. Where the songs of composers from Machaut to Josquin imply professional performance for a noble audience, by the 1520s simpler styles were emerging, suited to readers of Castiglione – readers who might well be members of the new urban bourgeoisie, and who would want songs that were fun to sing, either as solos with lute or among groups of friends taking the four parts. The philosophical humanism of the late fifteenth century became a more practical democratization, but with the same goals of expressivity and logic, the latter to be achieved by means of imitative polyphony. New were the possibilities of roughness and jollity, and the emphasis placed on a good tune. There are, of course, tunes in the songs of Machaut or Du Fay, but the tunefulness of the second quarter of the sixteenth century has a new directness, owed partly to its leaning towards major and minor modes, with their clearer harmonic relationships, and partly to its roots in dance rhythms.

Since Paris was the largest European city of the time, with a population of about a quarter of a million, it is not surprising that the new wave began with French songs, by composers including, besides Gombert, Clément Janequin (c. 1485 – c. 1560) and Claudin de Sermisy (c. 1490–1562), the former best known for the boisterous illustrative effects of his pieces about birdsongs and battle cries. A Frenchman, Philippe Verdelot (c. 1482 – c. 1531), went to Florence and became the main contributor to the first book of Italian songs that gave, in 1530, the new genre a name: madrigal. Another immigrant Florentine, the Netherlander Jacques Arcadelt (c. 1505–68), published in 1539 a collection of madrigals whose delicious tunefulness kept them in print for more than a century. The wave also journeyed on to Spain, where Mateo Flecha (?1481–?1553) created 'ensaladas', or medleys of tunes, put together for four-part singing, to German-speaking territories and to England, whose songs of this period include one attributed to the ruling monarch, Henry VIII (reigned 1509–47): *Pastime with good company*.

Inevitably the new style of song was absorbed by the church. Composers applied it to sacred texts and produced motets as lively and expressive as their madrigals; they also wrote masses based on such motets or directly on madrigals – not in the old cantus firmus way but rather by using the entire polyphonic fabric, adapted, repeated and extended as necessary. Such recomposition is known technically as 'parody', entirely without any sense of mockery, and Gombert, Morales and Clemens non Papa all wrote numerous parody masses, on their own works or those of others.

Only in Britain, again, did history go a different way, for British composers remained isolated, drawing on native traditions that went back through the Eton Choirbook to the mid-fifteenth century – traditions of florid writing for boys' voices, of textural complexity, of cantus firmus technique, of harmony still with the open-fifth flavour of the fifteenth century and of polyphony in exuberant free flow, largely independent of imitation. Outstanding in Scotland was Robert Carver (c. 1485 – c. 1570), whose *O bone Jesu* (O good Jesus) wields nineteen voices in chordal progressions of raw grandeur, making his native country seem as exotic an outpost of Christendom as Mexico. In England the most gifted composer among many was John Taverner (c. 1490–1545), who spent most of his life in his native Lincolnshire, apart from a few years (1526–30) at the Oxford college founded by Cardinal Wolsey. His three six-part masses, possibly written for the college, catch the great English polyphonic tradition just before religious change took it into the silence of uncertainty.

CHAPTER 6

Reformation and heartache

With the exception of chant, western music before around 1550 was engulfed by time to lie unheard until the twentieth century – in many cases the very late twentieth century. To that extent, all older music is new. The masses of Du Fay or the songs of Gombert – or, indeed, the wheeling constructions of Perotin – have not yet acquired the patina of the past. But with the music of the 1550s and 1560s a certain wear and familiarity, based on a longer continuity, begin to fade in. The works of the leading church musician of the younger generation, Giovanni Pierluigi da Palestrina (1525/6–94), were never entirely forgotten, at least in Rome, where he lived almost his whole life. They lent themselves to being remembered because, through the centuries, they remained comprehensible. And they remained comprehensible because, while immediately dependent on the euphonious polyphony of Gombert and Morales, they were harmonically conceived and their harmony was thoroughly that of the major and minor modes. To take the example of Palestrina's most celebrated mass, the *Missa Papae Marcelli* (Mass of Pope Marcellus), the music is underpinned throughout by chord progressions, moving often through richer harmonies: this mass is for choir in six parts; others by the composer have five or eight as well as the previously normal four. And while making sense in themselves, the harmonic phrases can be adapted to the words. In the sections with longer texts, the Gloria and Credo, it is as if the choir speaks each phrase with the colouring of melodic gesture and harmony, both explicable and expressive.

This mass by Palestrina, out of the more than a hundred he wrote, has a special place not only for its intrinsic virtues of verbal explicitness, economy and calm beauty but also for the legends attached to it: that it was written in a single night of angelic dictation and that it was composed in order to vindicate polyphony during the deliberations on church music that took place during the council of bishops convened at the northern Italian city of Trent (1545–63). These stories bear not on objective truth but on the classic status the composer was to acquire, even in his own time. He enjoyed the support of successive Popes and fellow musicians, and his style of declamatory polyphony had its effect on younger composers.

Palestrina's music is the sounding embodiment of the theoretical work of his contemporary Gioseffo Zarlino (1519–90), whose *Istitutioni harmoniche* (Musical Foundations, 1558) provided the age with its supreme treatise on music. Zarlino was a Venetian, had studied with Willaert at St Mark's (where he himself became director of music in 1565) and duly singled out for praise some of the madrigals and motets his master was shortly to gather under the imposing title *Musica nova* (New Music, 1559). But Willaert was not a lone innovator. What was new in this volume was arriving more widely: effective word-setting coupled to consistently consonant harmony in the major and minor modes. These were the means Zarlino set out to justify and explain, his criterion – in keeping with the Renaissance elevation of the human – being the ear: hence his distaste for the complexities of medieval rhythmic notation, which by his time was at last in decline, unneeded by the even flow of most music since the post-Josquin generation. His authority, backed yet again by reference to the ancient Greeks, gave the new style its intellectual support.

Institutional promotion came from the Roman church. The Council of Trent was called by Pope Paul III as a response to the breakaway denominations beginning to form around the teachings of such critics of Roman authority and practice as Martin Luther and Jean Calvin. What Luther and Calvin let loose, the Reformation, thus deeply affected the old Catholic order, for what emerged from Trent was a revised liturgy, with music that curiously accorded with Reformation ideals – ideals more generally those of the Renaissance. The single stipulation in the council's enactments concerning music was that the church should not admit 'any thing lascivious or impure', an injunction that may have helped bring about the decline in parody masses based on madrigals. This ruling also coincided with Calvin's wish, expressed in his preface to the Geneva Psalter (1542), for 'songs not merely honest but holy', avoiding what was 'in part vain and frivolous, in part stupid and dull, in part foul and vile and consequently evil and harmful'. In the background here, both for Calvin and for the bishops at Trent, was the idea inherited from Plato (to whom Calvin refers) that different kinds of music could be beneficial or deleterious. Equally important, and shared by Catholics and Protestants, was the value placed on music's expressiveness. Where a Du Fay mass is a building in time, with the words only a ground plan, a Palestrina motet, a Lutheran chorale (hymn in four-part harmony) or a Calvinist psalm tune is a presentation of the text.

Protestant music differed only in that, being intended not for regular choirs but for all believers, it was simpler in style and set texts in the language of the congregation. Here again the great Reformers were in touch with the temper of the time – with the Renaissance confidence in music as a skill all should master. And here again their Catholic contemporaries were not far behind them, developing the spiritual madrigal as a more popular genre of devotional music. The new, Reformation-period desire for church music that would exert an emotional grip on the listener or singer is also clear in the Iberian tradition, which remained decisively Catholic. Here too, as much as in Luther's Germany or Calvin's Geneva, religious feeling could be communicated in settings in the language of the people, whether that were Spanish, Portuguese or indeed Nahuatl, as in two short praises of the Virgin Mary attributed to Hernando Franco (1532–85), who was the first composer to cross the Atlantic, and who became head of music at Mexico City Cathedral in 1575.

Catholic–Protestant proximity, even when differences were being expressed in burnings and torture, is perhaps most apparent in music from sixteenth-century England, where ecclesiastical authority switched several times. During the long life of Thomas Tallis (c. 1505–1585) the English church became independent of Rome but still Catholic and Latin in its worship under Henry VIII, more aggressively Protestant under Edward VI (reigned 1547–53), who oversaw the printing of the first English prayerbook, Catholic and Roman again under Mary I (reigned 1553–8) and once more Protestant under Elizabeth I (reigned 1558–1603). Not much of Tallis's music can be dated, but it is clear he maintained certain elements of style all through. Honouring the English tradition he inherited from Taverner and the

Eton Choirbook composers, he often used boys' voices in exuberant high traceries and was more reluctant than continental contemporaries to abandon modes other than major and minor: hence the tones of plaintiveness and restraint that Anglican music inherited from him. If his settings in English are usually simple and homophonic (having all the parts move together in chords), the same is true of his beautiful Latin hymn *O nata lux* (O light born). And flamboyant polyphony to Latin texts remained an option under Elizabeth, as in his spectacular motet *Spem in alium nunquam habui* (I have not hoped in any), resoundingly laid out for eight choirs of five voices apiece and probably written in the late 1560s. Tallis seems to have composed this extraordinary work in response to the Italian tradition of polychoral writing that Willaert had instituted, but in other respects he and his colleagues in Elizabeth's chapel were following a wholly native path. The more pervasive influence of Italian music was to come a generation later, and not in motets but in madrigals.

Rather curiously, the Italian madrigal in mid-century was still dominated by foreign composers – by Willaert and by a new generation of Netherlandish composers who had followed the familiar path to Italy. Cipriano da Rore (1515/16–65) and Philippe de Monte (1521–1603) travelled as young men in the early 1540s; the somewhat younger Orlando de Lassus (?1532–1594) and Giaches de Wert (1535–96) arrived later in the same decade as boys, brought for their excellence as singers. Noblemen and bishops in both Italy and Spain still looked to the Low Countries as music's source, though these four composers were among the last in that crowded line going back to Du Fay – with the difference that their contemporary value as musicians depended not only on their voices and their presumed genes for polyphony but also on their Italian vitality and polish. Lassus was a prolific all-rounder who produced over two thousand settings of texts both sacred and secular, the latter including French and German songs as well as madrigals, but the other three musicians were famed above all as madrigalists. Moreover, Italian madrigals were required of Lassus and de Monte even during their long periods at the German-speaking courts of Bavaria and Austria respectively. All four moved the madrigal towards a greater seriousness, sometimes with words by noted poets (Petrarch, Tasso) and often with harmonies whose acute expressive effects came from disturbing the newly stabilizing major or minor tonality with chromaticism, i.e. using notes foreign to the scale.

The favourite subjects for such madrigals – the pains and griefs of love – were what they had been for the songs of Du Fay, Machaut and the troubadours. But now there was a fully coherent harmonic style against which dissonance could have the intensity of a bodily wound or an ache, as Zarlino recognized in advancing the possibility of harmonies that would be 'somewhat hard and harsh' or 'softer and somewhat more languid'. Italian madrigals of the mid-sixteenth century were beginning to speak directly of the emotions, to work on the listener's interior self with the same immediacy as did the music of the Reformation, Catholic as well as Protestant, which had, after all, learnt its new ways from secular song. Moreover, like church music this often poignantly private art was being voiced in public arenas. By now music printers were at work in many different cities in Italy, France and the Low Countries, with madrigals among their wares – along with dance music and, of course, French polyphonic songs where Parisian publishers were concerned.

Music suited to amateurs singing in domestic circumstances, and published as such, could also be courtly entertainment. Rore, Monte and Lassus were all court musicians,
and when the ruler of Florence, Ferdinando de' Medici, was
married in 1589, the event was marked with sequences of
madrigals and songs strung together as interludes within a
theatrical display, *La pellegrina* (The wanderer). The impetus
for this extravaganza came from groups of artists and connoisseurs who gathered regularly in Florence in the 1570s
and 1580s to debate the great Renaissance theme of ancient
Greek music. Similar discussions were taking place in Paris,
where the focus was on the rhythm of song (hence experi-
ments in applying classical metres, interpreted in terms of
short and long notes), but the Florentines were more directly
concerned with how music's fabled power could be restored.
Among them, Vincenzo Galilei (1520s–1591), father of the
great scientist, openly challenged Zarlino in his *Dialogo della
musica antica, et della moderna* (Dialogue on Ancient and
Modern Music, 1581). Ridiculing the madrigalian technique
of word-painting, whereby any affective word or phrase had
to be underlined musically ('false deceits', 'unyielding rock',
'cruel woman' are among his on-target examples of the
clichés of madrigal verse), he advised musicians to consider
rather how a great actor would declaim the words when in
character, and so find 'the accents and gestures, the quantity
and quality of sound, and the rhythm appropriate to that
action and to such a person'. Music was thus set towards a
new model, in rhetoric, and a new genre: opera. The Medici-
wedding interludes, rooted in the madrigal but with elements
of the new dramatic solo style, provided a starting point.
Their chief author, the poet Ottavio Rinuccini (1562–1621),
who had grown up in the circles of which Galilei was a
member, was soon to write the first opera libretto.

Spectacles of magnificence, whether staged in palaces, theatres or churches, were by now requiring the richest possible resources, and among the items in *La pellegrina* were several examples of the new sinfonia (symphony), a word coined to denote a concourse of instruments. The imminence of opera was thus also the imminence of the orchestra. Where church music is concerned, the great polyphonic masses, psalms and motets of composers from Gombert and Morales to Palestrina and Lassus were all published and copied as purely vocal compositions, but that is not necessarily how they were always performed. Groups of wind players were playing in Spanish cathedrals from the 1520s, and a manuscript collection of psalms by Lassus has an illustration showing a group of perhaps twenty performers on assorted instruments: keyboards, bowed and plucked strings, woodwinds. Possibly this was only a virtual orchestra, assembled to create a properly sumptuous effect in the reader's imagination, but certainly there were instrumentalists of diverse kinds performing regularly at St Mark's in Venice, where Zarlino in his last years was joined by a young musician who had probably studied with Lassus: Giovanni Gabrieli (c. 1555–1612).

Composing also from 1585 for the most prestigious of the city's benevolent societies, the Scuola Grande di San Rocco, and for its great hall sumptuously decorated by Tintoretto, Gabrieli wrote pieces for up to five groups, or choirs, of performers in different parts of the space: motets with singers and instrumentalists, and sonatas or canzonas for purely instrumental resources. The instruments available to him would have been as various as those in the Lassus illustration, and included one that, introduced early in the century, had until recently been used only for dance music: the violin. Thomas Coryat, an English traveller present for a ceremony at the scuola in 1608, was stupefied: 'Sometimes there sung sixteen or twenty men together, having their master or moderator to keep them in order; and when they sung, the instrumental musicians played also. Sometimes sixteen played together upon their instruments.' Such numbers of performers, all playing different parts, were evidently exceptional (if not for Gabrieli), but Coryat's amazement surely came also from the drama of this music – from how one group would seem to answer another, like an echo, or like a response in a dialogue. Just as the movement towards opera went along with increasing richness of colour and the arrival of the individual expressive voice, so Gabrieli's quite different kind of theatre was bringing music a new sort of continuity: not the old-style contemplative working of a theme in imitative polyphony but something more like conversation.

The composers of *La pellegrina* belonged to the same generation, among them Luca Marenzio (1553/4–99), who owed his fame to an astonishing output of thirteen madrigal books published during his eight years (1578–86) serving a d'Este cardinal in Rome. Lively in spirit and versatile in its response to words, his music found a wide audience: it brought him an invitation to Poland, and was instrumental in the founding of the English madrigal school at the hands of Thomas Morley (1557/8–1602). Morley was at the front, in England, of music's move from an aristocratic world of patronage into the bourgeois marketplace: he was principally an entrepreneur and publisher. Having set up shop in 1593, he brought out English-language arrangements of madrigals by Marenzio and others, composed songs himself, published a guide for amateur performers (*A Plain and Easy Introduction to Practical Music*, 1597) and stimulated a flurry of madrigal composition from younger musicians, notably

John Wilbye (1574–1638) and Thomas Weelkes (?1576–1623). The three volumes produced by the latter as a very young man (1597–1600) contain some of the most splendid items in this repertory, and though he died still in middle age, he outlived the genre, for the great flowering of the English madrigal was confined to hardly more than the last decade of Elizabeth's reign and the first of that of her successor, James I. It thereby coincided with Shakespeare's working life.

Nor were madrigalists the only musicians in Shakespeare's London – the city that had overtaken Paris as Europe's most populous – for among other contemporaries, if only as an occasional visitor, was John Dowland (?1563–1626). He, as much as Morley, looked back to old Italian genres, but in his case the lute song, of which he published his first volume in 1597, and the dance piece. Melancholy was his greatest theme – not so much the anguish of love as the grave wisdom of the solitary, who prefers contemplation to the shallow pleasures of society. Drawing on techniques developed in the madrigal, of expressive chromaticism and word-painting, he changed their effect. Where madrigals were by their nature social, Dowland's was a lone voice, in crucial ways his own voice, as poet, composer and performer. His most pessimistic songs, seeming to speak one to one, draw the listener into this pluriform subjectivity.

Meanwhile the doyen of English composers, William Byrd (c. 1540–1623), was moving towards a splendidly creative retirement. Like Dowland he was a Catholic, which made his life in London more arduous when, in the later 1570s, the legal sanctions against adherents of the old faith were enforced with greater vigour. He was an old believer, too, in his musical style, maintaining the polyphony of his youth, in music growing as if naturally from imitations of a pregnant motif. In 1575 he had collaborated with Tallis to bring out a volume of Latin motets honouring the queen. Now, around 1590, with his old friend and master dead and the new generation of Morley (a pupil of his) and Dowland about to assert itself, he gathered his works into several large collections, including two more of Latin motets, two of English settings (contrapuntal as ever, intended principally for a solo voice with viols) and one of harpsichord items (*My Lady Nevill's Book*, containing fantasias, variations and dances, especially pairings of slow pavane with quick galliard). Then he left the city for the country home of a Catholic nobleman, Sir John Petre, and devoted himself to writing music for celebrations of the mass that had, of necessity, to be clandestine.

Byrd in his later years was reflecting back on a time when music had been a commonwealth, a time when the masses of Palestrina, the motets and madrigals of Willaert and Lassus, and even the Anglican settings of Tallis had all spoken the same language of imitative polyphony, consonant major-minor harmony and expressive word-setting. By now that uniformity was breaking down from internal strains. Expressivity, which could only come from chromaticism and so from bendings or floutings of normal harmonic progressions, endangered the clarity and consistency of mid-century harmonic polyphony. The emergent system of major and minor keys would need another century and more of development before it was rich and resourceful enough to accommodate a fully expressive polyphony in the music of Bach. Meanwhile, the pursuit of expression was often a flight from polyphony, towards a new model of flexible melody for solo voice over an accompaniment essentially of chords, as in Dowland's songs or those of his contemporaries in Florence. The alternative, when polyphony was retained, might involve bringing the strains of the time to the surface: hence the music of Carlo Gesualdo (c. 1561–1613).

Gesualdo was notorious in his time, as he is still, for having murdered his wife and her lover together in bed. His music is hardly less extreme. Writing entirely for voices in five or six parts, he created harmonies of a very unusual type, dense with chromaticism and drifting free in their progressions. Stability has gone. The music seems to be melting as it considers the common topics of emotional and spiritual pain – not least in three volumes published in 1611: two of madrigals and one of music for the tenebrae services celebrated on the three evenings before Easter in commemoration of Christ's death. Long regarded as eccentric, such music did not begin to exert its spell until its world of intensely chromatic harmony had at last become normal: then its audience included Stravinsky, who in 1957–60 replaced lost parts for three Gesualdo motets and scored madrigals by the composer for instruments – having recently produced a response to Gabrieli in his *Canticum sacrum*. Stravinsky's ears may have been more acute than his contemporaries', but he shared the tastes of his time, and both Gesualdo and Gabrieli were among the composers whose rediscovery dates from the age of long-playing records.

In their own time they belonged to a world that was passing – that world of modal polyphony moving towards major-minor harmony. Perhaps the two greatest masters to reach maturity in the 1550s and 1560s, Palestrina and Lassus both died in 1594. Their younger colleague Tomás Luis de Victoria (1548–1611), who may have trained with Palestrina in Rome, had gone back to Spain to serve the royal convent in Madrid, and after composing a magnificent six-part

Requiem in 1603 for the dowager empress – a work whose harmonies blaze from a context of serenity – he wrote nothing more. Byrd, too, spent his last years in creative silence. The grand tradition of sacred polyphony continued at the outer edges of the western world, in the work of Manuel Cardoso (1566–1650) in Lisbon and of Juan Gutiérrez de Padilla (c. 1590–1664) in the Mexican city of Puebla. Then that sun went down.

CHAPTER 7

To speak in music

Maybe the great polyphonic tradition, which had developed continuously through the two centuries from Dunstable to Byrd, had aged, reached a natural conclusion, but its end was surely hastened by what was perceived at the time as a new style. Not for the first time in musical history, and certainly not for the last, the new way had its detractors as well as its champions, the former including in this case an Italian monk, Giovanni Maria Artusi, who in the epochal year of 1600 published a discourse on 'the imperfections of modern music'. His argument was mainly with harmonies and harmonic progressions that broke the rules, his implicit standard being Zarlino, though the authors he actually cited were the more prestigious ancients, including Boethius. By this date any amount of music might have fuelled his scorn, but the piece he chose to castigate — while preserving its composer's anonymity more out of contempt, one guesses, than delicacy — was a madrigal, *Cruda Amarilli* (Cruel Amaryllis), by Claudio Monteverdi (1567–1643).

Like many negative critics, Artusi aimed well. Monteverdi was far more industrious and professionally ambitious than the slightly older Gesualdo. Born in the northern Italian city of Cremona, he had published a volume of motets at the age of fifteen, and in his early twenties had gained a position at the highly musical court of nearby Mantua, under the much admired Wert. He was doing well, and looked like doing better. *Cruda Amarilli* was a good target, even if Artusi's objections were to musical strategies expressive of the text in ways that were half a century old: dissonances for 'amaramente' (bitterly), for example, or a sudden access of quick values for 'fugace' (evanescent) – exactly the kind of thing that Vincenzo Galilei had ridiculed nearly twenty years before, albeit from a very different point of view. For Artusi these mimetic moments created 'a tumult of sounds, a confusion of absurdities, an assemblage of imperfections'. Those responsible for such 'monstrosities', he averred, 'think only of satisfying the sense, caring little that reason should enter here to judge the composition'.

In that he was right. Writing to defend his brother, in a preface to a book of lighter madrigals published in 1607, Giulio Cesare Monteverdi explained that the intention was 'to make the words the mistress of the harmony and not the servant', which meant that rationality and rule would have to give way to verbal expressiveness. He too advanced a classical authority for his point of view, Plato no less. Music obedient to the rules of harmony he described as exemplifying a 'first practice' (*prima pratica*), which had been followed by composers from Ockeghem (extraordinary to find his name remembered into the seventeenth century, by which time his music was far further forgotten than it is now) to Willaert. But there was also a 'second practice' (*seconda pratica*), by which melody and harmony were bent to the text, and which the greater Monteverdi, according to his fraternal apologist, placed as having been instituted by Rore, with successors including Wert and Marenzio.

Two names Giulio Cesare also mentioned as adherents of the 'second practice' were those of Jacopo Peri (1561–1633) and Giulio Romolo Caccini (1551–1618), though their works were of a very different character from his brother's. Their speciality was not the five-part madrigal, of the *Cruda Amarilli* kind, but 'monody', or music for solo voice, for they belonged to the circle of Florentine musicians and connoisseurs that had been given intellectual leadership by Vincenzo Galilei. Caccini, who was a singer as well as a composer, waited until 1602 before publishing a volume of songs and madrigals for solo voice with instrumental accompaniment, a volume he was not too diffident to entitle *Le nuove musiche* (The New Music) and to back with a preface as proud and defiant as Giulio Cesare's. His idea of innovation turned out to be not so different from Willaert's in the last 'New Music', nearly fifty years before: he wanted, as he put it, to achieve 'the imitation of the ideas of the words'. But these songs were for a solo singer, enabled to 'almost speak in music'. Music was to be heightened speech, though Caccini also allowed for 'canzonettas for dancing' that would be distinct from expressive music. If this distinction was often elided (a good deal of Monteverdi's music, for instance, is dance-like and impassioned at the same time), the two ideals, to represent movements of the body and of the psyche, remained essential to music of the next century and a half, and the 'second practice' had as much to do with dancing rhythms as with the desire to, as Caccini's preface put it, 'delight and move the affections of the soul'. In that respect, too, there were precedents, for the same alternatives of dance and soulfulness exist in the madrigal repertory, both English and Italian, and in Dowland's songs.

The music of Peri and Caccini differed importantly from Dowland's, though, in that a fully composed accompaniment

was replaced by a 'basso continuo' (or, to use the com-
moner, briefer term, 'continuo'), a musical part indicating
just the bass line with numerals to show notes that must be
sounded in the harmony (e.g. '5' for a fifth). This continuo
might be rendered by a keyboard instrument, a lute or a
small ensemble, and the device was to be used with
much the same conventions by composers up to Bach and
Handel. It offered flexibility not only in instrumentation
but also in timing. An accompaniment that was a sequence
of chords, not a web of polyphonic lines, could be adjusted
more easily to the variable tempo (speed) a singer might
adopt in the effort to 'almost speak in music', whether
the topic concerned the joys and pains of love and self-
discovery, as in the solo songs and madrigals of Monteverdi
and the Turin-based Sigismondo d'India (c. 1582–1629), or
those of the spirit, as in the 'ecclesiastical concertos' – at
this date the term implied no more than music for several
performers together – of Lodovico Viadana (c. 1560–1627)
and the solo motets of Alessandro Grandi (c. 1575–1630),
who studied with Gabrieli and became an associate of
Monteverdi's. From the urge towards vocal expressiveness,
then, came a new texture, in both secular and sacred music,
of melody in primary position with harmonic support – the
texture of song as it would be known down to the present.
Also, by encouraging composers to think principally in
terms of chords, and most especially triads, continuo writing furthered the slow emergence of the major-minor
system.

   As Galilei had recognized, the new style allowed a singer
to be an actor, to express the feelings of a particular
character rather than, as in the madrigal, a general type
(mostly in that case the happy or languishing lover). Music,
in true Renaissance fashion, was becoming the possession of

the adequately endowed individual, just as time itself was, through the spread of the watch, of which the earliest dated example is from 1548. People now had personal relationships with time, and their music, too, was personal.

This representation of the personal by the personal, of a character by a singer, was what made opera possible, and here too Caccini and Peri were at the forefront, together with the poet Rinuccini and the Florentine patron of them all, Jacopo Corsi. Their first experiment, following up the 1589 interludes, was *Dafne* (1598) with words by Rinuccini set by Corsi and Peri. Two years later Corsi had his artists collaborate on *Euridice*, devised as a wedding gift for the Medici princess Maria and Henri IV of France. Peri and Caccini then rushed into print with rival settings of this same libretto. Both, though, were far outshone by the treatment of the same subject produced in 1607 in Mantua by Monteverdi, who may have seen the Peri–Caccini *Euridice* at the Franco-Florentine marriage celebrations.

Monteverdi's *Orfeo* is a marvellous marriage itself, of madrigal (where the chorus is involved), dance-song and the new expressive monody, which the composer seems to have been trying out for the first time. As he immediately recognized, the powers of passionate song are greatly increased by a dramatic context that places the character in a particular situation – a position of entreaty in this opera's most celebrated number, 'Possente spirto' (Powerful spirit), where Orpheus, sung by a tenor, persuades the infernal boatman Charon (a semi-comic bass role) to break with custom and ferry him, alive, into the empire of the dead. At other moments in the opera Monteverdi pursued, even more assiduously than Caccini himself, the ideal of music as tuned speech: a powerful example is the solo for the Messenger who brings Orpheus news of Eurydice's death. But 'Possente spirto' has to display, within the drama, music's powers in itself, over and above its capacities to enforce words. Orpheus changes the ways of the universe by the charm of his song, and accordingly his solo to Charon carries melodic grace and beauty — together with embellishments the composer wrote out — in addition to its underlining of verbal sense. Like the greatest songs, from the troubadours to the twenty-first century, it projects melody that is at once beautiful and urgently expressive.

Orfeo confirmed yet another innovation that sprang from the new monody: the possibility of a musical work of scale and weight outside the church. Where Byrd's songs or Palestrina's madrigals are inevitably less imposing than these composers' masses, after 1600 opera offered a large form that was thoroughly secular, and from this point church music became opera's daughter, emulating its solos and dramatic construction. Particularly was this so in Venice, where Giovanni Gabrieli's music had already provided an example of sound-drama; Monteverdi's arrival there in 1613 was almost a historical necessity. A century after Petrucci, Venice was still the main site of music publishing, and Monteverdi had been supplying the city's presses for three decades. Among the volumes so generated was one of music for the evening service of vespers, *Vespro della Beata Vergine* (Vespers of the Blessed Virgin), published in 1610 and containing clamorous psalms and other big pieces, in the Gabrieli line, interspersed with motets featuring a solo voice or duet. Just as *Orfeo* was the first great opera, so was this the splendid prototype of church music as quasi-opera, and it took its place firmly and fully in the concert repertory when the exploration of music before Bach began to accelerate in the late 1960s.

As master of music at St Mark's, where Willaert and Zarlino had served a long half-century before, Monteverdi produced further splendiferous settings for vespers and the mass. He also seized operatic invitations he received from back in Mantua and from Venetian magnificos, for one of whom he produced a compact opera for narrator, two characters and string group with continuo, *Il combattimento di Tancredi e Clorinda* (The Battle between Tancred and Clorinda), based on an episode from Tasso's epic of the crusades. This piece he published in his eighth book of madrigals (1638) — still so called, though the contents include duets as well as small-scale musical dramas, besides items more conventionally madrigalian.

In his preface to this volume, entitled *Madrigali guerrieri et amorosi* (Madrigals Warlike and Amorous), Monteverdi speaks of the 'principal passions' of our minds as three in number: 'anger, moderation, and humility or supplication'. Finding examples in earlier composers of temperate and soft music but not of agitated, he set himself to rediscover a kind of musical expression he concluded had been lost since Plato's time. By his own account his research was directed not only by reading the ancient philosophers but also by practical experiment, from which he discovered that rapid reiterations of a note would produce the effect of excitement he sought. Tasso's text, with its graphic depiction of a battle to the death, then gave him the opportunity to try out his new style, not just in the vocal melody but equally in the accompaniment. Early in the piece, for example, the strings eagerly indicate the movements of Tancred's horse as it paws the ground before galloping forwards.

Even so, Monteverdi's expressive means are principally vocal, and the *Combattimento* is a brilliant exposition of the new monody. Most of the piece is delivered by the narrator

in recitative (speech-like vocal delivery, often keeping to a
single reciting note), which allows the singer to introduce
inflections of rhythm and colour that will give the mono-
tone words expressive shape and value. But there are also
passages where melody carries the expression onto a new
plane. A striking example of the contrast comes near the
midpoint, where the narrator tells of the combatants'
exhaustion as night falls. His description is largely in recitative, but when he turns from surveying the present to
foreseeing the future of death and shame, he rises into
melody, and by the simplest gesture – an upward slur
through two notes on the exclamation 'O' – achieves the
utmost poignancy. For the printed version Monteverdi
added production notes, whose wording shows how novel
the concept of sung drama still was. He also recalled here
how the original audience, experiencing the piece during
the carnival season (which then lasted in Catholic Europe
from Christmas to Lent, and was the principal time for
spectacle and entertainment), 'were so moved to feelings
of compassion it was as if they would weep'.

Those incipient tears testify to the realization of a
Renaissance dream, that of making music able to speak of
the motions of a person's body and mind: of haste and
anger, of fatigue and sorrow, of stillness and fear. But the
means used by Monteverdi and his contemporaries –
monody, continuo, the texture of solo line with accompaniment, harmony directed by triads and the major and minor
scales, clear phrases and dancing metres – were, as the
Artusi controversy showed, rendering polyphony, the musical language of the Renaissance, more or less obsolete. That
point was made quite early, in 1607, in a manual of continuo
playing written by the Tuscan musician Agostino Agazzari
(c. 1580–1642): 'If anyone objects that a bass will not suffice

to play ancient works, full of fugues and counterpoints, I shall reply that music of this kind is no longer in use.' Monteverdi's fulfilment of the Renaissance has therefore been seen as, simultaneously, the beginning of a new period in music history, the Baroque – a term that entered common currency only when the music of the seventeenth century did, in the middle decades of the twentieth.

To the innovations of the early seventeenth century may be added the orchestra, the companion of opera. The kind of ensemble that was probably just a picturesque fantasy in Lassus's Munich, around 1560, was a reality half a century later, when Monteverdi, in the first edition of his *Orfeo*, printed in 1609, listed a similarly mixed grouping of thirty-nine players. Soon afterwards, and certainly by 1618, the first regular orchestra was instituted in Paris, the 'Vingt-quatre violons du roi' (Royal Twenty-Four Violins), that term embracing a full complement of string instruments whose players would accompany the partly sung ballets that were a speciality of the French court.

The development of the orchestra as a self-sufficient musical body had to await another, later seventeenth-century invention: the concert. For the moment orchestras were assembled for special occasions and always to accompany voices, whether in opera, court celebration or church music. However, the increasing demands such occasions made on instrumentalists – coupled with a wish these instrumentalists no doubt shared, to emulate the athletic display and expressive power of vocal music – brought greater attention to solo instrumental music and greater virtuosity, for where the lute and keyboard music of the sixteenth century had been written principally for amateurs, the early seventeenth century was the first great age of professional performers.

Among instrumentalists playing at St Mark's under Monteverdi was Biagio Marini (1594–1663), who might have led the violins when the *Combattimento* was first put on. He wrote sonatas for his instrument, with continuo, as interludes for liturgical celebrations, instituting a form that survived over wide areas of Catholic Europe to the end of the eighteenth century. Meanwhile the Amsterdam organist Jan Pieterszoon Sweelinck (1562–1621) and the Roman musician Girolamo Frescobaldi (1583–1643) were producing keyboard pieces in various forms: polyphonic inventions (often called ricercares or fantasias) that kept alive the old style to convey it onwards in the direction of Bach, toccatas (literally 'touched' pieces) exploiting the fingers' ability to move rapidly and evenly over the keys, and fantasias full of, indeed, fantasy. At a time when new standards of visual and sonorous beauty were being set by family firms of instrument makers – including the Amati, who established the great violin tradition in Cremona, and the Ruckers, building in Antwerp the finest harpsichords – Marini, Sweelinck, Frescobaldi and other composer-performers were following up the previous century's discoveries in matters of how an instrument's playing technique and sound qualities would suggest particular possibilities and challenges: songfulness through long phrases in high registers in the case of the violin, ingenuity under a lutenist's fingers or dazzling speed on the harpsichord. These instruments were, within the language of the early Baroque, gaining their own repertories and their own dialects.

Varieties of musical style were arising, too, in different cities and countries, for several reasons. Most importantly, music that was speech-like would obviously vary with the language, and since the mid-sixteenth century composers had been called upon increasingly to set texts in everyday tongues, as well as in the ecclesiastical Latin that had supported the great works of earlier times. Moreover, the division of Christendom – with a firm if disputed boundary established between Catholic states (in Italy, France, Spain, Austria and southern Germany) and Protestant (in northern Germany, Britain and Scandinavia) – now rendered the church music of one sphere useless in another. Monody, emphasizing the word, made linguistic differences more crucial, so that, for example, Italian melody, setting a language that already when spoken has pitch contours, marked accents and the possibility of extended vowels, developed differently from French, which is uttered in a much more even manner in terms both of pitch and of rhythm. Questions of culture, temperament and philosophy were also involved. For instance, French composers in the first half of the seventeenth century, writing lute songs and music for court masques (verse dramas incorporating song and dance), maintained a national concern with poetic quantities and accordance with nature, which in France meant having the sung words comprehensible, whereas what was natural in Italy was melodiousness and the enjoyment, for practitioners and listeners, of the act of singing.

National differences were noted by the German theorist Athanasius Kircher (1601–80) in his compendious *Musurgia universalis* (1650), but as he saw it, 'Italy justly appointed to itself the first place in music from the beginning.' Though that 'beginning' could hardly have been placed before the time of Palestrina, certainly by Kircher's time Italy was setting the tone for music throughout German-speaking Europe and beyond. The new continuo style, and the new expressiveness, introduced the possibility of quick changes in tempo and loudness, and these were marked with Italian terms that have survived in international use, such as presto (very fast), allegro (fast), andante (at walking pace) and adagio (slow), or piano (soft) and forte (loud). Also, instrumental music, in growing, inevitably grew into new kinds of musical form, and these gained Italian terms that similarly spread across western Europe: sonata, sinfonia, concerto – terms that as yet were malleable and almost interchangeable – as well as the more particular toccata and ricercare. Sometimes the new music and its terminology were learned by German composers at first hand. Heinrich Schütz (1585–1672), who spent most of his long adult life writing church music for the Protestant court at Dresden, studied with Gabrieli and returned to Venice in his forties, when he had discussions with Monteverdi. His friend Johann Hermann Schein (1585–1630) drew on Viadana in what he wrote as choirmaster-composer at St Thomas's in nearby Leipzig. And Michael Praetorius (1571–1621), in several published volumes, brought Italian style to Lutheran music and also made French dance music available in Germany.

From such dances came the form that was gaining dominance in consort music by the 1620s: the suite, a sequence of dance movements that would start with the pavane–galliard pairing of the previous century and regularly include another two pieces, similarly slow and fast. Schein wrote pieces of this kind for viols, while his contemporaries in Britain, such as Thomas Tomkins (1572–1656), preferred the more old-fashioned, more polyphonic form of the fantasia. Music for viols was music for home use, and quite without the pristine intensity of the new opera or the flashiness of the new Venetian church music. But in all these media of the early seventeenth century was the same slow continuing move from the old modes to a harmony based on scale and key. This turned out to be the period's most significant discovery – music that spoke not so much through verbal patterns, however urgently that principle was applied by Monteverdi, as through a new kind of tonality, a kind that would carry the art through the next three centuries.

PART IV

Time known 1630–1770

In concentrating on how music could speak, or dance, the first decades of the seventeenth century had found little alternative to the rapidly decaying, or positively moribund, Renaissance polyphony as a way of making music move of its own accord, without the support of words or dance themes. The period's instrumental music was still very often polyphonic in the old manner, if with a greater emphasis on a single guiding theme, examples ranging from Frescobaldi to Tomkins. Alternatively, the impulse could come from virtuosity, the constant achievement of the formidable conveying a sense of continuity. But the gradually increasing grip of the new tonality, of major and minor keys, reached a point around the middle of the century where new principles of purely musical form could be discovered. A piece in D major, for instance, gained stability from keeping more or less to the notes of the D major scale, but it also acquired dynamism. Whatever harmonic venturings it might undertake, the D major triad would have to be its ultimate goal. And in reaching that goal it could draw on harmonic forces fixed by convention and experience – such as the conclusive force of the perfect cadence, where a chord of D major (the tonic) comes immediately after one of A major (the dominant). So powerful was this effect that it was generally reserved for the endings of pieces and sections. Other chords and notes would similarly have their distinct functions, like words and phrases in a sentence. By utilizing these functions – normally along with a principal theme, or melody, to give a piece definition and character – composers could create music that moved through time with consistent purpose towards a clear endpoint.

This process was normally assisted by a more emphatic rhythm than in earlier music, within a consistent metre (e.g. three beats to a bar, in a strong–weak–weak sequence). The metres often came from dances, but they could be applied in music that did not follow the regular phrases of a dance. What they offered was pulse and pattern, a kind of internal clock to measure the progress of the harmony, out of which came a new logic, a reassuring sense for the listener of always knowing where the music was going and at what speed. Indeed, the importance now of the listener, and therefore of music's purely aural sense (as opposed to other sorts of sense it might make to performers), may have helped stimulate the arrival of key-based harmony, theme-based structure and metrical rhythm.

All these changes were noted at the time, not least by Schütz in a memorandum he drafted to his employer, the ruler of Saxony, in 1651, when he was in his mid-sixties. The old ways (which had been new ways half a century before) were boring the young. A colleague had been told to his face 'that a tailor of thirty years and a cantor of thirty years are of no use to anyone'.

This development was taking place during a period when time itself was becoming more cognisable. The pendulum clock – proposed by Galileo in 1641, and fully realized in 1657 thanks to the Dutch scientist Christiaan Huygens – gave people a measure of time accurate to within a few seconds in the day. Time was now as absolute and knowable as space. And it was to this absolute, knowable time – this clockwork time – that the music of the next century and more fixed itself. The great age of mechanical clock-making, up to the last of John Harrison's marine chronometers (1770), was also the era of music that proceeded through time with a mechanical elegance and constancy, and yet that found – in these same phenomena of harmony and rhythm that made continuous flow possible – the means for expressing anew divine grandeur and human joy and poignancy. This was the music of what was called, when it came to be known again in the twentieth century, the Baroque.

CHAPTER 8

Baroque mornings

Music's history during the half century from 1630 to 1680 was unusually complex, a diverse and crowded scene with no dominant figures such as, at least in retrospect, Monteverdi was in the decades before. While different genres and national traditions pursued their separate paths, and even intensified their differences, tangled interconnections led from one to another. For example, the German organist-composer Johann Jakob Froberger (1616–67) studied with Frescobaldi before becoming attached to the Austrian imperial court. He also listened to news from Paris in cultivating the suite, a form continuously refreshed by the favour shown dance music at the French court under Louis XIII (reigned 1610–43) and Louis XIV (reigned 1643–1715). This French touch Froberger may also have transmitted back to Paris through contacts with the first great harpsichordist-composers there: Jacques Champion de Chambonnières (1601/2–72) and Louis Couperin (c. 1626–1661). During the same period in Italy the preferred virtuoso instrument was the violin, while in British homes the viol consort maintained its sway, with the new-style suite adopted alongside the old-style fantasia in the music of such composers as John Jenkins (1592–1678), William Lawes (1602–45) and Matthew Locke (c. 1622–1677). Just about the only feature that was common internationally was the gradual stabilization of major-minor tonality, and here the suite, with its dance movements, may have helped. Suites were dances for the ear rather than the limbs, but still their dancing phrases, equal in length and closing in cadences of a few formalized types, brought greater clarity and direction to harmony. To that extent the keyboard virtuosos in Paris and the viol consorts in British country houses were moving in the same direction. At the same time the Italian violin, in its dash, was still remembering its dance origins and the same harmonic definition.

Recalling this period, the English musical polymath Roger North (1651–1734) wrote of the music-making in the household of his grandfather Lord North (1582–1666), when family members and servants would get together to play as a consort of viols supported by the house organ or harpsichord. But while the Norths were thus entertaining themselves at home, music was finding vastly larger audiences in the new opera houses of Italy. The first operas, such as Monteverdi's *Orfeo*, were private palace festivities, as were the court masques of contemporary Paris and London. Public opera started in Rome, thanks to the munificence of the Barberini family (including the ruling pope, Urban VIII), who in 1632 founded a theatre seating three thousand. From there, in 1637, the vogue sparked imitation in Venice, where Monteverdi, now in his mid-seventies, was available to contribute four scores, of which the two that survive are *Il ritorno d'Ulisse in patria* (The Homecoming of Ulysses, 1640) and *L'incoronazione di Poppea* (The Coronation of Poppaea, 1643), based respectively on Homer and on sordid events in the life of the emperor Nero. Unlike *Orfeo* these late operas have little to do with dance and madrigal, and presuppose modest instrumental resources, comprising perhaps only a small group of strings with continuo. Public opera was commercial opera; lavishness was restrained except where there was a demand for it, which was in the scenic devices and in the singers. Accordingly *Ulisse* and *Poppea* are composed largely of song, and the pattern of the *Combattimento*, alternating between recitative and melody, is more formalized. Another difference from *Orfeo* is in dramatic style. The innocent, pastoral, outdoors atmosphere of the earlier opera has been exchanged for complex social interactions and intrigues, involving individuals living lives of high passion in worlds that also include clown figures.

To realize these roles came a new kind of musician: the opera singer. As in all later ages, high voices were valued for their excitement, the voices of female sopranos and of castratos (male singers who had been castrated before puberty to preserve their voices unbroken). No sooner had public opera begun than the scarcity of such singers who could fill large theatres and large roles was apparent, so that remuneration and ego had to be on the same scale. Much of opera's extravagance and aura, therefore, dates back to this time. New, too, was another phenomenon opera helped further. The vast majority of people in the Barberini theatre were not singers, nor were they instrumentalists or stage hands. They were listeners. Where the secular music of the sixteenth century had been directed principally at those who would perform it – singers, lutenists, keyboard players and viol consorts, all making music at home – opera presumed a big audience of listeners. Similarly, Venetian church music, from Gabrieli to Monteverdi's successors, was made to amaze and delight those who heard it.

Such ostentation was spreading from Europe's most ostentatious cities, Venice and Rome. Schütz wrote the first

opera in German, *Dafne* (1627), to a version of the old
Rinuccini libretto. The first Italian opera performed abroad
seems to have been an *Orfeo* by the Roman composer Luigi
Rossi (?1597/8–1653), given in Paris in 1647 on the order
of the Italian cardinal Mazarin, who controlled France during the minority of Louis XIV. Antonio Cesti (1623–69)
learned his trade as an opera composer in Venice and went
on to produce an eight-hour feast of sumptuousness, *Il pomo
d'oro* (The Golden Apple, 1668), for the court in Vienna. In
London the first true opera, sung throughout, was *The
Siege of Rhodes* (1656), which most likely – its music is lost,
like Schütz's for *Dafne* – owed less to Venetian opera than
to homegrown and Parisian traditions of court masque. But
Paris style was about to be decisively altered by further
Italian immigrants. Francesco Cavalli (1602–76), who probably studied with Monteverdi and certainly took after him as
a composer of church music and opera, was invited to the
French court to create *Ercole amante* (Hercules as Lover,
1662). Surely present in the audience, since he held posts at
court, was another Italian who had been brought to France
as a boy and had Frenchified his name: Jean-Baptiste Lully
(1632–87).

Lully recreated opera in the French spirit, inventing a
new kind of gently melodious and rhythmically flexible
recitative suited to the language, emphasizing the dance
element (often the drama is got over as quickly as possible,
so that an act may flower in a sequence of dances), making
the onstage world reflect glory on that attending from the
other side of the footlights (with Louis XIV implicitly
addressed as primary audience member) and maintaining,
even through song, the poetry and acute expressivity the
French appreciated in the tragedies of the composer's contemporary Jean Racine. The librettist Philippe Quinault,

Lully's regular collaborator in the works he produced almost annually between 1673 and his death, was a joint creator. In other respects Lully's achievements were purely musical. His overtures (opening orchestral movements) established what has become known as the 'French overture', whose slow and imposing beginning is followed by lively fugal music (i.e. having a theme developed in imitation in the manner of a fugue). Not only did this kind of overture become the almost invariable norm in France, it was also a model for Purcell, Handel and Bach. So was another form to which Lully gave a standard aspect: that of the chaconne or its almost indistinguishable relative the passacaglia, either one consisting of variations over a repeating slow bass, and representing a peak moment in the grandeur and dignity of the opera.

Holding a licence from the king that gave him a monopoly of opera sung throughout, Lully was the most powerful composer in the Paris of his time, and his works held the stage for decades after his death (where Monteverdi's were almost immediately forgotten), defying successors. In other fields, though, composers of the generation after Lully maintained this as a gloriously creative period in French music, if a period almost forgotten until the late twentieth century. As in the Venice of Gabrieli and Monteverdi, music was an instrument of statecraft, a display of magnificence and leisure. And, again as in Venice, the message could be conveyed in church as much as in the opera house, as it was in the majestic sacred settings of Marc-Antoine Charpentier (1643–1704) and Michel-Richard de Lalande (1657–1726). There were also composers who created whole worlds writing just for their own instruments: Marin Marais (1656–1728) at the viola da gamba (cello-sized viol) and François Couperin (1668–1733) at the harpsichord. Their music, being mostly in suite form, honoured dancing as much as did Lully's operas – or, indeed, Charpentier's vivid church music.

Thanks to the political strength and cultural prestige of France at this midday of the Sun King's reign, French music had an influence outside the country, not least on composers in London under the Francophile monarch Charles II (reigned 1660–85), who founded a string orchestra modelled on that of his cousin in Paris. By far the outstanding composer in England at the time, right from his late teens, was Henry Purcell (1659–95). He was a striking personality, even in an age favouring brilliance and individuality, after something of a mid-century lull. In his case musical character came to some extent from the clash of styles, French (as also Italian) and English, bringing about corresponding harmonic mismatches. In England the glow of music from a century before was felt far more strongly than it was in France or Italy, partly because that had been a great age in English music, the age of Byrd, Tallis, Dowland and the madrigalists, and partly because the music of the national church had been formed then. Purcell, who wrote pieces for viols that looked back to the sixteenth century, had the old modes in his blood as he embraced the new tonality, and the result was a harmonic boldness unknown again until the later Wagner or even Stravinsky. Still another distinction he flagrantly ignored was that between the cultivated tradition and folksong. Most of his music is vocal, comprising theatre scores, Anglican anthems and odes for royal occasions, and often a number with a folksong's fresh simplicity will sit alongside a virtuoso showpiece or a skilfully tossed-off piece of counterpoint.

His short opera *Dido and Aeneas* (c. 1685) shows these incongruities and the effect they create, of a piece wrenched out with passion to portray passion. Dido, as befits a queen, is a noble character, and her contributions include two big numbers that, being solos, take Lully's chaconne form and make it movingly inward: 'Ah, Belinda' near the beginning and the great deathward lament 'When I am laid in earth' towards the end. Also French is the overture. But the piece includes as well many folksong-like episodes and others of broad comedy. Purcell probably wrote it for performance at a girls' school, whereas his other dramatic works were intended for the public theatre, which had no place for fully sung opera. Plays would include songs, and perhaps also dances and interludes for strings; more ambitious were the semi-operas, in which masque-like sequences of songs and dances were interposed into a spoken drama. As opportunities for music at court dwindled after the death of Charles II, Purcell became far more active in the public theatre, his semi-operas including *King Arthur* (1691) and *The Fairy-Queen* (1692).

London in Purcell's time was still the largest city in Europe, with a population of around half a million, accounted for in substantial part by young men and women who had come seeking work. Hence the demand, from the successful, for entertainment, and the opportunities for Purcell, as a composer of extraordinary fertility, to write not only music for court, church and theatre but songs and instrumental pieces that could be performed at home (from editions put out by a busy publishing industry in the city) or in new contexts: the pleasure gardens and concert rooms. Here he would have been writing for people of his own generation. John Banister (1624/5–79), an erstwhile member of the king's violin band, is credited with instituting the world's first public concerts, by 1672. By 1678 there was a purpose-built concert hall near Charing Cross. Also in 1678 the first German-language opera house was opened in another city that was developing as a commercial, bourgeois centre, Hamburg. Generally, though, throughout Europe the pattern of patronage was as it had been for centuries, support coming from monarchical courts, citified aristocrats or church authorities, with the last particularly important in north German cities (including Hamburg), thanks to strong choral and organ traditions in the Lutheran church.

That church possessed, unusually at this time, a kind of music that was popular in tone and well suited to congregational singing: the chorale. German composers could therefore depend on ready appreciation of – and, where appropriate, participation in – works that used chorales, including organ arrangements as well as cantatas (pieces for singers and instruments) for Sunday and holy-day worship. With these strong roots, defined partly by the language, German music gained an individual character that extended through the seventeenth and eighteenth centuries to be revived in the nineteenth (by Brahms) and twentieth. But German church musicians, who were often also organists, had another inheritance, which came from the contrapuntal expertise and instrumental virtuosity of Sweelinck. Through Sweelinck's German pupils a style of organ composition that combined learning with fantasy descended to the next generation of Dieterich Buxtehude (c. 1637–1707) in Lübeck, Johann Pachelbel (1653–1706) in Erfurt and Nuremberg, and several members of a musical family prominent in the central German region of Thuringia: the Bachs. Rather as in France and England, a rich mid-century culture of gifted but unexceptional musicians was giving rise, by the 1670s, to stronger talents. Pachelbel, though essentially an organ composer, was responsible for what has latterly become a Baroque hit, the canon from a piece for three violins and continuo. Buxtehude had the broader range, his output encompassing organ pieces, chamber music (music suited to domestic surroundings, requiring only a few performers) and sacred cantatas.

In Catholic areas of Germany, as in the Austrian and Spanish empires, music inevitably went in a different direction, open to composers and styles from Italy. Italian opera was maintained at the imperial court in Vienna (after Cesti) and also in Munich, while Italian manners affected the region's church music. However, the foremost composer was not an Italian. When music of this period in Germany and Austria started to be more deeply explored, around the end of the twentieth century, the two composers who came to seem most valuable were Buxtehude in the north and, in the south, his Bohemian contemporary Heinrich Biber (1644–1704), who spent almost his entire working life in Salzburg. Biber was a virtuoso violinist as well as a composer, and, besides church music in a magniloquent polychoral style descending from St Mark's in Venice, he produced a large quantity of violin music with continuo. With its flurrying scales and split triads, its multiple stops (chords made by playing on more than one string at a time) and altogether its bravado, this is music that springs from the nature of the instrument, while showing also how the instrument can voice passion and contemplation.

By the time Biber was writing his fifteen sonatas on the mysteries of the rosary (?1674) the violin was established as the principal non-keyboard instrument throughout Europe, with its main vehicle of display the Italian-born sonata, now commonly a sequence of movements contrasting in speed and character. Purcell in 1683 published a book of trio sonatas (sonatas for two violins and continuo), which his preface promised as 'a just imitation of the most fam'd

Italian masters', whose 'seriousness and gravity' he invoked. At the same time, in Cremona, Antonio Stradivari (c. 1646–1737) was bringing the art of violin making to what has long been acknowledged its peak.

Whether Stradivari's instruments travelled to London or Salzburg is uncertain, but they surely sounded in Rome and Venice, which remained the two leading musical centres in Italy. As Venice's importance had declined, so Rome's had increased, the music-loving cardinals joined as patrons by the exiled Queen Christina of Sweden, who lived in the city from 1655 until her death in 1689. Among musicians who wrote and played for her were Giacomo Carissimi (1605–74), better known for the opera-style narrative oratorios he composed for devotional performance in church, Alessandro Stradella (1644–88), the harpsichordist Bernardo Pasquini (1637–1710) and the violinist Arcangelo Corelli (1653–1713). Opera was still being produced in Rome, and Stradella and Pasquini composed such works, but Christina also associated herself with a different Roman tradition, of chamber music embracing cantatas and sonatas.

In an atmosphere of refined and repressed eroticism – for Christina was probably more celibate than the cardinals around her, all listening perhaps to a castrato singing a cantata of anguished love, or to Corelli performing with his pupil-lover in the duetting trio sonatas that formed the bulk of his output – music could speak of what could not be spoken. It would be hard to imagine circumstances more different from those of the theatres, halls and parks where Purcell was meeting his public. At the same time Corelli's music held the appeal of calm rationality, against which the sonatas of Biber or Purcell would surely have seemed outrageous and bizarre. He established two kinds of form, the church sonata (*sonata da chiesa*), most commonly having four abstract movements in slow–fast–slow–fast order, and the chamber sonata (*sonata da camera*), which took dance types from the suite and in some cases was composed entirely of such movements, prefaced by a prelude. Sonatas were indeed made for church or domestic use, though it is not clear that Corelli intended a distinction of function. His sonatas, of whichever sort, resemble in their elegance and lucidity the classical buildings of Rome, both the ancient and those rising in his own time. Phrases are even, and flow smoothly under the control of major-minor harmony and regular metre. The music is gloriously imperturbable, whatever joy or melancholy it may wistfully evoke. And it was fully in keeping with Corelli's disciplined creative nature that he should virtually confine himself to six published volumes, of twelve compositions apiece, it being quite normal through to the end of the eighteenth century to assemble instrumental works, whether printed or not, in groups of twelve or six. Of Corelli's collections, the first four (1681–94) are devoted to trio sonatas.

A late arrival in Christina's circle was the Sicilian-born Alessandro Scarlatti (1660–1725), whose career swung between Rome and Naples. He effectively founded the Neapolitan school of composers that was to dominate the next century; more than that, he stabilized the form that became inescapable for composers of Italian heroic opera everywhere: opera seria (serious opera). Like Corelli, he was an orderly artist, and made it his business to create rationality even in this most irrational form. His serious operas (he also wrote comedies) involve great personages in antique or exotic locations, and thereby summon situations in which immoderate behaviour – singing – is justified. Form, too, he clarified. In place of the fluid interweaving of simple recitation and song in earlier opera, his works

alternate strictly between recitative and aria, the former just
with continuo accompaniment (as became the norm), the latter
having vocal showiness set off by the orchestra. He also,
towards the end of the century, established an unvarying aria
form, the da capo (from the top), in which the opening section
is repeated after a contrasting interlude. This form lasted as
long as opera seria and, meanwhile, quickly entered instrumental music, a sphere that gained, too, from another Scarlatti
innovation. In 1687 he introduced a new variety of overture,
with fast–slow–fast sections, known as the 'Italian overture' in
distinction from the French. Here was the beginning of a genre
that would be taken up across Europe with the burgeoning of
concerts and concert halls: the symphony.

Italian music was disseminated through publications such
as Corelli's and in manuscript. There were also Italian
musicians, both immigrants and travellers, to be heard far
beyond the Italian sphere of musical influence, in Paris and
in London. The Neapolitan violinist Nicola Matteis, for
example, arrived in London in the 1670s and surely helped
Purcell towards his 'just imitation', while a little afterwards
Italian castratos were singing at the new public concerts.
Moreover, Italy was the regular destination for gentlemen
tourists from France and Britain, who could hear this music
on its home ground. Among them was François Raguenet,
who visited Rome in 1697 and published a comparison
between French and Italian opera, in which the former is
praised for the beauty of Quinault's librettos, for its majestic
bass voices and for its dances, though the author's enthusiasm for the vitality of Italian song and singing is undis-
guised. 'It is not to be wondered', he concludes, in a
contemporary translation, 'that the Italians think our musick
dull and stupifying.'

This antinomy between Italian music and French (German and English being of no account in Paris at the time) was to be argued in France for decades, and cross-fertilization was to affect the art in both regions. But, as was probably unknown to anyone outside England, the two cultures had already been brought into an exuberant fusion in the music of Purcell. And, in the even more remote sphere of Latin America, the spirit of the Italian Baroque, only lightly modified in passing through Spain, had been united with lively indigenous rhythms in the music of Juan de Araujo (1646–1712), working in the region of present-day Peru and Bolivia.

CHAPTER 9

Fugue, concerto and operatic passion

What music gained most immediately from Italy, right across Europe, was the mellifluousness and poise admired most of all in Corelli. The system of major-minor harmony, enmeshed with regular rhythm and phrase structure in smooth, clear forms, had fully arrived, and with it came music that sounds wonderfully straightforward – at least to those listening in a culture this music partly created. Notes seem to follow their courses with natural ease. A great period was beginning. Soon after 1700 there appeared – to join Corelli, Couperin and Alessandro Scarlatti – a brilliant new generation of composers who would ensure the triumph of the new harmony's lucidity and range through the first third of the eighteenth century. Johann Sebastian Bach (1685–1750), George Frideric Handel (1685–1759) and Alessandro's son Domenico Scarlatti (1685–1757) were almost exact contemporaries, and their lives overlapped closely with those of Antonio Vivaldi (1678–1741) and Jean-Philippe Rameau (1683–1764). From these composers, and from this period, came some of the earliest works in the basic classical repertory: the set of six Brandenburg Concertos, each for a different orchestral assembly, which Bach in 1721 dedicated to the ruler whose name they have perpetuated; Handel's *Water Music* (1717), also for orchestra, written to accompany a royal boating party on the Thames in London; and Vivaldi's set of violin concertos entitled *The Four Seasons* (1725).

People at the time recognized that a change had come. In 1726 a group of gentlemen amateurs in London set up an Academy of Ancient Music to keep alive the repertory of the sixteenth and seventeenth centuries, providing the first evidence of a taste for the past that was, by the mid-twentieth century, to overwhelm musical life. But the full extent of the change – the full richness of the high Baroque – may be visible only with three centuries of hindsight. Bach knew the music of Vivaldi – an unavoidable eventuality, the latter's concertos being so much in fashion – but took them as subject matter for improvement. Handel drank down Corelli and other Italians during the three years or so he spent in Italy as a young man, but he probably had little acquaintance with Bach's music and did not trouble to meet his most formidable musical contemporary. The two existed, though contemporaneous, in different worlds. Handel's operas, written for London, were hardly performed anywhere else. Most of Bach's music was similarly conceived for local conditions, within the Lutheran tradition he inherited from his family. Far better known was Georg Philipp Telemann (1681–1767), who worked in Hamburg, had connections with both Bach and Handel, published voluminously (as they did not) and drew on all available traditions, German, Italian and French. By contrast again, the younger Scarlatti, working from 1719 as music master to a Portuguese princess who became queen of Spain, largely constrained his abundant imagination to constantly varying a single form, the keyboard sonata, and published only one small volume – but not until 1738, when it sparked off an international Scarlatti craze but was too late to have any effect on Bach or Handel. Similarly little known, because created within an exclusively French tradition of keyboard playing and notation, was the music of Couperin — another late starter, or at least late finisher, since most of his publications date from after he was forty-five, memory allowing him to survey a whole range of human types and human behaviours with a benign irony. Still more patient, Rameau waited until he was past fifty before producing his great works, which therefore belong to a later period.

Working in separate cultures and circumstances, and composing for immediate needs that were very different, these composers are unlikely to have considered themselves colleagues in endeavour. Nor could they have imagined their music would be prized three centuries later, at a time as distant from them as they were from Ciconia and Dunstable — which is some measure of how comparatively close their music appears to us, simply because its new harmonic language was to prove so extraordinarily fecund and long-lived. Even so, their full familiarity is, in some cases, quite recently acquired. Some of Bach's keyboard music was known to Mozart and Beethoven as study material, but his biggest work — the St Matthew Passion (1727), a narration of, and contemplation on, the crucifixion of Christ written for performance in church on Good Friday — had remained unheard for almost a century when Mendelssohn conducted it in 1829, and it took another century before more than a very small proportion of Bach's music was at all regularly performed. Much of Handel, too, was neglected until the twentieth century. Even Vivaldi's *Four Seasons* was not much known before the arrival of the long-playing record, after the Second World War. And growing interest in the music of Bach's Catholic contemporary in Dresden, Jan Dismas Zelenka

(1679–1745), or in that of Domenico Zipoli (1688–1726), who spent his last years in South America, shows the period in a process of reappraisal that may be its constant feature.

Its music, though old, is thus also new. And those relatively few works of longstanding celebrity have gone on being renewed through changes in taste. Indeed, no music has changed more since recording began. Bach's Third Brandenburg Concerto, for example, was richly Romantic and symphonic when played by the Berlin Philharmonic under Wilhelm Furtwängler in 1930, but has taken on distinctively contemporary mixes of vivacity and antiquarianism in performances by any number of more recent outfits. The same score can be heard in a four-hand piano arrangement by the German composer Max Reger from 1904–5, and as music for virtual instruments thanks to the US electronic artist Wendy Carlos, whose version has its own historical perspective, since the original of 1968 was remade in 2000. Bach's music, it is often said, can survive any amount of transformation, but to the extent that this is true – and the Brandenburg examples invite us to think about what we mean by a 'work', about how performance and arrangement may convey, enhance or caricature a score – it is true also of Handel's, which provides similar examples. Equally, the music that Bach and Scarlatti wrote for the harpsichord happily suits the piano. Nor has Baroque music changed only in sound, for we listen to it (as to so much) under quite different circumstances – not, for instance, gathered in church on Good Friday as the original Leipzigers were for the St Matthew Passion, but perhaps seated in a concert hall or at home. Yet we may feel no less touched. Not only can the logic of the notes survive any alteration of the sounds, but this is still our language.

One result of the high Baroque relish for logic was the increased importance of standard formal types, such as the piece in two sections, each repeated, the second serving to mirror and answer the first – the principle of the Scarlatti sonata and of the dance movements so frequent in Bach's instrumental works. The combination of clear symmetry (repetition, mirroring) with systematic change (proposition–answer) was characteristic of the period, and may be found also in such vastly widespread and outwardly unalike forms as the da capo aria, the fugue and the concerto. Of these, the da capo aria was ubiquitous not only in opera seria but also in sacred works and cantatas. The fugue, too, could suit many purposes. Though today associated particularly with Bach, fugues were written by most composers from Germany, where the skills of combining old-style counterpoint with new-style harmony had been maintained through Sweelinck's pupil-progeny. The preferred genre for fugues at this point was keyboard music, and often such works would have a closing function, capping a prelude, toccata or passacaglia, by virtue of their culminative form. Baroque musicians, whether composers or performers, brought to their work an understanding gained from the science of rhetoric, and the projection of a fugue, from exposition to peroration, is like that of a speech.

Biology offers as apt a metaphor, for a fugue is like a process of growth, and – as in such a process, ideally – everything will unfold from the nature of the germinal material. A fugue starts with a melodic subject, which is more or less precisely imitated by the voices that enter in turn, nearly always to a total of four. Once all the voices are in play there will usually be a break from strict imitation, probably so that some element in the subject can be developed. Then the fugue proceeds, through imitative passages and episodes, all related to the subject, which in later stages will often be introduced in inversion (i.e. with all its intervals turned inside out, the rising ones falling and vice versa, so that the shape is recognizably the same and yet otherwise) and augmentation (with doubled note values, creating a grand slowing fitting for the approach to the end).

Bach's organ fugues generally have the amplitude to fill a large church, and perhaps to impress a large congregation with the composer-executant's double expertise, but the preludes and fugues he wrote for domestic keyboard are addressed to those whose fingers play them. He put together a book of twenty-four such pieces, in all the major and minor keys, and gave it the title *Das wohltemperirte Clavier* (The Well-Tempered Clavier, 1722) to draw attention to how a performer could indeed play in all these keys on an instrument that was suitably tuned. This was a problem because of a discrepancy in nature between different ways of dividing the same interval. For example, an octave should be equivalent to three major thirds (e.g. A–C♯, C♯–F, F–A), but if these latter intervals are tuned to their pure frequency ratio (5:4), their sum turns out to be a little less than an octave. The thirds thus have to be stretched to fit, and, as the major-minor system gained sway in the later seventeenth century, greatly enlarging the varieties of key and chord in use, so musicians came up with different temperaments, different ways of tempering the intervals so that all kinds of harmonies could be used. What temperament Bach favoured is a matter of dispute, but certainly his volume proves the value of some human intervention in the natural order. Despite that, whether the harmonic progressions are wondrously serene, as in the C major prelude that opens the book, or unsettled and unsettling, as in the G minor prelude and fugue, the effect is of nature being sounded, or sounding itself. Goethe felt this: 'I told myself it was as if eternal harmony conversed with itself, as perhaps it did in the bosom of God, shortly before the creation of the world.'

If the fugue was essentially a German form, the concerto was everywhere. Its origins were Italian, as the term implies: concertos, now more strictly defined, were pieces for instrumentalists concerting together. The first examples came around 1700, from composers including Giuseppe Torelli (1658–1709) in Bologna – whose immense basilica of San Petronio encouraged Baroque composers to fill it with the sounds of instruments, often including a solo trumpet or violin – and Tomaso Albinoni (1671–1751) in his native Venice, still one of the most musical cities. Albinoni is remembered now for a piece he did not write, an adagio in G minor put together in 1945 by an Italian music historian, Remo Giazotto, on the basis of a few bars. But he has a real place in history as the composer who, in 1700, published the first concertos adopting the fast–slow–fast pattern of movements Alessandro Scarlatti had brought to the operatic overture. His fellow citizen Vivaldi repeated the pattern hundreds of times, in works that circulated rapidly and widely. Bach made keyboard versions of several and wrote concertos of his own besides the Brandenburg set, adding something of musical interest to the vivacious alternations between soloist or soloists and full ensemble he inherited from his most notable Italian contemporary. Among composers in England, including Handel, the preferred model was Corelli, who codified in his last, posthumously published volume (1714) the concerto grosso, an expansion of the trio sonata in which two violins served as soloists, again alternating with the full ensemble.

The omnipresence of the concerto was partly due to the omnipresence now of its etymological relative the concert. Telemann in the early years of the eighteenth century founded a 'collegium musicum' as a regular forum for music-making in the university town of Leipzig, and this was still in existence in 1723 when Bach succeeded to the post of composer-choirmaster there. Bach's main duties were for the church, to write, rehearse and perform a cantata almost weekly as a contribution to the principal service, but he also found time to write for the collegium. In Venice concert-like services, including sonatas and concertos as well as settings of the sacred texts, drew fashionable audiences to the institutions set up for the city's large population of illegitimate children: Vivaldi held an appointment at one such refuge for girls from 1703. In Paris the most prestigious concert series was the Concert Spirituel, founded in 1725 and similarly devoted to mixtures of sacred and instrumental music. Meanwhile Handel, in London, had access to the richest concert life in Europe, which also brought to the city a succession of other foreign musicians, either on tour or to stay.

Composers and performers came to London, too, for the opera. Like François Raguenet, many English gentlemen had been enraptured by opera in Italy, and they wanted more back home. In 1705, therefore, a company was set up to present Italian opera, and it was this that took much of Handel's attention after his first arrival in 1710. Singers were imported from Italy, as were rival composers, all bringing with them the customary operatic trail of extravagance, egotism and intrigue, but stimulating also from Handel some resplendent scores. His librettos he took largely from the Italian repertory, having them adapted to suit him and his singers but by no means changing the conventions whereby, in particular, da capo arias were most commonly placed so as to provide dramatic exits. The repeating thrills of one solo number after another (if with recitative in between), flung out by gorgeously attired and emotionally electrified personages on the point of leaving the scene, were modified only at the end, when all the characters, including any who had died in the course of the action, would join in a chorus. As in Italy the principal male characters were sung by castratos, so that almost the entire piece would be a manifestation of high voices – voices that could express the rage, delight or pain that arias dealt in, and could express, too, the ambiguities and absurdities of self-presentation that Handel explored. Inordinately expensive (because of the fees paid to the star singers, all Italian), lampooned in the press and subject to ferocious backstage rivalry, opera in London swerved through its own operatic course of triumph and disaster, leaving behind many Handel works that, for the most part, did not return to the stage regularly until the 1980s, as sufficient counter-tenors arrived to take over the heroic roles written for castratos, and as producers and audiences came to appreciate an art that combined glamour with sublimity, imposture with intensity.

Bach's great essays in musical drama – his St Matthew Passion and its predecessor based on St John's gospel (1724) – come from exactly the time when Handel was busiest with opera, producing, for example, *Giulio Cesare in Egitto* (Julius Caesar in Egypt, 1724) and *Rodelinda* (1725). In some respects the contrast is extreme. Bach was telling a story in which each member of his audience – his congregation, rather – would feel immediately and openly involved, whereas the narratives of Handel's operas, as was the way in opera seria, were placed in outlandish locations from which the principal characters could strike back startlingly to arouse secret doubts and desires. To view the contrast differently, events in Bach's Passions are set in an immense frame of narration and commentary, whereas in Handel they take the stage. Furthermore, where Handel was addressing only the wealthiest in a wealthy city, Bach's Passions required no entrance ticket. Then again, in Bach the centre of gravity lies in the bass soloist singing as Jesus, in dialogue with the tenor Evangelist who presents the story, whereas in Handel the excitement is all at the top. Handel's arias are mostly fast and showy, and often they would have been made more so by the addition of a cadenza (a flourish the singer could add at will): after all, a star does not quit the stage without making sure of applause. Bach's singers, on the other hand, were not going anywhere, and ovations for them would have been out of place. Their tempos could accordingly be calmer – and should be, given the occasion.

But there were also similarities between the two types of work. The typical Handel opera is laid out for six singers, normally including two castratos and two or three leading women (*Giulio Cesare* is unusually rich in having eight roles), to be accompanied by a modest orchestra plus continuo, and the evidence suggests Bach's cantatas and Passions would have been sung by forces of similar size. Both Bach's arias and Handel's were sometimes cast as quasi-duets, with a solo instrument leading and shadowing the vocal line. Also, although the balance of recitative and aria is quite different in the two genres – for each of Bach's Passions is centred on the recitative, since this is where the sacred text is being pronounced – Bach's arias, like Handel's, are in da capo form and bring the unfolding narrative to a moment where time slows down. It does so for different reasons – expression in Handel, reflection in Bach – but it does so into the same musical form and with the same concentration on single kinds of emotion.

To take examples from works whose first performances were only six and a half weeks apart, the alto aria 'Es ist vollbracht' (It is finished) from the St John Passion shares with Cleopatra's 'Piangerò' (I will weep) in *Giulio Cesare* a contrast between slowness in the outer sections and speed in the middle part, corresponding to tones of lament that leads into active hope, from which the lament can be re-engaged with greater equanimity. Of course, the situations could scarcely be further apart. The alto in the St John Passion has just heard Christ's dying words, which he or she repeats (this might have been a boy in 1724, more likely a woman now), considers, and springs from in seeing the Saviour's death as a victory. Cleopatra is singing only of herself, at a point when she has been caught in a web of political-sexual manoeuvres she did much to promote, and what makes her speed up is the prospect of returning as a ghost to torment her enemies. Yet not only do both arias have the same formal shape, their outer sections share features that were widely recognized as proper to laments. Besides the slow even pulse, these characteristics include descending lines in the melody and particular keys: B minor in the Bach and E major in the Handel. Minor keys often imply melancholy or tragedy, not only in eighteenth-century music; similar associations for E major were more particular to the time in question. The music itself shows this, of course, but explicit support comes from the prolific theorist-composer Johann Mattheson (1681–1764), who as a young man was a close friend of Handel's, and who categorized E major as 'deadly sad'.

It is because music of this period makes so much of symmetry and repetition that any single section tends to have a certain kind of expression that is maintained through to the end. Indeed, the da capo aria's contrast depends on this, that the mood can be suddenly changed and instantly restored, almost at the flick of an emotional switch, and it is essential to the nature of Baroque musical drama, whether operatic or sacred, that the soloists express themselves in extended instants of constancy, even when what is constant is violently impassioned. This was more than a narrative convention, for the same singleness of expressive purpose is found equally in instrumental music, achieved by the same means of tonality, melodic figure and rhythm.

The expressiveness of rhythm was another subject Mattheson considered, particularly with respect to the dance rhythms that underlie so much of the age's music — not only its suites but also its choral numbers and arias. For example, he described the typical courante, a slowish but flowing dance, as 'directed towards a tender longing'. But he was fully aware, too, how musical feeling can fluctuate, despite the consistent tone conveyed by key and metre. Remarking on an old courante tune, he notes that at first 'there is something of the courageous in the melody', after which 'a longing is expressed', exactly as he earlier said was a mark of the form, but 'a little joy arises toward the end, especially in the last bar'.

There are courantes in the suites Bach wrote for keyboard, for solo cello and for solo violin, and they may indeed be felt to convey hints of longing, courage and joy. But they also insist that each piece has its own feeling and identity, that what it means is what it is.

CHAPTER 10

Rococo and reform

When Bach, writing to the Leipzig authorities in 1730, remarked that 'taste has changed astonishingly, so that the former style of music no longer seems to please our ears', he was thinking back to the music of the previous generation, and to how the full establishment of major-minor harmony had rendered earlier music strange. But taste was changing still, and in 1737 Johann Adolph Scheibe published a criticism of Bach's music as 'bombastic and confused', which it could only have seemed because its insistence on contrapuntal working – on fugue-like patterns of imitation ticking away whatever the context – had gone out of style.

Handel's variety of opera seria was going the same way. In 1728 the London dramatist John Gay (1685–1732), who had previously collaborated with the composer, produced *The Beggar's Opera* as a stinging corrective to Handel's works, its mode of musical speech more like that of folk-song, albeit with some of Handel's music included. Soon afterwards Leonardo Vinci (c. 1696–1730) and other young composers, trained in the conservatories of Naples, began gaining an ascent over opera in Italy, introducing a style that, again, resembled popular melody in its short phrases and tunefulness. In this new world Bach was too learned and Handel too sophisticated. The younger generation's music favoured lightness, simplicity and immediate pleasure, qualities that characterize the rococo style in the arts, though with reference to music the term *galant* is sometimes used, with its allusion to a civilized gaiety of French bearing. A few years after dismissing Bach as quite un-*galant*, Scheibe was able to announce the composers whom he saw as representing the future in Germany: Johann Adolf Hasse (1699–1783) and Carl Heinrich Graun (1703/4–59).

These two lived very different lives. Graun worked for the music-loving Frederick the Great of Prussia (reigned 1740–86), whose composers also included Bach's son Carl Philipp Emanuel (1714–88). Hasse was much more of a cosmopolitan figure. Like Handel before him, he began his career in Hamburg and went to Italy, but he found no settled home after that, moving back and forth between Italy, where he took note of the new Neapolitan style, and the courts of Germany and Austria as opportunity came. He, too, enjoyed the patronage of Frederick the Great. He also had the esteem of the man who was recreating opera seria, the Austrian court poet Pietro Metastasio (1698–1782), whose librettos were set again and again by innumerable composers from Vinci, Hasse and Albinoni to Mozart and beyond. Metastasio's great gift was for eloquent imagery that would render the extreme emotions of opera seria suitable for decorous musical expression as befitted the period. Hasse set nearly all his librettos, including *Artaserse* (Artaxerxes), two arias from which the castrato Farinelli (1705–82) is said to have sung every night for ten years (1737–46) to alleviate the melancholy of the king of Spain, Philip V – while in another room Scarlatti was perhaps playing for the crown princess.

The topic of music as comforter, of a solo musician performing for a solitary hearer, recurs often in the history and legend of this period. Another example is the possibly apocryphal explanation of Bach's Goldberg Variations, an hour-long sequence of keyboard pieces published in 1741, as having been written for a boy, Johann Gottlieb Goldberg (1727–56), to play to his employer as a distraction from insomnia. Behind such stories lies a change in how performing musicians were valued, not so much now for public dazzlement as for private consolation. According to eighteenth-century anecdote, Farinelli changed his style from bravura to sentimental sweetness at the suggestion of the Austrian emperor Charles VI (reigned 1711–40), himself a great lover of music and a composer, but the singer is much more likely to have been influenced by, as in turn to have influenced, the composers of his generation who came as he did from southern Italy. From his late teens he toured Europe as one of the most valued performers of his time, and for three years before going to Madrid he appeared in London – not for Handel but for a competing company which, inevitably, had engaged a composer of the Neapolitan school: Nicola Porpora (1686–1768), who later, in Vienna, was Haydn's teacher. Handel responded to the change in taste by including simpler, squarer tunes, such as the gently noble 'Ombra mai fù' (Never was the shade, also known as 'Handel's Largo') that opens *Serse* (Xerxes, 1738). However, he soon abandoned opera.

Meanwhile solo instrumentalists as well as singers were contributing to the age's pursuit of delight. High among them were two violinists, the Italian Pietro Antonio Locatelli (1695–1764) and the Frenchman Jean-Marie Leclair (1697–1764), both of whom had studied in Rome within the Corelli tradition and gone on to become performers of a kind that

survived to the end of the nineteenth century: virtuosos
touring with concertos, sonatas and showpieces of their
own composition. But the two were evidently divergent
spirits. When they were induced to display their talents
competitively in Kassel in the 1720s, an observer reported
that Leclair played like an angel, Locatelli like a devil, so
contributing to another musical myth, that of the demoni-
cally possessed violinist. However, Locatelli's music hardly
sounds satanic as it toys with the simple song shapes of his
Neapolitan contemporaries, and any astonishment due his
twenty-four unaccompanied capriccios (1733) is on the
grounds of their technical feats – fountains of notes spray-
ing up and down at speed, melodies sounding from one
string while a trill (rapid alternation of two adjacent notes)
is held on another – rather than their substance. Bach, as
ever, provides a contrast with his collection of three sonatas
and three partitas for solo violin (1720). Locatelli's music is
meaningless without an audience to amaze (he found his
admirers after 1729 in Amsterdam, where Vivaldi's concertos were rolling from the presses). In Bach's the notes
speak for themselves.

Leclair was one of many musicians attached to the court
of Louis XV (reigned 1715–74), though in his case only
briefly. Versailles was the model for other rulers, not least
Frederick the Great in Potsdam, and the centre for music of
grace and delicacy. That these qualities could coexist with
keen expressivity, exciting rhythm, characterfulness, colour
and even oddity was proved by Rameau as he came out of
his long near-silence. Like composers two centuries later
and more, Rameau composed only once he had made sure
of the disciplines at his disposal, and in 1722 he began a
series of theoretical publications with a treatise on harmony,
a study which, for the first time, laid out the relationships

among chords in the major-minor system. More than that, it showed in its author a constant sensitivity to expressive values. 'There are,' Rameau declared, 'chords which are sad, languishing, tender, pleasant, gay and surprising'; and he demonstrated his knowledge – of how chords work with each other and of how they work on us – when he turned from speculation to write the succession of stage works that started spectacularly with *Hippolyte et Aricie* (Hippolytus and Aricia, 1733), *Les indes galantes* (Exotic Courtship, 1735) and *Castor et Pollux* (Castor and Pollux, 1737).

Outwardly these works followed the forms set by the hallowed Lully and his successors, with episodes of sung poetic drama and a good deal of dancing. However, the incisive attacks, strong instrumental colourings and vigorous rhythms of Rameau's dances, coupled with a variety of tone that cheerfully embraced the comic, disconcerted admirers of Lully's works, which were still in the repertory. Nor were fixed minds mollified by Rameau's rationalizing of the harmonies that produced such a moving effect in, for example, the aria 'Tristes apprêts, pâles flambeaux' (Piteous rites, faltering flares) from *Castor*. The term 'baroque' was introduced in a criticism of *Hippolyte*, with entirely negative connotations of extravagance and misshapenness. Rameau was not abashed, any more than by disputes over his harmonic theories: like others of this philosophizing era in French culture, he thrived on intellectual debate. Meanwhile taste moved his way, and by the late 1740s he was so popular that the Paris Opera was instructed by the government to limit productions of his works to two per season.

Soon afterwards controversy returned, for in 1752 an Italian company arrived in Paris to present performances of opera buffa (comic opera), including the ancestral example of the form, the compact two-hander *La serva padrona*

(The Maid as Mistress, 1733), which its composer, Giovanni Battista Pergolesi (1710–36), had designed to go between the acts of an opera seria, as light relief. From this work and others like it had arisen a new tradition of works involving contemporary characters in lighthearted tests of contemporary morals and social distinctions, a tradition that by 1752 included pieces by the Venetian composer Baldassare Galuppi (1706–85) as well as by the Neapolitans. So different from Rameau's operas, not only in their subject matter but also in their simple tunes, which Paris had not heard before from the source, the Italian imports stimulated a public argument between supporters and detractors, a paper war known as the 'Querelle des Bouffons' (Quarrel of the Comedians). Not at all harmed by the publicity, Pergolesi's music was soon creating an international frenzy, and his melodious *Stabat Mater* for two soloists with strings and organ (1736) became the most frequently published work of the second half of the eighteenth century. The Russian court, alert to western fashion, brought Galuppi to St Petersburg in the later 1760s, and Italian comic opera is said to have reached as far as Beijing.

Besides advertising the immediate charms of Italian music, the Querelle des Bouffons refreshed the old question of which music was superior, Italian or French. Jean-Jacques Rousseau (1712–78), a philosopher for whom music was a central issue, had no doubt. For him the essential criterion was closeness to nature, which he thought he could determine not only by philosophical argument but also by practical trial, seeing which music would mean more to someone who was, musically, in a state of nature, unadapted to any particular national tradition. In the immediate aftermath of the Querelle he found his experimental subject in an Armenian encountered in Venice. He had someone sing to this man an aria by Galuppi and a monologue from Rameau's *Hippolyte*, and he watched for the results. 'I observed that during the French song the Armenian showed more surprise than pleasure, but everybody observed that from the first bars of the Italian air his face and his eyes grew soft; he was enchanted.' Rousseau's explanation was twofold, adverting to matters of spoken language and musical style. The Italian language was softer, more adaptable; Italian melody had bolder modulations (transitions from one key to another) and a more dynamic handling of metre. A few years later, directly confronting Rameau, he asked: 'What do chords have in common with our passions?' For him the expressive agent was melody, 'imitating the inflections of the voice'.

Italian comic opera in the Neapolitan style did more than encourage argumentation. It also provided new models of musical behaviour, in its jaunty solo numbers, formally and expressively simpler than the da capo arias of opera seria, and, even more importantly, in its numbers for several characters (a genre rare in opera seria), where short phrases supported quick, witty altercations. Adapted to the instrumental domain, such music could create an abstract effect of conversation and buoyancy in which the dialoguing parties were not characters on stage but musical themes. Hence the symphony, whose origins were not only in Alessandro Scarlatti's opera overtures but also in the vivacity of the newer Italian operatic style, and in the still increasing importance of the concert. Like operas, concerts were expected to start with symphonies, the first expressly written for that purpose coming from Giovanni Battista Sammartini (1700/1–75) in Milan in 1732. Soon afterwards the genre was taken up in Vienna, in Paris and in Mannheim, whose rulers were making one of the most musical cities in mid-century Europe. Chief among the initial generation of Mannheim composers was Johann Stamitz (1717–57), who seems to have been the first to write symphonies in the four-movement form that would become standard: lively opening movement, slow movement, minuet (a dance with three beats to the bar) and top-speed finale. He was also a pioneer in creating abstract dialogue with themes in regular four-bar phrases, as in Italian comic opera, with a harmonic simplicity that had the same origin.

At a time when symphony and comic opera were the coming forms, Handel and Bach looked elsewhere. Handel in the 1730s turned his attention more and more from opera to a genre of his own invention, the oratorio in English, in which he could exercise his dramatic powers, avoid the expenses of Italian singers and theatrical production, and set himself within the English tradition of choral music, as he had in writing splendid anthems for the coronation of George II (1727). With oratorio he could also adapt to a shift in English taste, brought by the consolidation of a bourgeois audience in London, one which could not tolerate (or afford) the sensuous thrills of Italian opera but was very much at home with music promising spiritual elevation, in which sensuousness might still be included, but under wraps. Like Rameau at the same time, and at very much the same age, Handel produced a series of works in which characterful action cascades into creative enjoyment, his choruses corresponding to Rameau's dances. Among those works was *Messiah* (1741), which he revived annually in London from 1749 to the end of his life, continuing to do so, and to play the organ in a concerto to complete the programme, even after losing his sight.

Bach, also suffering from failing vision in his last years, was devoting himself to musical monuments: the Goldberg

Variations, the B minor Mass — a work on the scale of Handel's oratorios, but with its drama in music's majestic unfolding through solos, duets and colossal choruses — and two compendia with no prescribed scoring, *The Musical Offering* and *The Art of Fugue*. The latter — a set of fugues and other essays in strict counterpoint laid out with didactic rigour and illuminated by mastery — seems to stand outside time, to be the supreme example of how Bach's notes are so strong that their means of performance (organ, piano, string quartet, brass ensemble, orchestra) becomes almost irrelevant. By contrast, *The Musical Offering* emerges more from its specific epoch and shows Bach accepting the possibility of a dialogue between his native solidity and the sweeter touch of newer music. The work was the result of a visit he paid to his son Carl Philipp Emanuel at the court of Frederick the Great in 1747. Frederick enjoyed music nightly — like his fellow monarch in Madrid, but more actively, taking part as flautist and composer. Bach had the opportunity while with him to try out instruments of a kind that, though invented several decades earlier, was only slowly gaining acceptance: the piano. He also had the chance to demonstrate how he could create counterpoint spontaneously, when Frederick gave him a theme on which to improvise. Back home he quickly got down to a sequence of inventions on the royal theme: compact studies of its contrapuntal potential, thorough elaborations in three parts and six, and a trio sonata, all recalling the musical graciousness of the Potsdam court through a mind made for musical logic.

The blindness of both Bach and Handel at the end — whatever sorrow it may have caused them, and whatever pain and disappointment at the hands of the same English surgeon, John Taylor — has an aptness as metaphor, for their musical world was vanishing. Whoever wrote fugues or oratorios after them did so in their image. Music in the 1750s and 1760s meant concert music (including concerts at such courts as those of Versailles and Potsdam as well as in the public venues of London and other cities, and encompassing instrumental music of all kinds, from solo exhibition piece to symphony and concerto) and Italian opera. It also meant, often, a new search for what was seen in Rousseau's terms as closeness to nature — closeness to the truth of listening (and hence a more compelling, dynamic style of orchestral writing) and to that of feeling. And though concert and operatic life was still supported by the court in most great cities, music was being addressed more and more to the bourgeoisie. Publishers went on putting out concertos and the new symphonies, which could have been used only in grand households or at musical gatherings, but the business, particularly in London, was turning more and more to what could be performed and enjoyed in the modest home: songs, chamber music and volumes for the piano as it continued its slow rise. In 1761 Johannes Zumpe, a London piano maker, introduced the small 'square piano' for the same market.

The following year Handel's place as the city's leading composer was inherited by another immigrant, Bach's youngest son, Johann Christian (1735–82). Having spent some years in Italy, he could combine the latest Italian fashion with a probity gained from his father's teaching, and though he wrote operas, he recognized that the public's appetite was more for symphonies and concertos, songs and chamber music, which he wrote, presented in concert and published. Symphonies were also produced by his half-brothers in Germany, the versatile and prolific Carl Philipp Emanuel and the enigmatic Wilhelm Friedemann (1710–84),

but otherwise the main centres for orchestral music were at
the Mannheim court, still, and in Vienna, which rose rapidly
in musical prestige as its many aristocratic families took on
house orchestras.

Several young composers born in the 1730s were ready to
supply these with material, and they contributed to a Viennese symphony boom in the late 1750s and 1760s. Among
them Joseph Haydn (1732–1809) was spotted quite early as
a front-runner, for in 1761 he was taken into service by the
stupendously wealthy Esterházy family. During long summers away with the family on one of its great estates, he was
obliged to provide musical entertainment. As he recalled
forty years later: 'I was cut off from the world . . . and so
I had no choice but to become original.' This is not quite
true. He was aware of what his Viennese contemporaries
were doing (if nothing else he would meet them again as
princely life returned to the great city for each winter
season), and he incorporated their innovations, such as
giving the first movement a slow introduction to focus
attention. But certainly his symphonies of the 1760s are
all quite individual, and suggest a constant pleasure in
finding what could be done with the new form.

During this time the court opera in Vienna was in the
care of Christoph Willibald Gluck (1714–87), who, like the
London Bach, had learned his trade in Milan. Metastasio
was still the Austrian court poet, and Gluck set some of his
librettos after assuming his Viennese appointment in 1755;
he had, inevitably, grown up with them. But there was a
new spirit in the air, and Gluck was listening. In the very
year of his Viennese arrival Francesco Algarotti (1712–64),
a Venetian writer who had spent time in London, Paris and
at the court of Frederick the Great, published an essay on
opera advocating reform. Alluding to the longstanding

argument as to the relative merits of Italian opera and
French, he invited his countrymen to learn from their
neighbours – but on the same grounds that had caused
Rousseau to vote the other way, in the interests of naturalness. Metastasio he praised; his real quarrel was with the
Italian opera composer, for allowing musical forms (the da
capo aria, the constant alternation between orchestrally
accompanied arias and recitative with bare continuo) and
the vanities of singers to come before expressive veracity.

Several composers took note of Algarotti, or were
already thinking roughly the same way, including the two
most prominent members of the latest generation to emerge
from the conservatories of Naples: Niccolò Jommelli (1714–
74), who was working at the Stuttgart court, and Niccolò
Piccinni (1728–1800), still in Naples at the time. But the
credit for reforming opera went to Gluck and his *Orfeo ed
Euridice* (1762, adapted for Paris as *Orphée et Eurydice* in
1774). He and his librettist Ranieri Calzabigi (1714–95) did
everything Algarotti had asked: maintained the nobility of
the subject, placed poignancy far above display or musical
luxury, included dance as part of the drama, and had the
orchestra accompany throughout. This was almost as far as
eighteenth-century opera could go in constraining song to
the drama at hand; only Gluck's later *Iphigénie en Tauride*
(1779), written directly for Paris, is even more an opera
without frills, unrivalled as such until *Wozzeck* almost a
century and a half later. Reform had come, and Rousseau's
hopes had been answered, but at a magnificent endpoint.
The future, as always, lay elsewhere.

PART V

Time embraced 1770–1815

It can be heard arriving in Haydn's symphonies of the 1760s, a sensation of roundedness, as if a new, third dimension of time were being added to the flatness of earlier music. Where the key had previously been affirmed throughout a piece, and digressions been made (usually to the dominant, a fifth above) only to heighten a coming re-emphasis of the basic tonality, Haydn's music was more enterprising. The music of the earlier eighteenth century, however erratic it may occasionally be, does not deal in surprise. Haydn's does. The idea of melody voicing a particular emotion, by virtue of its shape, metre and tempo, and then of that melodious emotion being sustained through a movement without essential change, has given way to the expectation of fluidity. As the Italian violinist-theorist Francesco Galeazzi (1758–1819) put it in the treatise he published in 1796: 'The merit of a composition consists . . . in the conduct and not in the initial melody.' In ways that even Rameau may not have foreseen, expression was being led by harmony, by shifts, slides and fluctuations in harmonic character. These changes were comprehensible because the music followed a grammar of modulation while always keeping its ultimate goal – the home key – in mind. In a closer sense than before, music could be understood, followed.

Because harmony was now the bearer, rather than the supporter, of meaning, the old convention of the continuo became obsolete. There was no longer any freedom as to the choice and timing of chords, and so performers lost their flexibility here. Parts were now written out exactly as they were to be performed. Also, musical form changed drastically. The two-part pattern found, for example, in Scarlatti's sonatas and Bach's dance movements was still there, but the second part was not now, in this more dynamic age, a mirror of or answer to the first. Instead it would begin by treating ideas from the first part in a turbulent fashion, cutting them down to essentials and moving them into distant keys, and then would return to the first part, repeated more or less complete. This was the principle of sonata form, so called because it was almost invariable for the first movements of sonatas and like works (symphonies, string quartets). There would be a first part (the exposition), which would nearly always include contrasting themes in the tonic and dominant (or, for works in the minor, the relative major, the major key a third above). Then in the second part would come the stretching and straining of one or both of these themes (the development), followed by their restoration, now both in the tonic (the recapitulation).

Where music of the earlier eighteenth century keeps pace with the clock, Haydn's seems, by means of directed harmony and sonata form, to seize time into itself, to embody not only our observation but also our experience of time, our experience of change and process. Clock time is still there, not least in the metrical rhythm. But the harmonic progressions and the developments of the themes give the music almost our own condition of living, sentient being. We do not so much listen to this music as meet it.

This thinking music, having what we would like to believe is our own temporal condition of purposeful growth, belongs to a period when rationalism, after two centuries, had won its place in every field of human thought, the period known as the Enlightenment. Aimed at spreading knowledge and the arts, the Enlightenment favoured commerce, providing opportunities, in the musical sphere, for piano making and publishing. Muzio Clementi (1752–1832) led both enterprises in London, while Haydn's pupil Ignace Pleyel (1757–1831) did so in Paris. The upright piano, introduced by John Isaac Hawkins of Philadelphia in 1800, was rapidly taken up by other firms and assured the piano's steady penetration of the bourgeois home.

With regard to its music, this is often known as the Classical period, a term it gained soon afterwards, when musicians of the 1830s began to recognize that an age had passed. It was short. A composer given a decent span, such as Antonio Salieri (1750–1828), could live right through it. But its significance was and is inexhaustible.

CHAPTER 11

Sonata as comedy

A survey of musical Europe in the emergent Classical period might follow the trajectory of a young composer who was learning his art on the road: Wolfgang Amadeus Mozart (1756–91). Put forward by his father, though with as much care and pride as ambition, Mozart played at the age of six for the ruler of Bavaria in Munich and at seven for the empress Maria Theresa in Vienna. Soon the family left their home in Salzburg for a trip that lasted over three years, including long periods in Paris and London, where the boy encountered Johann Christian Bach, possibly his model as a German composer who had learned from Italian music and French. After only a few months in Salzburg he was then back with his family in Vienna, from the age of eleven and a half to thirteen. But perhaps more important than any of these early travels was his first Italian journey, which he made with his father from just before his fourteenth birthday to just after his fifteenth, and on which he began conveying impressions in letters to family members back home. The Mozarts' purpose in Italy was to secure, and then accomplish, a commission for an opera seria to be given in Milan, which was within Austrian domains. But what mattered most for the future was the boy's familiarization with Italian musical culture, his being able to hear

Italian singers and Italian composers, including Jommelli and Piccinni, and to visit the places where Italian traditions were most alive: Naples for opera, Rome for church music, Bologna for scholarship.

Further theatre commissions took him back to Milan twice in successive years and then to Munich, when he was eighteen, but what he was looking for − what any eighteenth-century composer would have been looking for: a permanent position − was not to be had. There were plentiful opportunities for him in Salzburg, and he took them, writing symphonies and concertos for local concerts, church music for the cathedral (where he had a job alongside his father on the archbishop's musical staff) and much else. But to a musician who had been in Milan, Munich and Paris, Salzburg was a backwater. In 1777, aged twenty, he set out again, with his mother, for Munich (where the answer was still no), Mannheim and Paris.

On the way between Munich and Mannheim he stayed a while in Augsburg, with relations, and there gave a concert whose programme he outlined in a letter to his father, coincidentally providing some indication of what was expected of performers at that time. First, as usual, there was a symphony. After that Mozart and two colleagues were the soloists in his concerto for three pianos, following which he played a piano sonata, a solo concerto, a fugue and another sonata − a succession of showpieces in varied styles.

Once arrived in Mannheim he was impressed by the orchestra, which, by his account, included two each of flutes, oboes, clarinets and horns, four bassoons, and string sections on a matching scale (ten or eleven violins, four violas, four cellos, four double basses), together with trumpets and drums when necessary. Such descriptions have helped influence the size of orchestra used for late eighteenth-century music today. He was also struck by the music of the Mannheim composers Christian Cannabich (1731–98) and Ignaz Holzbauer (1711–83), and, perhaps even more so, by the singing and the person of the sixteen-year-old Aloysia Weber (c. 1760–1839). After more than three months in Mannheim, negotiating with court officials and waiting for the ruler to make up his mind about an appointment, the young composer was ready to abandon hope and return to Italy to write operas for Aloysia, whose capacities for spectacular virtuosity and sweetness he recorded in the succession of arias he wrote for her now and later. Close to this time he remarked how an aria should fit a singer like well-tailored clothing.

However, his father's reaction to the Aloysia prospect was explosive: Paris, rather, must be his destination. And it was. However, his experience there was just as frustrating. Slow, tentative offers came of posts he did not want; the opportunity to write an opera receded almost as soon as it appeared; and the first work he composed for the Concert Spirituel – a piece in the popular genre of the *symphonie concertante*, having multiple soloists (in this case four woodwind players) – failed to come off. He did not seek out his composer colleagues: 'I know what I am doing, and they know what they are doing, and that's just fine.' As a result he had nothing to say about the graceful music of André Grétry (1741–1813), which found favour with the queen, Marie Antoinette, or about the third of the century's operatic tussles in Paris, between the supporters of Gluck and those of the gentler Piccinni. His one moment of success came with the performance at the Concert Spirituel of his 'Paris' Symphony, his account of which suggests what passed for appropriate concert behaviour in 1778. He had taken care to put in the middle of the first movement a passage he knew would please, and sure enough 'there was a big *applaudissement*'. Then because he had heard that Parisian finales normally started with all the instruments together, he began his last movement with just a pair of violins for the first phrase. Just as he had hoped, people shushed one another to catch this delicate music, and clapped with relieved delight at the sudden access of gusto that followed. Shortly before leaving Paris, after six months of professional disillusionment, as well as personal grief at the loss of his mother, he was happy to meet up again with Johann Christian Bach, in town to write a French opera.

Mozart was departing at the insistence of his father, who now felt the young man's best hopes lay back in Salzburg, but he drew out his return journey with stays in Mannheim and Munich, partly in expectation of commissions, partly to see Aloysia Weber again. In both errands he was disappointed. Aloysia rejected him, and he failed to persuade the director of the leading German theatre company, in Mannheim at the time, to let him write a 'monodrama', a scene for actress with orchestra. The model examples of this genre were two recent pieces by Georg Benda (1722–95), *Ariadne auf Naxos* and *Medea*, and these impressed Mozart greatly. The great Mannheim orchestra, though, was now in Munich, since the ruler of Mannheim had succeeded to the Bavarian title. Mozart was at last to have the chance to write for them, but not for another year, after he had returned to Salzburg. Then the commission came for a work in which he could weld all he had learned in Mannheim, Paris and Italy into a glorious fusion, the opera *Idomeneo* (1780–1).

While Mozart lived so much of his youth on tour, Haydn, a generation older, spent these same years on the slow shuttle between Vienna for the winters and the Esterházys'

Hungarian palace for the summers. Perhaps learning most now from himself, he was also alert to the folk music he came across and to his colleagues in a musical establishment that was increasing. Around 1770 he wrote several unusually dark or melancholic symphonies, but after that for some years he was largely occupied with comic opera – both writing it and performing examples by Italian contemporaries for the Esterházys – and his instrumental music lightened again. If this effect of contact with comedy was nothing new or special to Haydn, no other composer of the time, or later, showed such an understanding of humour in music, across so wide a range of modes: the wry aphorism, the teasing surprise, the witty bon mot, the outburst of cheerfulness. Sonata form – which meant for him a dialogue of musical characters in the shapes of themes, a dialogue that might proceed through flagrant disagreements (themselves perhaps comic) but would have to reach a celebratory reconciliation – was essentially comedy, and his instrumental works of the 1770s are funnier than his operas of the same period.

Among those works, besides the symphonies, were sets of pieces in a new genre Haydn was to make just as much his own: the string quartet, for two violins, viola and cello. Quartets were symphonies for small rooms, usually having the same succession of four movements: their place was as music for amateurs to play at home, though they could also be concert material. The medium functioned rather as the trio sonata had in the hundred years before, exemplifying on a small scale the age's most characteristic musical behaviour, in this case the behaviour of independent parties engaging in discourse that might have its moments of dissent and shared sadness but would, at bottom, be good-humoured.

During the next decade Haydn gained a new associate in Vienna. In the summer of 1781, just a few months after the première of *Idomeneo*, Mozart at last released himself from the service of the Salzburg archbishop and settled in the imperial capital as an unattached musician. Haydn's principal work that year was a set of six quartets, which he published the year after as his opus 33 (the Latin term means 'work'), it being by now normal for publishers to number a composer's output in order to avoid confusion. Works, and sets of works, might not be printed and still gain a wide distribution, thanks to the efforts of professionals and pirates making manuscript copies. That was how much of Haydn's music had become known, for certainly he had produced more than thirty-two works or sets worthy an opus number before these 1781 quartets. But now he was often writing specifically for publication, partly because the music-publishing business was taking off in Vienna, led by the Artaria family, who had started issuing music in 1778 and were to be responsible for the first editions of several works by both Haydn and Mozart. In the case of these op. 33 quartets Haydn included a note saying he had written them in 'a completely new and special way', by which he seems to have meant especially that the two lower instruments are no longer subservient. The conversation was four-way.

One result was to stimulate a two-way dialogue, with Mozart. The two composers could have met during one of Mozart's earlier visits, but certainly they were now together from time to time, as when they played as members of an extraordinary Viennese composers' quartet comprising Haydn and Carl Ditters von Dittersdorf (1739–99) on violins, Mozart on viola (an instrument for which he had much affection) and Johann Baptist Wanhal (1739–1813) on cello. After one meeting, in 1785, Haydn told Mozart's father that his son was 'the greatest composer known to me in person or by name'. At that point Mozart had just completed a set of quartets in which he rose to the challenge of Haydn's op. 33, and which, in a wholly unusual gesture of respect, he dedicated to Haydn. They were, he said, 'the fruits of long and laborious endeavour', and indeed he had spent more than two years on them – he who could, on occasion, conceive a piece as fast as he was writing it down. Appreciating what Haydn had made of sonata form and quartet texture, he adapted both to his own penchant for almost continuous singing melody, and, in works of great diversity, put forward his own 'new and special way'. If he found quintets more comfortable, because of the greater harmonic variety available, his 'Haydn quartets', as they have come to be called, are testimony to what he rarely had cause to express: respect for a colleague.

Outside the quartet party, though, the two composers' worlds hardly overlapped. Haydn, while still in Esterházy service, was working in the 1780s mostly for other patrons and for publishers, and concentrating on the large abstract categories: the symphony (including six for Paris concerts in 1785–6), the string quartet and the sonata or trio (with violin and cello) for the burgeoning domestic piano market. That market was also being served by Carl Philipp Emanuel Bach, who, in his late sixties and early seventies, was publishing sonatas and fantasias that combined the majesty of his father's preludes with the virtuosity and expressiveness of mid-century opera. Mozart, too, wrote music for the home pianist: sonatas (for piano alone or with violin), innumerable sets of variations, duets (for two pianists) and trios and quartets with strings. Like Haydn he also wrote quartets for Frederick the Great's successor, the cellist monarch Frederick William II; unlike Haydn he created much of his instrumental music for his own needs as a performer, including the fifteen piano concertos he produced during his first six years in Vienna, when he was at his most popular in the city and could be sure of attracting an audience to a concert.

Otherwise his main concern was with opera for the court theatre. For a short while German opera was preferred, for which purpose he wrote his first Viennese opera, the comedy *Die Entführung aus dem Serail* (The Abduction from the Harem, 1781–2), one of a very few works in which he embraced music from beyond the range of his travels: the jangling sounds of Turkish military bands. In letters to his father he went into some detail about his operatic thinking here, not least in addressing the old topic, restored to favour again in the Enlightenment, of whether music is a language of the emotions – 'must contain the sort of sequence of feelings that would evolve by itself in a soul completely immersed in a passion', as the Berlin philosopher Johann Jakob Engel (1741–1802) put it in 1780 – or an appeal to the senses that 'pleases independently of all imitation', in the words of the French thinker Michel-Paul-Guy de Chabanon (1729/30–92), from a treatise published five years later. Mozart's letters, between these in date, are also between them in position, indicating that purely musical values must control the depiction of feeling: 'The passions . . . must never be expressed to the point of exciting disgust, and music, even in the most terrible situations, must still give pleasure and never offend the ear – that is, must always remain music.'

Court opera after *Die Entführung* reverted to Italian, the international opera language, and the repertory was dominated by Italian composers, who brought their culture not only of tunefulness on the stage but of intrigue behind it. Salieri, Gluck's protégé, held a court appointment; also favoured were pieces by the Neapolitan composers Pasquale Anfossi (1727–97) and, leading the new generation, Giovanni Paisiello (1740–1816) and Domenico Cimarosa (1749–1801), though the most frequently performed opera at the court theatre during Mozart's lifetime was *L'arbore di Diana* (Diana's Tree) by the Spaniard Vicente Martín y Soler (1754–1806). Mozart's big success came not in Vienna but in Prague, when his *Le nozze di Figaro* (The Marriage of Figaro, 1786) was given a production there. The Prague theatre commissioned his next opera, *Don Giovanni* (1787), where the central character's supper music in the final scene conveys a critical reaction to public taste. *Figaro* is duly quoted, as a note of thanks to the Prague audience, after more rueful selections from two recent hits in Vienna: Martín y Soler's *Una cosa rara* (A Strange Thing) and *Fra i due litiganti* (Between the Quarrelers) by Giuseppe Sarti (1729–1802).

However, there was one Italian whose presence in Vienna Mozart valued: Lorenzo Da Ponte (1749–1838), who wrote the librettos for *Figaro*, *Don Giovanni* and their successor *Così fan tutte* (Women are All the Same, 1789–90). He provided Mozart with integrated variety, wit and tight drama, but so he did other composers whose works have been all but forgotten, such as Martín y Soler. The music, as always in opera, is crucial, and Mozart's does not just tell us what the characters are feeling but seems to come from inside them. Attaining, by virtue of its harmony, a constant forward motion ever susceptible to subtle prevarications, it conveys the real-time experience of real people, and goes ever further into the ambiguities of human emotions, the uncertain boundaries separating real feeling from play-acting

their contemporaries and even of their immediate predecessors, the composers who had been highly valued in the mid-eighteenth century: Hasse, Graun, Jommelli, Carl Philipp Emanuel Bach. It was a harsh thinning, and its effects were to linger, for the operas of Cavalli have proved easier to revive than those of Hasse or Martín y Soler.

This is unlikely to change. However much the current valuation of Haydn and Mozart may have accrued posthumously, it is too real to be ignored. Only one composer of this period has ever been able to climb into their company, and he did so right away, a young man from the German town of Bonn who arrived in Vienna in 1792, a year after Mozart's death: Ludwig van Beethoven (1770–1827).

CHAPTER 12

Revolution's momentum

On 14 July 1789, the day the Bastille fell in Paris, Mozart was adding a postscript to a begging letter addressed to a fellow freemason while Haydn could have been working at a symphony for the French capital. Mozart died before the Revolution reached its most radical and bloody phase; his great colleague, working for aristocratic patrons in Vienna, public concerts in London and publishers in both cities, was little affected by it. But Beethoven, striving as a court musician in Bonn to support his faltering family, heard of the events in Paris at the ignitable age of eighteen, then matured to adulthood through the years of the Terror and the temporary salvation of the French republic at the hands of his near contemporary Napoleon (1769–1821). His mind was formed in this era of radical change, which, however disastrous in political and human terms, raised a flag for hope.

The change emanating from Paris affected – though not all at once – music's sound, its subject matter, its audience and its professional basis, at first in France and then right across the western world. The Revolution brought great events onto the streets, and its commemorations likewise took place out of doors, not in the palaces of a moribund monarchy or the cathedrals of a repudiated religion.

Military bands, made for outdoor performance, gave the Revolution a sound world of fanfares, marches and solemnity, with some borrowing from how grandeur had been portrayed in Gluckian opera. Meanwhile new kinds of opera were giving more attention to the bourgeoisie, who had gained most from the Revolution and could now see depicted on stage their feelings and their heroism. One such work was *Lodoïska* (1791), by the Italian composer Luigi Cherubini (1760–1842), who had arrived in Paris five years before. *Lodoïska* took up a theme that had already occurred in French opera but was now very much to the point: the defeat of oppression dramatized as a heroic rescue from enslavement or imprisonment, effected by one person on behalf of another – a proud display of liberty, equality and fraternity. This was to be the theme also of Beethoven's single opera, *Fidelio*.

In the longer run the Revolution's most significant musical achievement was the Paris Conservatoire, founded in 1795 as a state institution for the training of musicians, to replace the diverse opportunities that had been provided before, and were still provided elsewhere, by the church, aristocratic patrons, older relations and the tradition of apprenticeship. Cherubini was on the founding faculty and became director in 1822, the year in which a similar college was opened in London: the Royal Academy of Music. Other such conservatories and academies gradually appeared throughout Europe, reshaping musical practice as a profession, entry into which required the acquisition of particular skills in a particular musical language.

Beethoven's education was within the contrastingly heterogeneous and haphazard system of earlier times. Like many musicians of all periods, he was born into a musical family, his father and grandfather having been singers at the court in Bonn. With the memory of Mozart still fresh (Beethoven was only fifteen years younger), his father seems to have hoped to produce a prodigy, and had the boy performing at seven. Beethoven's development, though, was slower. From his father he passed to the local organist and composer Christian Gottlob Neefe (1748–98), who recognized his potential and gave him a grounding in Bach. Vienna, the city of Haydn and Mozart, was his obvious goal, and he went there at sixteen, but had to come back almost immediately to see his dying mother, and stayed on to look after his family. At twenty-two he returned to Vienna with the support of a Bonn nobleman, Count Waldstein, who sent him to 'receive Mozart's spirit from Haydn's hands'. He duly studied with Haydn, for just over a year, and then for a similar period with another Viennese composer of the same generation, Johann Georg Albrechtsberger (1736–1809), who was said to write a fugue a day. Meanwhile, as a virtuoso pianist, he won attention and help from the city's leading musical aristo- crats, who just a few years before had been assisting Mozart. In the summer of 1795, his education complete, he put out his first publication: a set of three trios for piano with violin and cello. With this collection as his op. 1 he initiated the habit of reserving opus numbers for impor- tant works, the first composer to do so. Another sign of his creative self-assurance came three years later, when he started writing his sketches into bound books.

The short time Haydn spent teaching Beethoven was an interlude between two lengthy periods of residence in Lon- don, in 1791–2 and 1794–5, which confirmed his assumption of a role that was new in the world. Under the old dis- pensation composers were local figures, serving a court, church or city. But in the new bourgeois Europe – where commerce meant communication, so that music could be disseminated widely in printed form and everyone wanted the best – attention could fasten on a composer from regions far-flung. Vivaldi had felt this. Haydn in London, though, applauded at concerts and sought after as a dinner guest, was the first composer to enjoy the full glow of international fame. Had Mozart lived only a few more years, he might have had it too.

Haydn travelled at the invitation of Johann Peter Salomon (1745–1815), who came from Bonn – Beethoven, as a boy, had known him – but since 1781 had lived in London, where he succeeded Johann Christian Bach as the prime instigator of musical life. The city still led the world in terms of concert activity, and in 1775 the London Bach and his associates had founded a new concert hall, the Hanover Square Rooms, where patrons could lounge on sofas as if in a private drawing room. This was the venue to which Salomon lured Haydn, whose works, widely published and admired, were laying the foundations of an international concert repertory. Haydn wrote a set of six symphonies for each of his visits, as well as quartets and English songs that could also feature in Salomon's concerts. The orchestra, with about forty players, was unusually big, and this factor, together with the public ambience, surely contributed to the richness and splendour of the London symphonies (Nos. 93–104). Perhaps, too, their sound is that of a composer enjoying his triumph at the centre of the music trade, praised and needed by performers, publishers and pupils.

Once back in Vienna Haydn almost abandoned the instrumental genres that had been his mainstay (there were no further symphonies and just two more quartets) in favour of masses, which he wrote almost annually for his last Esterházy employer between 1796 and 1802, and two oratorios: *The Creation* (1796–8) and *The Seasons* (1799–1801). Both of these were based on English texts and aimed partly at the English market, where they soon joined Handel's oratorios as favourites of the emerging choral societies. So they did too in the United States, where the Handel and Haydn Society of Boston, established in 1815, was only the first of many such organizations paralleling developments in England and Germany. Haydn in his last creative decade thus fulfilled his obligations as an old-style court composer and simultaneously proved his mastery of the composer's new function as commercial supplier.

Beethoven's course during this period remained closer to the Mozart model, to the life of a composer-performer who would dazzle in concerts or at private soirées – though, unlike Mozart, he made no venture towards opera. Most of his works of the 1790s – of his twenties – revolve around the piano, being sonatas, sets of variations, trios and concertos. But he seems to have set himself to complete, by the end of the century, examples of what Haydn had made the two big instrumental forms. And he did: his first collection of quartets, comprising six works, was published in 1800 as his op. 18, and in the same year he called a concert to introduce his First Symphony. That in itself was new, that a composer should create a concert for a symphony rather than a symphony for a concert, as Haydn and Mozart had done. Beethoven showed his ambition, too, in his music's dynamism and intensity.

Even so, his First Symphony and op. 18 quartets give little sign of how far he was to develop in just the next three years, bringing to music its own revolution a decade after Paris's. The connection is more than a metaphor. Beethoven admired Napoleon for saving the republican ideal by assuming responsibility for it as First Consul from 1799, and four years later he wrote a symphony, his Third, which he dedicated to his hero – then tore out the dedication when, the following year, Napoleon declared himself emperor. Eventually he published the work under the title 'Sinfonia eroica', to which he added the epigraph: 'to commemorate the memory of a great man'. The piece also has links of substance with what had been happening in France, for in 1802 Beethoven was able to hear Cherubini's music when *Lodoïska* was performed in Vienna; not only did he gain a lasting regard for the composer, he borrowed his colleague's broad brush.

Much bigger than any predecessor, the 'Eroica' Symphony has a first movement that alone lasts almost as long as a Haydn symphony. The work is, too, urgently progressive throughout its great length. Beethoven understood sonata form not as fundamentally comic or lyrical, in the way of Haydn and Mozart, ending in a reconciliation of dissimilarities, but rather as heroic struggle, in which an essentially single musical force, defined by a guiding motif, would push towards a triumphant conclusion in the principal (major) key. Hence the increased importance of the development section, as the chief scene of challenge and conflict – though development is happening in Beethoven's movements almost from the beginning, in keeping with their forward-driving character. Hence, too, the might of the coda (tailpiece), as victory celebration. Moreover, the separate movements were no longer altered moments of tension or repose but phases in a continuous process, and an innovation dating back to Haydn's op. 33 quartets – that of replacing courtly dance, in the form of the minuet, with a 'scherzo' of more robust exuberance – was vigorously embodied. A work would now address itself to humanity in general, and its voice – not the singing voice of Mozart's instrumental music – would be that of an orator.

Probably the most celebrated Beethovenian oration is his Fifth Symphony (1807–8), in which everything seems to be impelled by the short, forceful idea that opens the work, in which the scherzo unfolds into the finale as the music turns from C minor to C major, and in which this C major is loudly and lengthily affirmed at the end. The first performance took place at an extraordinary concert Beethoven presented in Vienna on 22 December 1808, when the four-hour programme – entirely of his own music, and most of it recent – began with his Sixth Symphony (the 'Pastoral') and continued with an early setting of a solo scene from a Metastasio libretto, the Gloria from a mass written for the Esterházy prince who had commissioned Haydn's last six, the most recent piano concerto (No. 4), then the Fifth Symphony, the Sanctus from the Esterházy mass, a fantasy improvised on the piano and, finally, another fantasy for the full assembled forces of orchestra, choir and solo pianist (Beethoven himself). Yet even this was not all he had composed in the five years since the 'Eroica'. There had also been, besides the Fourth Symphony, two other concertos, three newly spacious string quartets, three piano sonatas in this new heroic style, and an opera, *Fidelio*, based on the libretto of a French opera on the popular rescue theme.

By this point Beethoven had definitively succeeded Haydn as the most esteemed composer internationally. He was dealing regularly with publishers in Germany, Switzerland and England as well as Vienna, and his music was being played by pianists and orchestras wherever these were to be found. The year after his monster concert a group of Viennese noblemen, wanting to keep him in their midst, guaranteed him an income as long as he stayed in the city, which he did. It may seem odd that music growing from the Revolution, and sharing the Revolution's zest for change and optimism as to its outcome, was supported by people of ancient family. But Beethoven's patrons, like their cherished composer, saw it as the duty of the gifted and well placed to serve the common good.

The French Revolution, a far greater stimulus to European culture than its American pre-echo a decade or so before, projected the possibility of change. The social order could be revised; Christianity could be banned, and then unbanned; even the calendar could be reinvented – and all towards human betterment. Time was becoming motion, progress, and this was the time that Beethoven made sound. It was the time, too, that Mozart had felt, before the Revolution, in writing to his father how music had to keep changing until it reached perfection (a state that some would feel it achieved in him). And it was the time that was recognized by the German writer Johann Nikolaus Forkel (1749–1818) in *A General History of Music*, whose publication spanned the period from the year before the storming of the Bastille to early in the new century, and which saw music history as a gradual development (though for the author the peak had come even sooner, in Bach). Politics, composition and scholarship were in agreement: time was change.

By a melancholy irony Beethoven could feel change within his own physical person, for he was aware at the latest by 1801 of the gradual onset of deafness. This, to his great regret, curtailed his social interactions, and was responsible for his becoming solitary and often gruff. It also caused him to withdraw from the concert platform. After his 1808 concert he wrote just one more concerto for himself, and he made no important appearance after 1814. His interest in other musicians seems understandably to have declined during the same period; besides, he was uninterested in the pleasantness coming into fashion. Also active in Vienna at this time were Johann Nepomuk Hummel (1778–1837), a pianist-composer who kept up an enormous output of amiable music for the home and concert hall, and Louis Spohr (1784–1859), whose instrument was the violin, for which he wrote concertos and quartets shaped as miniature concertos, alongside his symphonies and operas. These engaging and fecund junior contemporaries drew much more from Mozart, reinvented now as the smiling master of charm and delight, than from Beethoven, whose influence, even on his pupils, was surprisingly indistinct – or whose language was just too complex for imitation. As to the reverse effect, Beethoven may well have felt he had nothing to learn from those around him (Cherubini always excepted) and that, in any event, he had absorbed enough: Bach and Handel, not Spohr and Hummel, were to be the conversational partners of his later music.

Deafness may have been one reason for his slowing down as a composer in his early forties, especially after his Seventh and Eighth symphonies (1811–12), which he seems to have conceived as a pair, the one large and athletic, the other compact and full of sly humour. Economic conditions also played a part. One of his patrons died and the others were affected by the growing hardships of the war against Napoleon, in which Austria was one of the battlefields. Obliged to accept rather miscellaneous commissions, he produced, for example, a curious postscript to the 'Eroica' in the form of *Wellington's Victory*, a musical picture of the defeat of Napoleonic forces at the Battle of Vitoria, in Spain, in 1813.

Though successful in Vienna at the time as an orchestral piece, this was created for a mechanical instrument built by Johann Nepomuk Maelzel (1772–1838), who in 1815 began marketing another invention, the metronome, for defining musical tempos. The Maelzel metronome was a clockwork device with a stick which could be set to swing back and forth at different speeds, accompanied by a clicking noise. A composer could now prescribe a tempo by precise measurement (so many beats per minute) rather than by a more or less vague Italian term (e.g. allegro non molto, 'fast but not overmuch'), because performers would be able to set their metronomes in rehearsal to the indicated speed and adapt their performance accordingly. On the face of it, the metronome brought to an apotheosis music's assimilation to clock time. However, its judgements have always been disputed. Beethoven became an enthusiast, but the metronome speeds he marked have often been felt to be too fast, in keeping with a general tendency among composers to overestimate what is practical and musically convincing as a quick tempo.

Napoleon, for his part, may never have heard the symphony that extolled him (though as if he were already deceased) or the battle piece that noisily celebrated one of his great setbacks. His taste, to the extent that he had time for music, was for Italians, though not so much for Cherubini as for Paisiello, Ferdinando Paer (1771–1839) and Gaspare Spontini (1774–1851), all of whom he brought to Paris for their ability to provide music properly imperial but tuneful and not too long. It was a much younger composer, though, who was decisively on the rise during the last years of the emperor's reign: Gioachino Rossini (1792–1868), whose early triumphs, presented first in Italy and rapidly taken up elsewhere, included *L'italiana in Algeri* (The Italian

Girl in Algiers, 1813). A Rossini comedy was like an elaborate clockwork mechanism itself, spinning brightly lit characters through farcical situations to the tick-tock of regular rhythm and clear harmonic drive.

Also in 1813, in London, Salomon and others founded the Philharmonic Society to establish a concert series with a repertory founded on Beethoven's symphonies. Works embodying change were thus coming to represent permanence. And their value was duly reinterpreted, for it was in the same year that the Berlin writer-musician Ernst Theodor Amadeus Hoffmann (1776–1822) – known now almost exclusively for his fantastical tales, but in his time a respected composer and critic – published an influential essay on Beethoven. Ridiculing the efforts of composers of instrumental music to 'represent definite emotions, even definite events' (*Wellington's Victory* he could not yet have encountered, or probably even suspected), he immediately set himself against the view that went back through Rousseau to Plato. But he also repudiated the notion of music as delectable and comprehensible in its own right, as sound and form. Rather, 'music discloses to man an unknown realm, a world that has nothing in common with the external sensual world that surrounds him, a world in which he leaves behind him all definite feelings to surrender himself to an inexpressible longing'.

That, at any rate, was the effect of the greatest instrumental music, of which there were, for Hoffmann, only three composers. Haydn and Mozart were 'the first to show us the art in its full glory'. Then came Beethoven, whose music 'opens to us also the monstrous and the immeasurable', 'sets in motion the lever of fear, of awe, of horror, of suffering'. Grandiloquent, this positioning of Beethoven was also a transformation. The great composer's works were not to be seen as bringing world forces into combat for the vanquishing of tyranny and the exaltation of freedom. And in the specific instance of the Fifth Symphony, whose unified progress Hoffmann was the first to acclaim, the author was to be understood as addressing not the multitude but the individual listener, led 'imperiously forward into the spirit world of the Infinite'.

Hoffmann had a new name for this artistic programme: Romanticism.

PART VI

Time escaping 1815–1907

The Romantic period in music, generally reckoned from Beethoven, introduced something new to the art: tragedy. And to the extent that earlier music was tragic (Gluck's, Mozart's, even Monteverdi's) it was incipiently Romantic. Tragedy is loss. Loss is the inevitable concomitant of change. In venerating Haydn, Mozart and Beethoven, and keeping many of their works in frequent performance, the nineteenth century created an ideal that could never be recaptured. Greatness was gone.

That was one aspect of music's loss, but there were others that came as the shadows fell over what had been so optimistic in Beethoven's works of the century's first decade. Faith in progress became harder to sustain. The complexity that Beethoven developed from what he found in Haydn and Mozart, a complexity essentially of harmony and form, appeared to demand a continuing extension, at least of the chords and key relationships that could be used, to the point where it became impossible to achieve an affirmative conclusion that tied up all the ends. Beethoven arguably reached that point with his Eighth Symphony, whose gestures are so often ironic. A decade passed before he completed another symphony; meanwhile his music grew ever wider-ranging and more open-ended. Change was continuing, as if driven by an unstoppable historical engine, but directions were unclear, and henceforth they rarely, even in Beethoven, featured triumphant arrival.

There were doubts, too, about music's purpose. Hoffmann's essay placed musical understanding in a metaphysical realm, and some post-Beethoven Romantics were happy to see their work in that numinous light. For many others, though, music was a language of feeling, which the growing harmonic resources were making at once more precise and more ambiguous. This was a great age for song and instrumental lyric, and for opera as emotional drama. Less prevalent was the moral urgency with which Beethoven had spoken to his audience rather than of himself.

Many listeners, though, were seeking exactly that resolute confrontation with eternal truth, that path to Hoffmann's 'Infinite'. For the nineteenth-century audience, now thoroughly dominated by the bourgeoisie, music was a new religion – perhaps *the* new religion – replacing those whose claims were being undermined by scientific inquiry and biblical scholarship. The great concert halls of the age's latter part suggest a sounder confidence than the cathedrals: the Musikverein in Vienna (1870), the Concertgebouw in Amsterdam (1888), Carnegie Hall in New York (1891). Orchestras by this stage had been established in major cities throughout Europe and the Americas, and one could go to their concerts every week in the season, as if to church. Music at home was often entertainment, but it could also be close to prayer.

Yet the nineteenth century, so diverse, also appreciated music as relaxation and jollity, along the historical path from Rossini's comedies to the waltzing operettas of Vienna and the parlour ballads of the English-speaking world. Music could be a pastime. On grander levels its evocation of passing time could alternatively be consolatory. One effect of the memorialization of the classics — with Haydn, Mozart and Beethoven joined soon by Bach — was to maintain the integrity of major-minor tonality, long after the late works of Beethoven had strained that system to the edge of disintegration. Indeed, the promise of resolution, of ultimate concord, was central to music's power. The universe was becoming ever more complicated as nineteenth-century science began uncovering its age and its extent. But a symphony could, for an hour, grant an experience of wholeness, continuity and comprehensibility, or at least a deeper knowledge of how those things were escaping.

CHAPTER 13

The deaf man and the singer

For all that the definitive defeat of Napoleon at Waterloo in 1815 restored and stabilized the old monarchies, the real victors were the bourgeoisie. Court music dwindled in importance: there would be no more Haydns, great composers cheerfully writing for appreciative princes. The demand for music came now wholly from concert and opera audiences, from the choral societies that were emerging in English-speaking and German cities with the growing presence of sacred music in the concert hall, and from amateur performers at home. This was the commercial world in which Hummel and Spohr throve, and which Rossini mastered. From the year of Waterloo his base was Naples, which remained the dominant source of Italian opera, and from there his works subjugated a larger area of Europe than had Napoleon's troops. He knew his audience. With a teasing wit and an imaginative flair that would be fully present right from the overture, he combined humour with sentiment in his comedies, among them a remake of *Il barbiere di Siviglia* (1816), and in his serious operas treated subjects that had the warranty of history, as in *Elisabetta, regina d'Inghilterra* (Elizabeth, Queen of England, 1815), the Bible, as in *Mosè in Egitto* (Moses in Egypt, 1818) or great literature, as in *Otello* (after the Shakespeare play, 1816),

Ermione (after Racine's *Andromaque*, 1819) or *La donna del lago* (after Walter Scott's poem *The Lady of the Lake*, 1819). In 1822 he travelled to Vienna, where his Neapolitan impresario was staging six of his operas. He met Beethoven, and his music was heard by a young man still hoping to make his own mark as a theatre composer: Franz Schubert (1797–1828).

While Rossini was conquering the world, Beethoven and Schubert had their sights on domestic ambiences that became, in their compositions, world-sized. Both composers, living separate lives in the same city, were devoting themselves largely to piano music and songs. The works that Beethoven completed during the first few years of post-Napoleonic peace included his song cycle *An die ferne Geliebte* (To the Distant Beloved) and his last five piano sonatas, though by 1822 he was working on a symphony commissioned by the Philharmonic Society of London, while also moving towards completing a great mass, the *Missa solemnis* (1819–23), which he had started as a gift to his friend, pupil and colleague Archduke Rudolph (1788–1831), the brother of the Austrian emperor and a cardinal of the Roman Catholic church. Schubert during the same period was producing hundreds of songs, to verses by great poets and close friends. Among these compositions, swiftly done, were such classics of the repertory as *Erlkönig* (Elf King), which he wrote when he was eighteen and six years later, in 1821, made his first published work.

In many respects the two composers were far apart. They belonged to different generations and are said to have met only once, when Beethoven was on his deathbed – though the vines of myth-making have long obscured the facts of their connections. Their musical differences, though, are clear. Schubert had none of Beethoven's dynamism. Always his own man in songs, he moved quite abruptly in his instrumental music from a Mozartian ease to a darkness and strength of purpose – even within meandering uncertainty – that owed only a little to Beethoven. This new style arrived in an unfinished quartet (1820) and the 'Unfinished' Symphony (1822), the latter comprising just first and slow movements, and voicing a resignation that – extraordinary in so young a person – leaves nothing to be added. An unfinished Beethoven symphony, if such existed, would be looming into the future. Schubert's music is haunted by the need to prevaricate, repeatedly to consider harmonic knots that could lead in any number of directions: not for nothing are themes of night, doubt and anxious separation frequent in his song texts. Also, Beethoven enjoyed international esteem. His new piano sonatas, though complex and difficult to perform, were published as soon as they were written. Schubert's works, until he started having them printed, circulated only among a circle of friends, gathering together for musical evenings. His efforts at wider notice, centred on the theatre, came to little, and many of his larger works, including the 'Unfinished' Symphony, were unknown and unheard until long after his death.

But there were also ways in which Beethoven, around fifty, and Schubert, half his age, were close. Both were out of tune with the times. In the peace that followed Napoleon's fall and completed the bourgeoisie's rise, people wanted Rossini, frivolity and entertainment. The sonatas that Beethoven was writing – most especially his almost hour-long 'Hammerklavier' (op. 106 of 1817–18; the name implies nothing more than 'piano') – were an embarrassment that had to be tolerated on account of the symphonies of the decade before, already keystones of the concert repertory.

Also, both composers created sacred music not so much to hymn the almighty as to animate those who would be singing and listening. Beethoven wrote on the score of his *Missa solemnis* that it came from the heart and was intended to touch hearts, surely those of performers as much as listeners. Fiercely stretched (especially the sopranos), the choral singers cannot but project the work with intensity, though there are passages that settle into the sweetness of the epoch and others where the composer's study of Handel, Bach and earlier music produces astonishing harmonic turns or vigorously polyphonic textures. The same are to be found, and from the identical sources, in the piano sonatas composed alongside the mass: op. 106, for instance, ends with an enormous fugal movement, as if the interlocking of fugue could once again, as in the previous century, give concluding solidity.

What settles the ending of the *Missa solemnis* is not fugue but a quiet confirmation of peace that clothes the words of the Agnus Dei and is given actuality by the memory of battle noises from earlier in the movement – a confirmation particularly meaningful to people who had just lived through the Napoleonic wars. This is just one example of Beethoven's critical reinterpretation of the sacred text in terms of the here and now, and of the divinity of mankind. The phrase in the Credo that is most forcibly affirmed is that proclaiming Jesus's humanity, and the entire work, in its scale and in its address, seems destined much less for the church than for the concert hall. It thereby continues a line from Beethoven's earlier mass, from Haydn's late masses, which were instantly repeated as concert pieces, and from Mozart's Requiem, which had featured importantly in the concerts that established its composer's posthumous status. Schubert's masses similarly belong to this beginning phase in the sacralization of the concert.

The two great Viennese composers of the era were alike, too, in their intermittent success in the theatre. Both of them had studied with Salieri, Beethoven for a short period in 1801–2, Schubert through his teens. But Salieri's regime at court was over and Viennese opera was now in German, taking place predominantly in suburban theatres, which was how Mozart's *Die Zauberflöte* had been presented in 1791. As in Mozart's time so it was most often still, in German opera and in English, that there was no recitative, the arias and other numbers arising within spoken dialogue. This was how Beethoven wrote *Fidelio,* and rewrote it and rewrote it again for subsequent productions. And this was how Schubert wrote most of his theatre music. Beethoven dreamt of an opera based on Goethe's *Faust*, which he never began; Schubert completed three full-length operas, which joined the piles of his unheard manuscripts.

No-one in the German musical theatre could hold a candle to Carl Maria von Weber (1786–1826), a cousin of the Aloysia Weber of whom Mozart had been enamoured, and of her sister Constanze, whom he had loved next, more maturely, and married. The whole extended family was involved in music and theatre, and Carl Maria grew up on the road with his parents' troupe, taking part in plays and operas. In this world there was little room for the sophistication demanded by Rossini's scores, and Weber absorbed the energy of the rough-and-ready, while developing also a keen ear for instrumental sonorities – especially for the evocative darkness of low woodwinds and horns, which he used to introduce picturesqueness to the early Romantic orchestra. The combination of melodrama with sonorous magic made his *Der Freischütz* (The Freeshooter, 1821) the most successful German opera of its time. His next works, also his last, were commissioned for Vienna (*Euryanthe*, 1823) and London (*Oberon*, 1826).

Meanwhile, Beethoven's efforts after the *Missa solemnis* were to write a set of piano variations and finish his Ninth Symphony. The variations were prompted by the leading Viennese publisher, Anton Diabelli (1781–1856), who had invited every composer he could think of to spin variations on an unpretentious waltz of his own invention. His wish was for one variation from each composer, producing together a kaleidoscope view of the musical world, and most of those invited obliged him, among them Schubert, whose songs he had issued, and the eleven-year-old Franz Liszt (1811–86), whose parents had brought him to Vienna to complete his education. Liszt too studied with Salieri, as well as with Beethoven's pupil Carl Czerny (1791–1857), a one-man piano-music factory who was to reach op. 861 in his output of studies, sonatas and much else, and who also provided a Diabelli variation, plus a coda for the set. In 1822 Liszt made his spectacular debut in Vienna; the next year, after a second concert, he received, as he would always remember, Beethoven's kiss.

Touched though Beethoven may have been by a child he could not hear, the ageing composer recognized his distance from the music business as represented by Diabelli, Czerny and, in due course, Liszt. To Diabelli's collection he contributed not one variation but thirty-three, creating an hour-long work that completes its own circle in arriving back at the waltz: the gesture is a homage to Bach's Goldberg Variations, but it also neatly excludes the other variations Diabelli had assembled. A process of musical investigation is set in train, with the waltz as both object of inquiry and means of detection, and though what comes out may be humorous or angry, it can happen, too, that simplicity opens a window onto awestruck contemplation.

If there is similar variety at times in the Ninth Symphony, this work recalls much more the heroic Beethoven of a decade or two before, and indeed two essential elements in it reach back to his youth: the idea of setting Friedrich Schiller's 'Ode to Joy' – a celebration of human comradeship, written four years before the fall of the Bastille – and the melody found for those words, a melody that had appeared in different versions in the choral fantasy of 1808 and even in a song from thirteen years before that. As in *Fidelio*, a cantata of irresistible optimism – in this case the 'Ode to Joy' – takes over from an old world (opera, symphony) and instals music as a living force, present not so much in the work as in the performance, a force that is being made to live by people exhorting an audience.

Once again, for the last time, Beethoven presented a concert to bring the Viennese public up to date with his symphonic output: the date was 7 May 1824, and the symphony was followed on the programme by a recent overture (*Die Weihe des Hauses*, The Consecration of the House) and three segments from the *Missa solemnis*. After that Beethoven concentrated on string quartets, stimulated by the return from St Petersburg to Vienna of the violinist Ignaz Schuppanzigh (1776–1830) and by the commission Schuppanzigh brought from a Russian prince. In Vienna Schuppanzigh led chamber music concerts, at which, in 1824–6, he introduced new works by Schubert as well as Beethoven. Most of these works appear to have baffled contemporaries (allowing for the fact that Beethoven's music was noticed much more by the new musical magazines of the day than was the little known Schubert's), and they remain challenging, to play and to hear. Even more than in his late piano sonatas, Beethoven's moves in his last quartets are often abrupt, his textures dense and his forms dependent much more on the music's immediate conviction – the force of the Beethovenian voice – than on the period's convention. The C sharp minor Quartet, op. 131, has seven movements that can also be understood as forming one; the Quartet in B flat, op. 130, has six full movements, of which the last, in the original plan, is again an encounter with Bach, the *Grosse Fuge* (Great Fugue), where contrapuntal energy compels the drive through harmonies of extreme dissonance.

Schubert's last three quartets, and the three piano sonatas he wrote near the end of his life, are all conventionally expressed in four movements. In other ways they are more alarming than Beethoven's masterpieces, for where Beethoven remained positive to the last, grappling to embrace and give order to the full range of musical possibility in his time, much of Schubert's late music gives voice to hopelessness. *Winterreise* (Winter Journey, 1827), a sequence of twenty-four songs, provides an experience of interior theatre, access to changing states of mind in a solitary traveller who, rejected in love, sees his distress reflected all around in the winter landscape through which he is going. Acutely expressive as the vocal line is, the work depends equally, as usual with Schubert, on the piano, which offers the singer its own landscape of support and imagery, and at times disregard or illusion. The work's weird ending allows various interpretations, none of them easily consolatory. So it is with the late instrumental works, that their ultimate messages are sombre, disquieting. They can even hurt, as the anguished cries of the G major Quartet do, or they can convey an unrelievable despair. The sonatas' slow movements sing sad songs, that of the A major tearing into a frenzy that has the musical continuity broken by slamming chords, that of the B flat moving at a slow walking pace to arrive repeatedly at the brink of collapse.

This is not music made for success – certainly not for success in a world that wanted to be either charmed or astonished. Many were there to provide charm. The astonishers belonged to a new breed of virtuosos, of whom one of the earliest and most celebrated was Nicolò Paganini (1782–1840), beginning his world conquest in Vienna in the last year of Schubert's life. Haggard in appearance, and drawing from his violin sounds that spoke of barely plausible dexterity, he provoked audiences to ecstasy and generated myths that he had made a pact with the devil – myths he was loath to disown, and even promoted by conspicuous bad behaviour as a gambler and womanizer. People in Vienna are said to have taken their seats for his concerts two hours ahead of time in order to beat the crush. Goethe was mystified: 'I lack a base for this column of sunbeams and clouds. I heard something simply meteoric and was unable to understand it.' Nevertheless, Paganini's concertos, his twelve solo caprices and other works – which he delayed publishing in order not to reveal his secrets – exist to indicate some of his remarkable feats, such as playing notes almost simultaneously in very fast music with the bow and pizzicato (plucked with the fingers), or producing extremely high notes, an octave above the instrument's regular range, by making the string vibrate twice as fast as normal.

Paganini and Schubert, the public musician and the private, showmanship and intimacy, pride and fear: here was another contrast of the musical 1820s, but also another conjunction. The admired virtuoso and the ignored composer, who must both have spent much of their time at work, were without a place within the bourgeois society that was forming after 1815. They were outsiders, by virtue of acclaim or neglect. Paganini was one of the first to benefit (if he did) from the nineteenth century's cult of the musical genius, the cult that had appropriated Mozart (but as saint rather than demon) and would happily have adopted Beethoven, had he not been determined on continuing his exploratory course – continuing, indeed, to insist that the essence of music is in change, not conservation.

But it was possible for other composers to find comfortable niches, as the amiable Rossini had always done, and did so again when, in 1824, he settled in Paris. One of his first efforts there was an opera of showpieces for the coronation the next year of Charles X, in whose brief authoritarian reign (1824–30) a new tradition was instituted at the Paris Opera, of works ample both in length (five acts was the norm) and stage resources: grand opera. The tradition is generally reckoned from *La muette de Portici* (The Mute Girl of Portici, 1828) by Daniel Auber (1782–1871), which can hardly be faulted for its scenic effects, since it ends with the heroine, portrayed by a dancer, casting herself into lava flowing from the eruption of Vesuvius. Rossini added to this repertory with *Guillaume Tell* (William Tell, 1829), but then, with the fall of the king his contract was curtailed, and he wrote no further operas.

Born to comfort, and also to intellectual stimulation, a boy in Berlin was starting his creative career just as Weber, Beethoven, Schubert and Rossini, in successive years, were ending theirs: Felix Mendelssohn (1809–47). In his A minor Quartet (1827) he achieved a determination and a vividness that make the work seem to be rushing after the recently departed Beethoven, but other youthful works of his are serenely supreme, including his buoyant Octet for strings (1825) and his overture for *A Midsummer Night's Dream* (1826), of which the latter added more colours to the atmospheric palette of Romantic orchestration. On 11 March

1829, in Berlin, he put on the first performance of Bach's
St Matthew Passion since the composer's lifetime; he had
been given a copy of the score by his grandmother.
Restoring Bach's great work to circulation, but now in the
concert hall rather than the church, he was responsible for a
further step in music's assumption of religion's status. He
was just twenty when he did so, and yet already a mature
and esteemed composer. If anyone was to succeed to
Beethoven's (or Schubert's) place in the musical world,
here surely was the leading candidate. But there was to be
no immediate succession.

CHAPTER 14

Angels and other prodigies

What happened next was the sudden arrival of a whole range of diverse talents. Just in the signal year of 1830 – the year when Louis Philippe took over in Paris as 'citizen king' and Belgium achieved independence after riots brought on by *La muette de Portici* – the new generation's achievements were extraordinary. On 17 March, in Warsaw, Fryderyk Chopin (1810–49) gave his first important concert, including on the programme his F minor Piano Concerto. Six days earlier Vincenzo Bellini (1801–35), one of the last major composers trained in Naples, had seen his treatment of the Romeo and Juliet story, *I Capuleti e i Montecchi*, brought to the stage in Venice. Meanwhile Mendelssohn, back from his first British tour, was putting some travel impressions into his overture *Die Hebriden*, also known as *Fingal's Cave*. In December came two notable events. On the 5th, in Paris, Hector Berlioz (1803–69) presented his *Symphonie fantastique* (Fantastic Symphony), and on the 26th, in Milan, Gaetano Donizetti (1797–1848) sat as his international stock rose through the première of *Anna Bolena* (Anne Boleyn).

The following year a work of Chopin's was considered in the leading German musical paper, the *Allgemeine musikalische Zeitung*, by a young musician who, just three months younger than the colleague under review, was writing his first article and had yet to make his mark: Robert Schumann (1810–56). A line from this notice has gone down in history: 'Hats off, gentlemen, a genius!' But this is only one element in a brief but elaborate imaginary dialogue, in which Schumann speaks in many voices, and hears many in the piece he discusses. The work is a set of variations on an aria from Mozart's *Don Giovanni*, and Schumann describes it as a sequence of scenes in itself, with the piano supplying not only the voices of four characters from the opera but also the sounds of their minds and of the atmospheres around them. Nothing could indicate more clearly another side of Romanticism from the Hoffmannian sublime, one that delighted in compact and intense definitions of mood and character.

Schumann also reveals a lot in his seemingly casual remark that Chopin's variations 'might perhaps be by Beethoven or Schubert had either of them been piano virtuosi'. Beethoven and Schubert, only a few years after their deaths, set the measure. But the reference to virtuosity implies that Chopin falls short – as Schumann was to feel himself falling short. The French critic François-Joseph Fétis (1784–1871) clarified the point the following year, when, reviewing Chopin's Paris debut, he distinguished between Beethoven's 'music for the piano' and the young Pole's 'music for pianists'.

But composers of this generation did not want to be the next Beethoven. They wanted to be themselves. None of them, except possibly Mendelssohn in his dreams, wanted to emulate Beethoven's breadth in tackling all the genres of the period: opera and symphony, quartet and song, big choral piece and piano miniature. Individualism was part of the Romantic ethos, the individualism of self-expression and of self-determination in choosing a particular musical world. Bellini and Donizetti took after Rossini in concentrating almost exclusively on opera. Chopin wrote no music that did not involve the piano, and very little that was not in the form of the short solo piece. Schumann's pattern of composing through the 1830s was to be much the same, as was Liszt's, except that Liszt at this point in his life was concerned more with his contemporaries' inventions than his own. In 1833 he produced a piano arrangement of Berlioz's symphony, followed during the next few years by versions of Beethoven symphonies, Schubert songs and the latest operas. With electronic means of disseminating music still decades away, Liszt offered the means for a vast repertory to travel widely. By contrast again, Berlioz composed nothing for the piano, and nothing that was not as original and distinctive as he could make it.

He also, at least in these earlier years, composed nothing that was not all about himself. The *Symphonie fantastique*, which he subtitled 'episode from an artist's life', is explicitly an attempt to describe (for an audience) and live through (for himself) the highs and lows of love as he had felt them on being initially rejected by the Irish actress Harriet Smithson. To the first audience Berlioz distributed his programme for the work, detailing the events of the five movements as if they had been scenes in an opera, though gallantly without naming the object of his hope and despair. She had been visiting Paris with a British Shakespeare company since 1827, and it is hard to know whether Berlioz was enamoured more of her or of the roles she played, just as it is hard to know where the borders lie in the symphony between real feeling and dramatization. Indeed, blurring that distinction was part of the Romantic enterprise. Berlioz's music has nothing of the confessional tone that arises uncompelled in Schubert's sonatas, songs and quartets. Like Schumann in this respect, he showed in his writings and in his music a selfconscious ability to marshal his resources and manipulate his expressive voice. What he has to say, for instance, about the storm music in Beethoven's 'Pastoral' Symphony is evidently done for effect – if splendidly: 'It is no longer an orchestra that one hears, it is no longer music, but rather the tumultuous voice of the heavenly torrents blended with the uproar of the earthly ones, with the furious claps of thunder, with the crashing of uprooted trees, with the gusts of an exterminating wind, with the frightened cries of men and the lowing of the herds. This is terrifying, it makes one shudder, the illusion is complete.'

A key word here is the final noun. Berlioz's reach for the extraordinary, the macabre, the jubilant, the menacing – a ball, a pastoral scene and a 'march to the scaffold' are the middle movements of the *Symphonie fantastique* – produced an unceasing inventiveness in harmony, gesture and orchestral colour, all to the ends of magnificent illusion. Though not a performer he was evidently a remarkable listener (the first great music critic) and he absorbed all he heard in the works of Gluck, Beethoven and Weber at the Paris Opera or the orchestral evenings presented from 1828 by the Société des Concerts du Conservatoire. He used a full orchestra in almost everything he wrote, and eventually compiled a treatise on orchestration. He also exemplified a new kind of musician, the conductor, though he placed the *Fantastique* at its first performance in the hands of François Habeneck (1781–1849), who ran the Société.

Orchestras in the seventeenth and eighteenth centuries had generally been led by a keyboard or string player, a practice that has been widely revived for music of this period since the 1970s. Change came early in the nineteenth century, when conductors included composers such as Weber and Spohr and, among the first musicians to make conducting their main activity, Habeneck and Michael Umlauf (1781–1842), who was responsible for the première of Beethoven's Ninth Symphony. Conducting gave composers a means of maintaining their economic status in a commercial world, and where most composers since the mid-seventeenth century had been instrumentalists, most from the early nineteenth to the early twentieth were conductors. A conductor was needed from this point partly because ensembles were growing (the *Fantastique*, keeping pace with developments in the Paris Opera orchestra, required four harps, four sets of timpani, deep bells and a cor anglais, all used with a keen sense for positioning on the platform as well as for colour), partly because the sense of voice in music since Beethoven demanded a visual stimulus, an instigator.

That sense of voice was conjured not only by the immense orchestral apparatus of Berlioz but just as much by the lone piano of Chopin or of Liszt, both of whom were living in the same city as Berlioz, Paris, in the early 1830s. A regular visitor there was Paganini: Berlioz wrote a work for the great virtuoso to play on the viola – characteristically not a formal concerto, for he wrote no abstract music, but another symphony with a programme, *Harold en Italie* (Harold in Italy, 1834), after Byron – and received for his pains no performance but a handsome fee. Other lustrous moths drawn to the city of lights included Bellini and the German-born Giacomo Meyerbeer (1791–1864), of whom the latter gave the Paris Opera two model examples of grand opera in his *Robert le diable* (Robert the Devil, 1831) and *Les Huguenots* (The Huguenots, 1836), which became staples of the repertory while he worked carefully on his next piece, *Le Prophète* (The Prophet, 1849). Berlioz, whose attention to audience requirements was always modified by his own urgent expressive desires, had no success at the same theatre with his first opera, *Benvenuto Cellini* (1838). One reason may have been that the score, intended for a different company, did not include a ballet, which, as the composer had noted in a review of Rossini's *Guillaume Tell*, was an absolute requirement at the Paris Opera, 'even in a representation of the Last Judgement'.

The theatres of Paris, among which the Théâtre Italien rivalled the Opera, drew all the great singers of the time. Bellini, writing *I puritani* (The Puritans, 1835) for the Italien, could write with confidence for a central cast entirely of stars. Also prominent in the city were two daughters of the Spanish singing teacher Manuel García (1775–1832): Maria Malibran (1808–36), who died young as a result of a riding accident, and Pauline Viardot (1821–1910), who lived to cast her spell on a leading writer (Ivan Turgenev) and on composers of another generation (Brahms among them). All these singers, brought up on Rossini, adapted themselves to the greater force and dynamism required by Bellini, Donizetti and Meyerbeer – required not so much because the orchestra was bigger (for often it was not) but because the roles were. Five-act grand operas required a new stamina; Romantic opera in general demanded a stronger investment from the performer in heroes and heroines who were themselves living Romantic lives, taking charge of their destinies along courses that would lead, especially for the heroines, to death.

As they went they sang, and their songs went into the instrumental music of the period – directly in the case of

Liszt's operatic fantasies (e.g. *Réminiscences de Lucia di Lammermoor*, 1835–6, after Donizetti's latest hit), indirectly in other instances, as in the correlation between the long, limpid melodies of Chopin and of Bellini. Chopin was not only a great melodist, nor was he only a composer of 'music for pianists', however far-reaching his understanding of piano textures, on instruments of newly increased size and power. His harmonic venturings went as far as Schubert's, and his gestures could be as terrifying as anything in Berlioz, as at the close of the G minor Ballade (c. 1833). Soon after arriving in Paris he abandoned concert-giving (until 1848, near the end of his life), able to support himself by giving lessons and publishing his music. One must wonder at the large numbers of amateur pianists in the 1830s who could contemplate music so difficult and, at times, unsettling.

Linked by their feeling for music's expressive power (in Mendelssohn's view, music was a language more exact than words), by their search for that power in harmony and colour as well as melody, and by their projection of it as music's voice, the Romantics of the 1830s were allied also in their opposition to anything that smacked of rule or authority. Berlioz chafed under the jurisdiction of Cherubini at the Conservatoire; Schumann in 1836 wrote that the musical world was divided between Romantics and classicists, the latter party for him perhaps including Hummel and Spohr. Both these emerging composers no doubt overstated the case. Cherubini's Requiem in D minor (1836) is fully Romantic in its sombreness, even if it lacks the theatricality of Berlioz's setting of the same text made the next year. There are also Romantic features in Spohr's music. But the energy of the Romantics in the 1830s was a youthful energy, an energy of revolt.

There was, however, an exception: Mendelssohn. In a way he was the eldest of his generation (though in fact Berlioz was five years older), having begun his professional career in the early 1820s, when Beethoven and Schubert were still living. He had already shown his attachment to traditional forms, to the Classical style and to Bach before Berlioz had been heard of. The two composers met in Italy in 1831 and got on; at that time they were both taking advantage of the concert overture, a new form, for its openness to descriptive orchestral writing (Mendelssohn's *Die Hebriden*; Berlioz's *Waverley*). But where Mendelssohn thereafter moved increasingly towards types from the past, whether Classical (the three op. 44 quartets, 1837–8) or Baroque (the oratorio *St Paul*, 1836), Berlioz was constantly reinventing the concert, creating a strange assemblage of narrated fragments (*Lélio*, 1831–2) as a second part to the *Symphonie fantastique*, or a hybrid of symphony and oratorio in the 'dramatic symphony' *Roméo et Juliette* (1839).

The dilemma was one that has faced generations of revolutionaries on achieving power, whether to work within the existing system or overturn it. Mendelssohn by the mid-1830s had achieved power. His 'Italian' Symphony – another collection of musical traveller's tales, from the time he met Berlioz – was commissioned by the Philharmonic Society of London, and he conducted the first performance in 1833. Music in England was still dominated by guest composers, who also included Spohr; Mendelssohn's visits were almost annual, and in the 1840s he became a particular favourite of the new monarch, Victoria, and her German husband. Meanwhile, in 1835, he took charge of one of the most venerable German orchestras, the Leipzig Gewandhaus (so called from the Cloth Exchange in which they gave their concerts). There, besides introducing new works (including his own and his friend Schumann's), he performed the music that had meant most to him from his childhood – Bach, Handel, Haydn, Mozart, Beethoven – and added Schubert's 'Great C major' Symphony, which Schumann had recently discovered. He also founded a conservatory in the city, of immediate and lasting importance in the training of musicians within what were becoming, oxymoronically, Romantic traditions.

Mendelssohn's way, embracing the past, proved to be that of the future. In New York, for example, Beethoven's Fifth Symphony was on the programme of the Philharmonic's first concert, in 1842. Soon one could speak of an international repertory, a canon. The same operas could be seen in New Orleans as in Paris or Milan, the same symphonies heard in London, Leipzig and Copenhagen. They would not be the symphonies of Berlioz, but they might well be those of Mendelssohn or Schumann.

Schumann's works of the 1830s, all for piano, had included three sonatas or sonata-like compositions but a great many more sets of short pieces, in which he could play with shifts of tone and voice. Among them are *Carnaval* (1834–5), in which the figures at a masked ball include girlfriends, fellow musicians (Chopin, Paganini) and the composer himself in two of his favourite personae, the poetical Eusebius and the vital Florestan. His delight in masquerade extended to musical code: *Carnaval* is based on four notes that, in German musical nomenclature, spell out the name of a girlfriend's home town, Asch, these being letters that also appear in his own name. Marriage in 1840 – not to the Asch maiden but to Clara Wieck (1819–96), the match having been, in properly Romantic fashion, fiercely opposed by her father – may have reduced Schumann's need or taste for subterfuge. He spent most of that year writing songs, then moved on to orchestral scores ('Spring' and D minor Symphonies, 1841) and chamber music (Piano Quintet, Piano Quartet and three string quartets, all 1842).

If these chamber and orchestral works are outwardly conventional, they also explore new possibilities. The D minor Symphony (revised as his Fourth) has the normal four movements played as a single continuity, and the 'Rhenish' Symphony (No. 3, 1850) matchlessly finds symphonic space for evocative sound-pictures, notably of a ceremony in Cologne Cathedral; both initiatives were to be taken up by composers later in the century. More generally Schumann found ways to make Romantic songfulness work within the great forms. Of course, the accommodation was easier when there was a singing subject within the piece: a soloist. Hence the superb fluency of Schumann's Piano Concerto (1841–5), as of Mendelssohn's Violin Concerto (1844), both of which were introduced in Leipzig.

The two composers also shared family proximity to fellow composers of the opposite sex, for both Mendelssohn's sister Fanny (1805–47) and Schumann's wife Clara were creatively active. Their lives, somewhat parallel, indicate some of the problems facing a woman in what was formally a man's world – however much music, not least Schumann's and Mendelssohn's, may express sexual prevarication and frontier-crossing, as happens explicitly in Schumann's song cycle *Frauenliebe und -leben* (Womanly Love and Life, 1840). Both Fanny Mendelssohn and Clara Schumann contributed songs to sets published under their menfolk's names, hesitating to disturb society's fiction that composers were all male. Fanny died quite young; her death hastened her brother's. Clara long survived her husband's decline into madness and death, but her creativity she suppressed.

Or perhaps silence simply overcame her, as it seems to have been overcoming Chopin in his last years.

Romanticism, like a centrifuge, had spun music to the edges, in several ways. Vienna, which had been the chief fount of European music for half a century, was now dominated by a composer whose waltzes, unlike Chopin's, definitely were made for dancing: Johann Strauss I (1804–49). Leading composers were coming not only from Poland but also from Russia, from Denmark. Mikhail Glinka (1804–57) drew on firsthand experience of Bellini and Donizetti, in Italy, as well as on Russian folklore and literature in his operas *A Life for the Tsar* (1834–6) and *Ruslan and Lyudmila* (1837–42), hailed by subsequent Russian composers as foundation stones. Niels Gade (1817–90) became the Scandinavian Mendelssohn, and similarly a regionally venerated prototype.

Chopin's nationalism was more ambiguous. In his youth he was applauded both in Warsaw and abroad for his Polishness, but, having left his native country at the age of twenty, he made only one return visit, and his mazurkas and polonaises are no different from his waltzes, nocturnes and other series in offering inexhaustible models of tone, rhythmic character and form. Like Bach's dances, Chopin's belong much more to their composer than to anywhere on the map. The comparison is apt in other ways, for Chopin – if within a quite different style, of extended moments and precipitous trajectories – was equally a contrapuntalist. What he might have done if, like Schumann, he had turned to the orchestra is unimaginable. Instead he drew to a halt.

Schumann did not. He went on to ever larger genres: opera and oratorio. Both he and Berlioz took up the Faust theme at almost the same time, producing respectively *Scenen aus Goethes Faust* (1844–53) and *La Damnation de*

Faust (1845–6), both concert-length scores for solo singers, choir and orchestra, but otherwise thoroughly dissimilar. The Berlioz work, almost cinematic in its vividness and its shifts from closeup (song) to longshot (symphonic and choral sections), is like his earlier music, full of sound and fury, and wonder and strangeness. Yet he was now having much more trouble composing, his *Faust* being a burst in a long period of creative darkness. Schumann, composing much more steadily, had arrived at oratorio through his belief in art's transcendence, and his treatment of the subject is driven much less by the demonic Mephistopheles than by the promise of benediction in the second part of Goethe's poetic drama, which Berlioz did not touch. And while Schumann was drafting this ceremony for the religion of art, Mendelssohn was supplying the religion of religion – and of hallowed, Handelian form – with a vehicle in his oratorio *Elijah* (1846), which he wrote for one of the choral festivals that were such a feature of nineteenth-century British musical life: the Birmingham Triennial. When Berlioz turned to sacred narrative it became children's story, with the reversion to smoothened and sweetened adaptations of earlier styles he produced in his oratorio *L'Enfance du Christ* (The Childhood of Christ, 1850–4).

Mendelssohn and Chopin both died in their thirties, as had Bellini before them; all three were sanctified by immediate posterity as graceful beings lifting off into heaven before their time. By the end of 1853 Schumann had written his last sane note, and Berlioz might have seemed to be running out of steam, while Donizetti was also in his grave. But Romanticism was far from over. Liszt was entering his most creative period, and two other composers, only three years younger than Chopin and Schumann but slower to start, were moving into high gear. Giuseppe Verdi

(1813–1901) had made his name with *Nabucco* (Nebuchadnezzar, 1842) and in 1847 alone saw new works staged in Florence (*Macbeth*), Paris and London. And *Der fliegende Holländer* (The Flying Dutchman, 1841) had introduced the world to Richard Wagner (1813–83).

CHAPTER 15

New Germans and old Vienna

In 1853, twenty-two years after he had saluted a contemporary in his first article, Schumann in his last gave his weakened blessing to a member of the next generation: Johannes Brahms (1833–97). Brahms, only twenty, was already the author of three piano sonatas, songs and chamber pieces, the works of a young Romantic. Schumann must have recognized his youthful self in this music, and in his short essay he looked forward to the time when Brahms would be where he, Schumann, was now, writing compositions for chorus and orchestra that would open 'still more wondrous glimpses into the secrets of the spirit world' — words recalling Hoffmann's on Beethoven and suggesting a prospect very different from the play of masks he had discerned in Chopin's music and placed in his own earlier works. Brahms, a little ahead of Schumann's schedule, was to strive for something suspiciously like these wondrous glimpses in his Alto Rhapsody (1869) and *Schicksalslied* (Fate Song, 1868–71). But his immediate future was that of a pianist-composer and song writer, and he found himself, as a German musician, in a world dominated not by Schumann's ambitions but by those of Liszt and Wagner.

Liszt, in one of his periodic self-reinventions, had settled in 1848 in the central German town of Weimar, Goethe's old home, where he was court music director but, in keeping with the democratic times, pretty much running his own show. He made Weimar in the 1850s what Leipzig had been in the 1840s and Paris in the 1830s, a musical hotspot, and he developed a network of colleagues and pupils that became known as the New German School (with Berlioz as honorary member). But, ever generous, he presented operas by his great contemporaries across whatever divides of nationality and aesthetic philosophy, including works by Schumann and Donizetti, Berlioz and Verdi, and, in 1850, the first performance of Wagner's *Lohengrin*. (Wagner, having sided with the socialists in one of the many revolutions that sputtered across Europe in 1848, was in exile in Switzerland.) At the same time he went on producing quantities of piano music, including his fearsome *Etudes d'exécution transcendante* (Transcendental Etudes, 1851) and B minor Sonata (1852–3), the latter going beyond Schumann, Schubert and Beethoven in welding four movements into one.

By now his days as a touring virtuoso were over, but he had many successors on the circuit, as the spread of the rail network in the middle decades of the nineteenth century, coupled with the development of transatlantic passenger shipping, was opening the age of the intercontinental star. One of the first was the soprano Jenny Lind (1820–87), who, as 'the Swedish nightingale', was presented throughout the United States and in Havana in 1850–1 by the impresario Phineas T. Barnum. Later in the 1850s, and in the 1860s, the US pianist-composer Louis Moreau Gottschalk (1829–69) criss-crossed the country by rail, taking with him an extraordinary compound of European and Caribbean heritages. But surely the most remarkable traveller of the period was the Norwegian violinist Ole Bull

(1810–80), who also traversed the United States in the 1850s and, on his sixty-sixth birthday, played from the top of the Great Pyramid.

Liszt in Weimar, stationary while Lind, Gottschalk and Bull wowed their US audiences, was not only remembering the piano but also discovering the possibilities of the orchestra, as Schumann had done a decade before. He completed two piano concertos that had long been in progress. More than that, he invented a new form: the symphonic poem, or orchestral movement having a narrative or illustrative meaning. This was an innovation waiting to happen. Opera overtures had been used as concert pieces since the early eighteenth century, and from Gluck onwards had often been made to include some reference to the coming drama. Among the four overtures Beethoven completed at different times for *Fidelio*, those now known as *Leonore* Nos. 2 and 3 (after the opera's original title) are effectively symphonic poems, transmitting almost the whole action of the opera in a few minutes. After that, concert overtures, whether telling stories or describing scenes (in defiance of Hoffmann's highest hopes), had come from many others besides Mendelssohn and Berlioz. Liszt's symphonic poems just went the next step, expanding the dimensions and liberating the descriptive impulse from the formal and functional expectations of the overture as a genre.

In the 1850s Liszt produced twelve symphonic poems, at first taking help with orchestration from his assistant Joseph Raff (1822–82), who was later to create whole symphonies picturing the seasons, the alps and the forests. Here again Liszt, in some ways the most Romantically self-expressive of the Romantics, showed his sense of composition as a collaborative act. That was the way with his many piano arrangements and paraphrases of orchestral or operatic scores, which he continued to make. It was the way, too, with his B minor Sonata, which he wrote as a blueprint for other pianists to complete in playing it: the first public performance he entrusted to his pupil Hans von Bülow (1830–94), who married his daughter Cosima.

If all these works question the notion of lone artistic invention, Liszt's *Faust Symphony* (1854–7) looks forward in a different way, beginning with a theme that uses all twelve notes of the chromatic scale and so presages the atonality of half a century later. No less striking is how the work simultaneously fulfils its Faust programme and symphonic expectations. The first movement, with its twelve-note theme, conveys Faust's endless yearning; the second brings balm in a character study of his beloved Gretchen; the third restores the Faust and Gretchen themes but in grotesque form, to create an image of Mephistopheles; and the finale finds redemption in heaven. Liszt dedicated the symphony to Berlioz, just as Berlioz had dedicated his 'dramatic legend' on the same subject to Liszt.

Not surprisingly, Liszt's works of the 1850s reflect two of the New Germans' key ideas. The consolidation of the repertory had given musical progress a particular actuality: Beethoven's symphonies were self-evidently not only bigger than Haydn's but harmonically richer and texturally more involved. Further evolution along all those same lines was probably not to be looked for, but evolution there must be. (Darwin's *The Origin of Species* was first published in 1859.) From the perspective of the 1850s it was hard to see much evolution in Mendelssohn's symphonies or Schumann's. Berlioz's were different. Indeed, they were differently different, for they included a purely orchestral score (the *Fantastique*), a concerto (*Harold*) and a potpourri (*Roméo*), though they shared the crucial feature – and here was the second idea – of embracing poetry, whether voiced in song or present as a programme, communicated instrumentally. Liszt's symphonic poems and symphonies (on Dante as well as Faust) did the same. Progress must continue: that was the artist's transcendent duty. On the more mundane plane of compositional practice, Liszt came to feel that each new composition must include a new chord.

That criterion was most conspicuously met by Wagner's opera *Tristan und Isolde* (1856–9), in the '*Tristan* chord' that appears in the opening phrase of the prelude, to use a term Wagner preferred to 'overture' in respect of pieces that belong to the whole work's continuity. 'Opera', too, was a term he felt most of his works had outgrown: they were 'music dramas' or, in the case of *Tristan*, an 'action for music'. What they projected was, in his view, not just passionate drama sung from the stage (though certainly they work that way) but 'deeds of music made visible'. And though the '*Tristan* chord' was not in fact original, for it had appeared in a symphonic poem by Bülow (*Nirvana*) and has even been detected in Mozart, its place right at the start – and the shadow it casts right through the piece – gave it an utterly new significance. Dark in sound and uncertain in its harmonic meaning, it is a disquieting problem waiting to be resolved. The entire action can be construed, exactly as Wagner hoped, as a four-hour musical process in which this hovering chord's resolution is demanded, prepared, delayed and ultimately supplied – supplied, as commonly in Wagner, by a woman's redemptive death.

In his essay 'The Artwork of the Future' (1849) Wagner set out the paths which, as a master of the manifesto and of self-promotion, he made the paths of his age, elaborating on the ideas that were current among the New Germans. Music was not to be invented but discovered. It was an immense sea — a sea of harmony, murky in the depths, bright on the surface — washing the shores of two continents: dance, from which it gained rhythm, and poetry, which gave it melody. Among those who had navigated these waters before, Beethoven had taken instrumental composition as far as it could go. His Ninth, breaking out of the instrumental category in its finale, was the last possible symphony. Now music would have to absorb movement and speech in order to manifest itself. It would have to become music drama, with the composer taking care of both text (as Wagner always did) and production.

Most unusually for a German composer, Wagner wrote nothing but operas, except for some early efforts, the occasional minor piano piece and a couple of works bearing on operas in progress (a set of songs to poems by Mathilde Wesendonck, who was the object of his affections while working on *Tristan*, and the *Siegfried Idyll* for chamber orchestra). For him music drama was not a choice but a necessity, compelled by the human thirst for knowledge — in this case, of music, which he saw as a natural element, like space or time — and also as a marker of a future society whose art would be communal, made by all and understood by all. He was a long way from talk of 'illusion'. His great model for the future came from the distant past, from what had served Gluck and the Renaissance Florentines in very different ways: ancient Greek theatre. In that spirit he planned a sequence of three music dramas plus a 'fore-evening' that would, all together, reach for the sources of German culture and expose the contrary materialism of the present: *Der Ring des Nibelungen* (The Nibelung's Ring), which he began in 1851 and finished twenty-three years later. *Tristan* was an interlude in that project.

He composed the four parts of the *Ring* in order, but wanted to hold them in reserve until the cycle was complete. The first performance of *Tristan*, in Munich under Bülow in 1865, was therefore the world's first opportunity to hear what he had been talking about through fifteen years of pamphleteering. (His *Tannhäuser* had divided audiences at the Paris Opera in 1861, but that was in essence an old piece.) The world took note (as did Cosima von Bülow, about to leave the conductor for the composer). Though Wagner's earlier operas had revealed his unparalleled capacity to engross, to let forth a stream of music that would seem to take its own course, moving through solo passages, choral scenes and orchestral breaks with superb command, *Tristan* was quite new in its chromatic harmony and in the depth of expression thus summoned. Moreover, the stream seems to be the sound of thought and emotion proceeding in some entity – the world, perhaps, in which the characters are locked and resounding. For generations afterwards, the prolonged love scene that forms the second act, and the similarly protracted agonies of the third, before the appeasement brought by Isolde's expiration upon Tristan's lifeless body, were precisely what Wagner said they were: the sounding of the human heart.

They are also supremely well crafted stage music. Verdi, who had no philosophical ambitions for his art, was dealing during the years of *Tristan* and the *Ring* with other topics: the old topics of conflicted loves (amorous and paternal), deceit, sacrifice and mistaken identities in the three works that, coming in rapid succession, made him an international celebrity – *Rigoletto* (1851), *Il trovatore* (The Troubadour, 1853) and *La traviata* (The Woman Led Astray, 1853) – and new ones, still rooted in personal feelings and relationships, in those that followed more slowly. In *Don Carlos* (1867), for example, themes of love and jealousy are interwoven with the workings of statecraft, all handled with greater depth than in the usual run of Romantic historical opera. Particularly powerful is the scene for two bass voices, those of Philip II of Spain and the Grand Inquisitor — a scene Wagner surely took note of when composing a similar moment in the last *Ring* opera, where again a bleak personality is addressed by one no less dark but more percipient. The two composers were not, after all, so very far apart. They both wrote family dramas. And Verdi, too, strove to achieve a continuous musical-dramatic flux in each act, even though he kept such conventions of Italian opera as the aria in three parts: a slow and melodious opening, a reaction to some change, and a fast conclusion.

Don Carlos, like the revision of *Tannhäuser*, was made for the Paris Opera under the Second Empire (1851–70), the theatre that rejected Berlioz's glorious epic *Les troyens*. Such younger composers as Charles Gounod (1818–93) and Georges Bizet (1838–75), like Berlioz, experienced only disappointment within this gilded cage, and found the environment more conducive at the Théâtre Lyrique. Works presented there included Gounod's *Faust* (1859) and *Roméo et Juliette* (1867), and Bizet's *Les Pêcheurs de perles* (The Pearl Fishers, 1863), all of which demanded little of their audiences but the ability to relish fine singing and good tunes. During the same epoch Jacques Offenbach (1819–80) established an alternative operatic tradition at the Bouffes Parisiens, where he presented such sharply satirical and briskly ironic yet generous-spirited pieces as *Orphée aux enfers* (Orpheus in the Underworld, 1858).

Wildly favouring opera at this point in its history, Paris produced one of the great masterpieces in Bizet's *Carmen* (1875). The work stands out not only for its string of great songs and its brilliant orchestration but also for its handling of chromaticism in a way utterly different from Wagner's, not to extend the traditional system but rather to reconform it, along new routes coming from Spanish dance. What is expressed in this world is not so much individual psychology – Carmen's self-searching is confined to one devastating moment, when she tells the man who has left everything for her: 'I don't love you any more' – as the brutal incompatibility of Romantic love with the drive of sex. The subject was to return in Italian operas of two and three decades later, but sentimentalized as Bizet's harshly clear vision was not.

Had Bizet been a Spaniard *Carmen* would be renowned as a nationalist piece, among many others at a time when nations were being defined not by their rulers but by their peoples. Italy, hitherto dappled with kingdoms, dukedoms and city states, was largely unified by 1860, and Verdi, whose operas had been totems in the process, became briefly a member of the country's first parliament. Elsewhere nationhood was being gained not by fusion but fission. What Verdi was for Italy, Liszt became for his native Hungary: a national hero, albeit absent since he was nine. He revisited Budapest in 1871 and founded an academy of music there in 1875. To the northwest, still within the vast Austro-Hungarian empire, Bedřich Smetana (1824–84) was bringing a national verve to music in Prague. Admiring Liszt, he wrote symphonic poems in his thirties, but made his national reputation with a comic opera set to the lively rhythms of Czech dance: *The Bartered Bride* (1866). Cooler national colour entered in the works of Edvard Grieg (1843–1907) – his Piano Concerto (1868), lyric pieces for piano and music for his compatriot Ibsen's play *Peer Gynt* (1874–5) – filtered through his training in the Mendelssohn–Schumann traditions of the Leipzig Conservatory. Like Liszt and Smetana, he became the musical symbol of a country lacking identity as a state, Norway being attached to Denmark.

Russian musical nationalism had a different goal, that of creating indigenous work in a country whose composers had hitherto been foreigners (as they still were in Britain, where Gounod was among those to fill the vacancy left by Mendelssohn's demise). Verdi, for instance, had written *La forza del destino* (The Force of Destiny, 1862) for the splendid Mariinsky Theatre in St Petersburg, opened two years before as one of several imposing new houses of this opera-busy period: others included the Bolshoy in Moscow (1856), the Teatro Colón in Buenos Aires (1857) and Covent Garden in London (1858), all of which were built for an imported repertory that was largely the same in Argentina as in Russia. Soon, though, the Mariinsky was being filled with the music of native composers: Aleksandr Dargomyzhsky (1813–69), Aleksandr Serov (1820–71), Anton Rubinstein (1829–94), Modest Musorgsky (1839–81), Petr Tchaikovsky (1840–93) and Nikolay Rimsky-Korsakov (1844–1908). The key figures were Rubinstein and Mily Balakirev (1837–1910), who came to represent traditional alternatives in Russian culture: to westernize or to develop from Russian roots. When Rubinstein in 1862 founded the St Petersburg Conservatory to educate students in the great western tradition, Balakirev immediately opened his Free Music School, with a less dogmatic curriculum. Yet their approaches were not mutually exclusive. The group that formed around Balakirev – known as 'The Mighty Handful' and including Musorgsky, Rimsky-Korsakov and Aleksandr Borodin (1833–87) – took influences not only from Russian folklore and chant but also from Berlioz (who made two visits), Schumann and Verdi.

Differences were personal as much as aesthetic. Rubinstein was an energetic composer (of twenty operas among much else) and authoritarian, whereas Balakirev wrote slowly, revised at length, and generously gave some of his best ideas to others.

One of his ideas was a programme for a symphonic poem on a subject already treated by Berlioz and Gounod: *Romeo and Juliet*. This was a gift to Tchaikovsky, for it appealed to his taste for tragedy urgently expressing itself as dynamic form – the sound, indeed, of time running out – and the resulting piece (1869) was his first triumph. The same year Musorgsky, after several abandoned attempts, for the first time completed an opera, *Boris Godunov*, telling the story of a Russian usurper of the early seventeenth century. Orchestrated with a grim beauty all its own (the score was lovingly given more colour by Rimsky-Korsakov after his friend's death), the work is deeply Russian in its musical references and creates a vocal style close to the sounds and rhythms of the language. Musorgsky had recently experimented with modelling sung lines on the melodies of speech, following Dargomyzhsky's example, and he made powerful use of the technique in portraying the tsar's attack of guilt. No less potent here is the orchestra's part in conveying the tsar's nightmarish hearing of a clock, and there is a telling disregard of formal effect: Boris leaves the stage to end the act, and the music simply breaks off. However, the work was refused performance until the composer had insinuated a substantial female role.

Musorgsky wrote no abstract music. His one major instrumental work is a set of character pieces for the piano – dazzling, weird, funny, touching: *Pictures at an Exhibition* (1874). But Tchaikovsky, Balakirev, Borodin and Rimsky-Korsakov all wrote symphonies in the 1860s and early 1870s, at a time when the genre was almost moribund elsewhere. By 1875 there had been no notable symphony in western Europe for nearly twenty years, since Liszt's pair.

This was when Brahms broke in. He had waited a long while, for he had found larger responsibilities than to Schumann and Liszt. From the latter he had distanced himself; the two were on different courses, which gained a physical reality in their virtually simultaneous moves across the power map of Europe. In 1861 Liszt, increasingly concerned with religious subjects, had settled in Rome, where four years later he took minor orders (allowing him to fulfil various ecclesiastical functions but not to say mass). The next year Brahms had taken up residence in Vienna, the city of Beethoven.

It was a good time to arrive. The centre was being rebuilt, gaining a new opera house (1869) as well as concert halls, whose construction teams were surely whistling the latest waltzes of Johann Strauss II (1825–99): *The Blue Danube* (1867), perhaps, or *Wine, Women and Song* (1869). Brahms, wishing he had written the former, did indeed compose waltzes, notably his *Liebeslieder* (Love Songs, 1868–9) for four singers and piano duet, and the funeral waltzing of *Ein deutsches Requiem* (A German Requiem, 1865–8), setting biblical texts for soloists, choir and orchestra. But the work he felt bound to write, the work his friends were expecting and the work he was waiting to complete right from his arrival in Vienna, was his First Symphony – which, when it came, coincided with another project long prepared and long anticipated.

CHAPTER 16

Romantic evenings

In August 1876 an audience heavily laden with genius, wealth, position or luck travelled to a small town in Bavaria where a composer had built a theatre: Bayreuth. Among those who came to this first complete performance of the *Ring* (for a few years earlier Wagner had acceded to the wish of his patron, the Bavarian king Ludwig II, to hear the first two parts in advance) were Liszt, Grieg, Tchaikovsky, the composer's ardent admirer Anton Bruckner (1824–96) and two Frenchmen: Camille Saint-Saëns (1835–1921) and Vincent d'Indy (1851–1931). Saint-Saëns was amiable and various in his affiliations, to Mozart as much as to Liszt and Wagner; d'Indy was to become a forceful proponent of orthodox form. At the end, as flames leapt from the hero Siegfried's funeral pyre to engulf the fortress of the gods while Brünnhilde, like Isolde before her, attained the ecstasy of cognizant death, many of those present must have felt the world had changed. And so it had. There had been nothing like this before: a work a quarter-century in the making, occupying four evenings of a week, performed in a theatre specially built for it. But the full grip of Wagnerism came a little later, after the composer had written his swan song, *Parsifal* (1882), and his widow Cosima (née Liszt, formerly von Bülow) had created for him a lasting memorial, the Bayreuth Festival, at which his works, and only his, were presented each summer. In 1876 it was still possible to take Wagner or leave him.

Tchaikovsky left him. He was more thrilled by *Sylvia*, the ballet score by Léo Delibes (1836–91), which he had heard on the same trip at another, more imposing new theatre, that of the Paris Opera, and which he wished he had heard before composing his own recently finished *Swan Lake*. Grieg also found more stimulus elsewhere, in Norwegian folk music, which he began studying in the field in 1877. And though Bruckner was ravished, apparently sitting with his eyes closed to enjoy the music the more, his ravishment went into a form Wagner had declared redundant almost three decades ago: the symphony.

Suddenly symphonies were everywhere again. Brahms's First, so long in the making, was launched into the world within three months of the *Ring*. The next year came his Second and Bruckner's Third, the two works introduced in Vienna just a fortnight apart, though only one of them (the Bruckner, to be sure) carrying a dedication to Wagner. It was almost as if the conflagration at the end of the *Ring* had destroyed music drama and enabled abstract music to be reborn – though neither Brahms nor Bruckner would have seen it that way, the one because he would not have wished to owe anything to the master of Bayreuth, the other for reasons of simple humility. Clearly, though, symphonic music was moving forward once more – music for the enlarged resources of the *Ring* (an ensemble of ninety musicians or more) that was being played by an ever-increasing number of orchestras. Among the most prestigious, then and now, the Boston Symphony was founded in 1881, the Berlin Philharmonic the next year and the Chicago Symphony in 1891.

Bruckner, like Brahms, was a non-native Viennese: he had arrived a few years after his junior colleague, in 1868, to take a teaching position at the conservatory. Also like Brahms, he had reached his early forties before completing a symphony he felt worth dignifying as his No. 1. Much more curiously, both composers' first symphonies are in C minor, though that — except for the fact that both are in the expected four movements — is where resemblances end. Bruckner's opening allegro starts with characteristic ostinatos (repetitions of short figures), as if winding up some great machine, but is almost immediately on to solid statement, whereas the Brahms symphony emerges from the dark, seeming to enact the uncertainty from which it took shape. Of the slow movements, Bruckner's is a solemn adagio, such as he wrote in nearly all his symphonies. Brahms, who composed no full-scale symphonic adagio, supplies something more fluid and congenial. Nor did Brahms ever write a bald symphonic scherzo, whereas Bruckner's is as bald as they come, another piece of machine music set to repeating units and a strong pulse. Even so, there is something stationary about Bruckner's music, as if the segments, often separated by pauses, were architectural sections being put together, while Brahms's music is constantly on the move. Also, the whole sound is different. Brahms's textured orchestration clothes music of ambiguity and regret; Bruckner's choirs of instruments sound out certainty and faith.

Having spent much of his early life as a musician at the great Austrian monastery of St Florian, Bruckner was imbued with piety, church music and the resonance of an organ in a great building. He wrote his symphonies as hymns of praise, and they became his central endeavour for the rest of his life, though he also produced some startling choral pieces. The endeavour was arduous. Lacking self-confidence, he accepted the advice of well-meaning friends to revise his scores, so that while composing his Ninth Symphony (1887–96), which he was planning to dedicate to God but failed to finish, he also had his First, Second, Third, Fourth and Eighth on his worktable. Brahms had no such problems once his First Symphony was out of the way. He completed virtually his entire orchestral output during the next eleven years – three more symphonies, three concertos, a pair of overtures – then returned to what he always loved best: chamber music and songs.

Brahms and Bruckner concurred at least in making their music self-sufficient, feeling no pull from the Wagnerian shores of poetry and dance. However, their concord in this was disputed by the leading Viennese music critic of the second half of the nineteenth century, Eduard Hanslick (1825–1904). He, too, considered musical beauty to be 'a beauty that is self-contained and in no need of content from outside itself, that consists simply and solely of tones and their artistic combination', repeating the view articulated a century before by de Chabanon. But where Brahms's music, for him, was sublime in its entire behaviour, Bruckner's only expressed sublimity. In Brahms he found internal consistency and motivation from within (he perhaps underestimated the composer's indebtedness to what was by now the concert hall's familiar tradition, from Bach through Mozart, Beethoven and Schumann to the present). Bruckner asked for justification from outside (or simply owed much less to the great tradition), though what may have annoyed Hanslick most was Bruckner's allegiance to Wagner, whose artistic philosophy placed him wholly beyond the pale. Emphatically contradicting Wagner, and voicing his insistence on musical validity as the only criterion of excellence, he was even prepared to criticize the finale of Beethoven's Ninth Symphony as only 'the vast shadow of a titanic body'.

If Hanslick had qualms when Beethoven introduced words, he was scathing when Tchaikovsky brought life's experience into his symphonies. Yet the autobiographical – always to be understood as containing elements of knowing self-dramatization and self-mockery – was one of that composer's strongest modes. On returning from Bayreuth he took up again the theme of doomed love, in his symphonic poem *Francesca da Rimini*. The next year he abruptly leapt into marriage and, when he found heterosexuality decidedly not to his taste, out again. During this period of desperation and shock he was working on an opera, *Eugene Onegin* (1879), and a symphony, his Fourth (1877–8), both of which seem to express aspects of his situation and feelings – most especially in the case of the symphony, for which he disclosed a programme having to do with the dread power of fate. Yet the work imposes itself as urgent form: the fate theme, however fierce in effect, has its place as the symphony's agent of dynamism, and also of coherence, for it comes back in the finale, making this another of those nineteenth-century works of symphonic unification, where the entire composition is exposed as growing from the same musical genes.

Among Tchaikovsky's contemporaries in Russia the zest for nationalism had abated. So it had in Prague, where Smetana's set of six symphonic poems *Má vlast* (My Homeland, completed 1879), like the Slavonic Rhapsodies and Slavonic Dances (both 1878) of Antonín Dvořák (1841–1904), spoke more of celebration than embattlement. Nationalism now was simply an option. French composers were continuing to write Spanish music: Edouard Lalo

(1823–92) in his *Symphonie espagnole* (1874), Emmanuel Chabrier (1841–94) in his joyous *España* (1883), Jules Massenet (1842–1912), who had succeeded Gounod as leading French opera composer, in *Le Cid* (The Cid, 1885). They could also write Russian, Norwegian, Polish and Moroccan music all in the same piece, which Lalo did in his ballet *Namouna* (1882), a great crossroads not only in space but also in time, anticipating the syncopations (offbeat rhythms), simultaneous different tempos and spatchcock design, with fairground elements, to be found thirty years later in Stravinsky's *Petrushka*. As in Chabrier's *España*, ostinato and pulse provide motive forces in music whose harmony is more colourful than progressive.

Other composers, too, were eager to hear from beyond Europe. They could travel to do so, or they could study anthropological reports, or they could attend the great trade exhibitions of the period, which, amid the wealth of the globe, brought Asian and African musicians to the major cities of Europe. By one or other of these means arrived the Nile dances of Verdi's *Aida* (1871), the intoxicating bacchanal of Saint-Saëns's *Samson et Dalilah* (1877) and the picturesque effects of operas by Delibes and Massenet, as well as, in Russia, Balakirev's symphonic poem *Tamara* (1867–82), Rimsky-Korsakov's heady symphonic suite *Sheherazade* (1888) and the Polovtsian Dances from Borodin's *Prince Igor* (1890).

Orientalism's appeal was not universal. It meant little to Tchaikovsky, who found his lands of lost content in the eighteenth century or the fairytale. It certainly meant little to César Franck (1822–90), who provided a French parallel (though he was born in what was to become Belgium) to Bruckner, for here was another slow beginner who adapted Wagnerian harmony to create an original symphonic language – in his case of grand themes that, as with the otherwise very different Tchaikovsky, could reappear in later movements. Like Bruckner, too, Franck was an organist, serving in that capacity for much of his life at one of the French capital's great churches, Ste Clotilde, and founding the school of Parisian organist-composers that went through the next century as far as Messiaen. Again like Bruckner, he was a charismatic teacher, in person and by example. At once formally solid and yearningly expressive, his great works are nearly all in abstract instrumental genres, beginning with his Piano Quintet (1879).

Everywhere the old forms were continuing to flourish as at no time since the 1840s. Four of the epoch's greatest symphonies were introduced within twelve months of one another in 1884–5: Bruckner's Seventh, Tchaikovsky's *Manfred* (a programme symphony after Byron's poetic drama of a young man wandering the alps assailed by unnameable guilt), Dvořák's Seventh (written for England, where he was the next favourite musical import after Mendelssohn and Gounod) and Brahms's Fourth, his most comprehensively retrospective, having a Baroque-leaning passacaglia as its finale. Such fecundity might have implied new growth, but not now. There was a sense, not only in this Brahms symphony, of an age moving towards its glorious end. Verdi's *Otello* (1887) was the last big Italian Romantic opera, which could be followed only by the warmly mature ironies of his comedy *Falstaff* (1893), again after Shakespeare. Wagner's death in 1883 was commemorated by Liszt in a piano piece, *R.W. – Venezia*, for indeed that master of theatre had set his leavetaking in Venice, the city of dissolution. Liszt had foreseen his son-in-law's passing in another watery memorial, *La Lugubre Gondola*, also for solo piano and again, like other piano pieces of this time by him, cast in severe harmonies that have almost relinquished allegiance to a key, as if to end not only the Romantic interlude but the whole era of tonal music. Liszt himself died in 1886, in Bayreuth.

Yet, in this twilight, other, younger composers were coming to the fore. For them, Wagner could not be ignored, however mixed their feelings about him might be. Chabrier's reaction was not uncommon. In 1880 he went to Munich to hear *Tristan* and wept. A few years later, though, he sniffed back his tears and let out a snort – a piano duet arrangement, *Souvenirs de Munich*, in which themes from the exalted opera are smartly realigned as quadrilles. Soon after that another two French musicians, Gabriel Fauré (1845–1924) and André Messager (1853–1929), visited the Bayreuth Festival and returned to do the same for the *Ring*. But young composers, even French ones, were not always so disrespectful. For Claude Debussy (1862–1918) visits to Bayreuth in 1888 and 1889 seem to have helped him overcome the infatuation with Wagnerian sounds and subjects he showed in his cantata *La damoiselle élue* (The Blessed Damozel, 1887–8) and a set of five songs to poems by Baudelaire (1887–9). What he retained from Wagner, very productively, was freedom of form and the lucidity of orchestration he specially admired in *Parsifal*, the sense of an orchestra 'lit from behind'.

Fauré was nearly a generation older than Debussy, but he was another late starter, and the two composers began their careers almost simultaneously, in the 1880s, and in the same genres: songs, piano pieces and chamber music. These were the genres of the Parisian salons, often weekly gatherings of artists and intellectuals that would take place in the home of one of them or of a wealthy patron. Here, in a musical world where opera houses and concert halls had by now become organs of routine, younger composers, above all in Paris, were finding an alternative forum. Where songs were concerned, the poetry helped. Fauré and Debussy both learned through setting the verse of their coeval Paul Verlaine that lightness could be heavily freighted with expressive ambiguities, and Debussy created his first orchestral masterpiece as a response to a poem by another contemporary, Stéphane Mallarmé: *Prélude à 'L'après-midi d'un faune'* (Prelude to 'A Faun's Afternoon', 1892–4).

Like Liszt, Debussy seems to have heard in Wagner the ending of the major-minor system as it had existed: Wagner was, he once wrote, 'a beautiful sunset that was mistaken for a dawn'. The dawn, then, must be found in other directions, and Debussy was helped towards them by his memories of church music, which preserved the old modes, and by his encounter – at one of the international exhibitions, in Paris in 1889 – with musicians from Java and Indochina. Of course, anyone brought up as a Catholic would have been familiar with plainsong, and its modes had lent a touch to the harmony of Franck and, still more so, Bruckner. But though Franck was an important influence on the young Debussy, Franckian solidity of development was not. Debussy wanted the modes not to consolidate a harmonic system in danger of becoming outworn but rather to levitate his harmony, release it from the forward motion of the last two centuries. At the same time, his experiences of Asian music suggested other kinds of expression, of texture, of colour and, again, of modality.

The result, in the orchestral *Prélude*, is an orientalism very different from that so recently expressed by Saint-Saëns or Borodin in their thrilling scores, an orientalism not of image but of essence. The image is western: a French poem and, beyond that, a long tradition of situating languor and sensuality in an Arcadian landscape. What Debussy had learned from the east, and perhaps most deeply from himself, was how to give the faun's erotic reverie shape as a piece in which the principal idea – the opening flute solo – is constantly held in the music's memory. This is not music that steers the flow of time as Beethoven had, or grasps after its escape in the way now of Brahms or of Tchaikovsky, writing his last symphony (No. 6, the 'Pathétique'). Instead it finds a place from which it can observe time going by, a place of stillness and repose.

While Debussy was listening to the faun's flute and Tchaikovsky penning his 'Pathétique', Dvořák was spending long periods in the United States. The country was at last gaining professional composers, who would go to Germany for their training and come back to fill niches similar to those of their European elders. Thus Edward MacDowell (1860–1908) became the Grieg of the western hemisphere, John Knowle Paine (1839–1906) and George W. Chadwick (1854–1931) leading 'New England symphonists' with their roots in Schumann and Brahms, and Horatio Parker (1863–1919) the local Mendelssohn. All these composers also taught at universities and conservatories, as had some of their European predecessors from Mendelssohn to Franck and Tchaikovsky. The role of the composer-professor was becoming a clear alternative to that of the composer-conductor, and it was as a professor that Dvořák went to New York in 1892–5.

He also found himself learning there, from the songs of a black student, songs 'distinguished by unusual and subtle harmonies, the like of which I have found in no other songs but those of old Scotland and Ireland'. US composers, he concluded, should listen to this music from nearer home than Leipzig and Berlin, including the music of native

Americans as well as the songs that had become part of the
US black heritage. This was not a matter of patriotism. For
him, as for other composers of his generation interested in
folk music, folklore was an international source, and it was
possible for a German-Austrian (Brahms) to write Hungarian dances just as it was possible for Dvořák himself, from
Bohemia, to absorb black and native American melodic
styles into the work he wrote for the new Carnegie Hall:
his Ninth Symphony, subtitled 'From the New World'
(1893). As that work makes clear, what particularly appealed
to him was the discovery of music using the pentatonic scale
(of five notes rather than the normal seven, e.g. C–D–E–
G–A–C), through which the major-minor system could be
refreshed. Other composers found that same scale in European folk music, but it is particularly common in eastern
Asia, and rapidly became a cliché of musical orientalism.

Still other composers were looking at alternative scales:
Erik Satie (1866–1925) took up the old modes in his *Trois
gymnopédies* for piano (1888), the neologism of his title
appropriately suggesting ancient Greek callisthenics. New
scales could also be found not in folklore or the past but in
recent developments in chromatic harmony, notably the
whole-tone scale of major seconds (e.g. C–D–E–G♭–
A♭–B♭–C), much used by Debussy, and the octatonic scale
of alternating major and minor seconds (e.g. C–D–E♭–F–
G♭–A♭–A–B–C), appearing in Liszt and Rimsky-Korsakov. Yet there was still room for development within the
central harmonic system. Among contemporaries of
Debussy, those who chose, unlike him, to centre their
creative lives in opera house or concert hall were thereby
bound to maintain and extend the old resources, and in
November 1889, within ten days, two symphonic poems by
members of this generation had their first performances: in

Weimar Richard Strauss (1864–1949) conducted his symphonic poem *Don Juan*, then in Budapest Gustav Mahler (1860–1911) introduced *Titan*, a symphony he later numbered as his First. Both Mahler and Strauss used a language of chromatic harmony and quasi-vocal expression that had come to them through Wagner from Beethoven; they both also increased the size of the orchestra, in the interests of more varied colour and greater dynamic range. They would go on doing so.

Among young composers in Italy were Pietro Mascagni (1863–1945) and Ruggero Leoncavallo (1857–1919), names locked together in perpetuity by the success as a double bill of their short operas *Cavalleria rusticana* (Rural Chivalry, 1890) and *Pagliacci* (Clowns, 1892). By a process not so different from Dvořák's, both these works achieve a new simplicity and directness by bringing into opera the frank appeal of contemporary popular song. Often the term 'verismo' (realism) is used for this style, but such operas are realistic only in that their modern-day characters express themselves in music their real-life counterparts had taken to heart. The commerce of music had come some way since the mid-century waltzes of the Strauss family, the operettas of Offenbach and the songs of the US composer Stephen Foster (1826–64); 'light music' had deviated further from the paths of the acknowledged greats than had been the case when Brahms expressed his appreciation of *The Blue Danube*. Mascagni and Leoncavallo brought these streams together. So did Giacomo Puccini (1858–1924) in *Manon Lescaut* (1893), whose orchestral score pushes chromatic harmony as hard as any of the contemporary works of Mahler or Strauss.

In 1896–7, within six months of one another, Bruckner and Brahms reached their last days. Tchaikovsky and

Franck had died before them; Verdi was finishing his last work, a group of four sacred choral pieces; and Dvořák was completing his career with operas. Ernest Chausson (1855–99), a disciple of Franck and master of post-Wagnerian harmony glowing with evening light, had recently put his age's sense of approaching closure into the mouth of the eponymous hero of his opera *Le roi Arthus* (King Arthur, 1886–95). Hugo Wolf (1860–1903), working in the Vienna of Brahms (his bête noire) and Mahler (his friend), produced over two hundred songs and an opera within a decade, as if rushing to beat not only the madness that overtook him in 1897 but also the ending of Romantic lyricism.

Wolf apart, most of these composers had reached maturity late and produced their greatest works in their forties, fifties and sixties – even their seventies and eighties in Verdi's case. After them music was again, as it had been in the 1830s, in the hands of young giants: Puccini, Mahler, Debussy, Strauss and others who were soon to compound their local reputations, such as Edward Elgar (1857–1934), Carl Nielsen (1865–1931), Jean Sibelius (1865–1957) and Ferruccio Busoni (1866–1924). This time, though, there was no common cause.

CHAPTER 17

Nightfall and sunrise

With the nineteenth century about to reach its end, many composers seem to have felt, as Beethoven had a hundred years before, that a major symphonic statement was due. It was at this moment that Sibelius produced his First Symphony (1898–9), still following in the path of Tchaikovsky. Debussy, already wary of traditional forms, offered a kind of symphony without a first movement, a set of three symphonic poems suggesting the drifting of clouds (*Nuages*), communal celebration (*Fêtes*) and mermaids at seductive play (*Sirènes*), collectively entitled *Nocturnes* (1897–9). Elgar's symphonic debut was with a set of variations, *Enigma*, each a character study of one of his friends (1898–9). As for the leading representatives of what the orchestral repertory had made seem the central tradition, Strauss's symphonic poem *Ein Heldenleben* (A Hero's Life, 1897–8) was soon followed by Mahler's Fourth Symphony (1899–1900).

These two composers – conscious of their responsibilities to that tradition, as Brahms and Bruckner had been before them – maintained and developed two strong aspects of Austro-German orchestral music since Beethoven: the sense of a voice coming from the orchestra and the unification of symphonic form. Strauss's *Ein Heldenleben* is in six sections, varying in tempo and tone but all drawing on the same supply of thematic material, especially on the theme of the 'hero', and played without a break. Mahler's symphonies, by contrast, are all in separate movements, which often approximate to regular types (sonata allegro, slow movement, scherzo, upbeat finale), but they are strongly linked by connections not so much of material as of narrative. In his Third Symphony (1893–6), and again in his Fourth, Mahler included sung texts to help clarify his story, as well as to supply added variety and invoke the magisterial example, contra Hanslick, of Beethoven's Ninth. He had done the same in his Second Symphony, where the progress is from funeral march to choral finale, the latter expressing confident hope in resurrection. (Christian themes ran through this Jewish composer's music in his expression of a multifarious self.) Texts for the Third and Fourth he found in *Des Knaben Wunderhorn* (The Boy's Magic Horn), a collection of folk-style verses put together early in the nineteenth century.

In the case of the Fourth Symphony, the naive poem is sung by a soprano in the finale, projecting a child's vision of heaven. This is preceded by three movements that also have touches of the childlike in their imagery of sleighride, alphorn, dance and nursery rhyme, all set forth with characteristic complexity in a voice that can be frank or ironic or both at the same time. Using techniques of parody he perhaps learned from such works of Liszt as the *Faust Symphony*, Mahler encouraged ambiguity and doubt in his music, either by guying themes that had previously been taken at face value or by introducing crude styles (tavern dance, military march) with an accent on their crudity. Bringing such sources into the concert hall, the music creates a sense of being in the world, and specifically of being Mahler in the world, identifying with the persona so powerfully if variously presented.

Strauss's music, too, can seem to be about himself, and indeed there is no doubt as to the identity of the hero of *Ein Heldenleben*. Even so, the protagonist here is seen totally from outside; his deeds are described and illustrated but not felt. Mahler, using borrowed texts and often borrowed musical material, and without assigning his work a personal programme, produces an intensely autobiographical effect. Strauss, nominally writing about himself, does so with objectivity and humour. Where they agree is only in their acceptance of the longstanding Romantic assumption that music has to be about an individual's feelings: love, generosity, anxiety and aspiration. They both understood music as passionate voice.

That voice depended importantly on the system of major and minor keys, and in particular on the manifold possibilities therein of meaningful chord progression and key modulation, all within an experience of time as continuous unfolding. Perhaps the force of such late Romantic music — persisting into the present — is to be found here, in a sense that time, if passing, is passing in an orderly fashion, and that, whatever difficulties and diversions are encountered, in due course there will be an ameliorative end. Mahler unsettles this prospect, in that bridges in his journeys may be traversed by means of kitsch and arrivals may still be tinged with doubt, but this only heightens his relevance to listeners in a later world.

To go on enforcing harmonic logic, in music that could use a vast range of chords, composers felt the need for large volumes of sound. Mahler in his maturity wrote nothing but symphonies and songs, the latter often with orchestral accompaniment. Strauss, too, favoured orchestral music and songs in the 1890s, and amalgamated the genres in the operas that became his main concern in the new century. And both composers built onto the orchestra established by Wagner's *Ring*. Outside Austria and Germany, though, such enhanced ensembles were less used because they were less needed. Instead of shoring up the major-minor system, composers were exploring alternatives, including, as before in Lalo and Chabrier, the use of ostinato and an essentially rhythmic drive to power harmonically complex music. This was the way of Paul Dukas (1865–1935) in his brilliant short orchestral piece *L'Apprenti Sorcier* (The Sorcerer's Apprentice, 1897), where a resilient motif, repeated persistently, is shot through a wide range of harmonies and colours, maintaining a compulsive forward motion for which Goethe's parable, of a young magician whose magic gets out of control, provided the perfect metaphor.

So powerful was the hold of the major-minor system that even the period's most freethinking musicians – Debussy and, in New York, Charles Ives (1874–1954) – looked for other frameworks that were still fundamentally harmonic. In 1902 Ives made several choral settings of psalms, bending away from an old US tradition into, for example, chords of five notes that would superimpose the triads of two different keys. That same year Debussy was asked by a periodical to speculate on music's future – an invitation itself expressive of a widespread unease, surely occasioned partly by the novelty of Debussy's own music – and he began with a dream related to harmony: 'The best thing one could wish for French music would be to see the study of harmony abolished as it is practised in the conservatories.' Where Bach's chorale arrangements were by now being taken as models of harmonic rule, Debussy provocatively challenged this academic veneration, if in terms that point not so much to Bach's music as to his own: 'He preferred the free play of sonorities whose curves, whether flowing in parallel or contrary motion, would result in an undreamt-of flowering.'

Such free play, which Debussy contrived largely by building harmonies on scales of whole tones or others related to the modes of medieval music, folksong and Asian ensembles, he had by now sufficiently mastered that he could write a full-length opera – *Pelléas et Mélisande*, based on a widely staged drama by the Belgian poet Maurice Maeterlinck and first performed in the same year of 1902. The piece is in some ways a Wagnerian opera: the setting is medieval-legendary, and the focus, as in *Tristan*, is on an adulterous liaison with sea and night as components of the backdrop. But where Tristan and Isolde sing out their love through much of their opera, Pelléas and Mélisande declare themselves only briefly, almost surreptitiously. Much more often their feelings are concealed – not just deliberately, from the surrounding characters, for fear, but also, more affectingly, because the opera catches them at a moment when they are only beginning to know what their feelings are. Debussy said he wanted to reach 'the naked flesh of emotion', and arguably he did. But that flesh is supple, and constituted not only of passion but of prevarication and uncertainty.

Apparently unaware of Debussy's opera, Arnold Schoenberg (1874–1951) produced his own version of the story in a symphonic poem, *Pelleas und Melisande* (1902–3), in which he characteristically united diverse aspects of recent music: the sonic opulence and detailed story-telling of Strauss, Mahler's expressive inwardness and the developmental urge in Brahms. Living most of the time in Vienna – as did Mahler during the time he was chief conductor of the opera there (1897–1907) – Schoenberg was very aware of his inheritance. His previous symphonic poem, *Verklärte Nacht* (Transfigured Night, 1899), similarly brought post-Wagnerian harmony into the Brahmsian medium of the string sextet, adding a second viola and a second cello to the normal quartet: Brahms, who had died only two years earlier, had written a pair of works in this rich chamber form. Another feature of these symphonic poems, as of Schoenberg's music generally, is an overabundance, the pressure of expression at the boundaries of form.

What helps the form hold, very often, is an access of strict counterpoint, which, like ostinato in Lalo or Chabrier, served to maintain onwardness. Brahms, a great admirer of Bach, offered an example here, not least in the passacaglia finale of his Fourth Symphony, from which tracks led not only to Schoenberg but also to the latter's German near contemporary Max Reger (1873–1916) and to Busoni. In the very early years of the twentieth century Reger held a more conspicuous place in Austro-German music than Schoenberg; certainly he was far more productive, especially of instrumental music. Several of his works are sets of variations culminating in a fugue, but contrapuntal energy is almost omnipresent, driving through dense harmonic textures. He acknowledged his source in making piano arrangements of Bach's music, as indeed did Busoni, a musician of mixed German-Italian background best known at this period as a virtuoso pianist.

Nor was Busoni the only performer to take a renewing interest in Bach. What would much later become known as the 'early music revival' can be dated to 1890, when the French musician Arnold Dolmetsch (1858–1940), living in London, gave his first concert. A pioneer not only as a performer but also as an instrument maker, he retrieved sounds that had been virtually forgotten for generations:

those of the harpsichord, lute, viol and recorder. Soon after him, in 1903, Wanda Landowska (1879–1959) made her debut as a harpsichordist and so began her long career as a popularizer of the 'modern' harpsichord, an instrument unknown to the seventeenth and eighteenth centuries, having more the scale and strength of a grand piano. As she verbalized it, the rediscovery of older music was a reaction to the present state of composition: 'If sometimes we tire of grandiosity and if we lack air in the thick air of exaggerated Romanticism, we need only to open wide the windows on our magnificent past.'

Evidence of what she might have meant by 'exaggerated Romanticism' is not hard to find in this period. Puccini's operas *Tosca* (1900) and *Madama Butterfly* (Madam Butterfly, 1904) move efficiently to moments of full emotional delivery, made trenchant not only by his gift for the big tune but by the dramatic verisimilitude in which such moments are embedded, with recitative replaced by a fluid and melodious vocal style adaptable to many different kinds of dialogue, from love scene to interrogation. Strauss learned something from this in his first operatic masterpiece, *Salome* (1905), where decadent emotions and a decadent setting are laid out in extraordinary detail. So did Leoš Janáček (1854–1928) in his, *Jenůfa* (1904), an opera of a very different sort, taking its melodies from Czech speech rhythms and folk music. There was 'exaggeration', too, in orchestra size, with perhaps the upper limit – in terms of what can be accommodated on a concert platform and controlled by a conductor – being reached in Schoenberg's massive cantata *Gurrelieder* (Songs of Gurra), mostly written in 1900–1 and calling for a body of around 135 instrumentalists, including eight flautists and ten horn players.

But the richness of this period's music was a richness, too, of variety. Schoenberg and Mahler were by no means the only composers working in Vienna: this was also the golden age of operetta, of works more smoothly sumptuous than those of Johann Strauss II but still led by the charm of the waltz, works such as *Die lustige Witwe* (The Merry Widow, 1905) by Franz Lehár (1870–1948). In the United States a whole new popular form was coming into being in ragtime, as exemplified by the enormously successful *Maple Leaf Rag* (1899) of Scott Joplin (1867/8–1917). In Paris and Berlin at the same time a new kind of musical entertainment was emerging: cabaret, with songs having sophisticated lyrics and often a political, moral or social-critical edge. Satie and Schoenberg both contributed to this repertory, briefly.

For Satie, striking out against traditions of form and genre as well as harmony, cabaret gave a speedy exit from what Landowska had called 'grandiosity', but there were other ways, even within the Paris of the time. Debussy's continuing work with drifting harmonies, after the success of *Pelléas* had brought him to the centre of French music, resulted in a second quasi-symphony, *La Mer* (The Sea, 1903–5), whose central movement, *Jeux de vagues* (Wave Play), slips easily from one wave-shaped melodic idea to another, each seemingly generated by the underlying harmony, as waves are by underwater tensions, and the sequence of chords following no progression but drifting and circling, again like marine currents. In 1907, in a letter to his publisher, Debussy wrote how he was feeling 'more and more that music, by its very essence, is not something that can flow inside a rigorous, traditional form. It consists of colours and rhythmicized time.' *Jeux de vagues* agrees with that description, as do many of the piano pieces the composer was writing during this period, not depending, as Mahler and Strauss were, on huge resources to maintain a strong harmonic direction. Among these pieces were three triptychs: *Estampes* (Prints, 1903) and two sets of *Images* (Pictures, 1901–5 and 1907). As these titles imply, the imagery is often pictorial, but only so as to suggest a particular musical concern with some aspect of texture, as in *Reflets dans l'eau* (Reflections in Water) from the first set of *Images*, or of harmony, as in *Pagodes* (Pagodas), which opens the *Estampes* in Chinese pentatonic style. Scales drawn from eastern Asian and Spanish traditions were as fruitful as they had been in the 1880s, not only for Debussy but also for such contemporaries as Puccini (*Madama Butterfly*) and Maurice Ravel (1875–1937). Ravel wrote the period's most languorous orientalist masterpiece (the song cycle *Shéhérazade* for soprano and orchestra, 1903) as well as some of its most vital Spanish music: the orchestral *Rapsodie espagnole* (1907–8) and a brilliant comic opera about a clockmaker's wife who has to organize her romantic life like clockwork, *L'Heure espagnole* (Spanish Time, 1907–9). The arrival in Paris in 1907 of a composer from Madrid, Manuel de Falla (1876–1946), was almost a homecoming.

Debussy's use of unusual scales was also an important example for a young Hungarian in the city at the same time: Zoltán Kodály (1882–1967), who took back some of the French composer's music to show his friend Béla Bartók (1881–1945). The two of them had started collecting folk music in 1905, and the lessons they were learning in the villages of Transylvania and Slovakia were supported by Debussy's music: vast possibilities were to be found outside the major-minor system. That same discovery was being made elsewhere, notably in Britain, where the Australian composer Percy Grainger (1882–1961) began collecting, studying, arranging and departing from folk music in the interests of greater freedom in every musical dimension, of harmony, rhythm, instrumentation and form. This freedom meant, for him, ignoring the western notion of the finished art work: many of his pieces exist in numerous different forms, for quite different performing means. Evidently he was an inspiring colleague. But though English contemporaries, such as Frederick Delius (1862–1934), Ralph Vaughan Williams (1872–1958) and Gustav Holst (1874–1934), shared his passion for folk music, they all kept a much stiffer idea of what a composition should be.

Mahler's adoption of the folk tone was a little different, being ironic and forming only a part of his musical world. It was, too, a decreasing part after his *Wunderhorn* songs and song-symphonies, if still present in the purely orchestral symphonies that followed (Nos. 5–7, 1901–5) and their colossal successor (No. 8, 1906–7), whose two choral tableaux set the hymn *Veni Creator Spiritus* (Come Creator Spirit) and the closing scene in heaven from Goethe's *Faust*. This last symphony, for whose first performance Mahler summoned over a thousand performers, represented the extreme in musical gigantism, outdoing the choral strength of Schoenberg's *Gurrelieder*. The latter had already reacted by concentrating on smaller genres in his First Quartet (1904–5) and First Chamber Symphony (1906), but there was no let-up in his harmonic daring, his insistence on counterpoint or his formal elaboration. Powering ahead on all these fronts, and playing continuously, the quartet and the chamber symphony both set up highly complicated musical situations that require an arduous drive towards resolution. Their composer's evolution since *Verklärte Nacht* is more than a young artist's entry into solid maturity; it is as if this music were being made by – and making – history.

Others, though, did not feel time's arrow, or felt it differently. No such onrush sounds through the works of Sergey Rachmaninoff (1873–1943), who had been trained in Moscow in the Tchaikovsky tradition. No ineluctable force leads from his Second Piano Concerto (1900–1) to his Second Symphony (1906–7); both are, rather, supreme products of a Romanticism continuing without strain from the nineteenth century. And Sibelius's Violin Concerto (1903) shows how the old modes could be used not to dissolve traditional harmony, as in Debussy, but to strengthen it. The dispute Schumann had witnessed, between radicals and conservatives, was being rerun, but now within a much more complex musical world, lacking agreement even about the nature of the sides. Schoenberg always thought of himself as a traditionalist, doing what such predecessors as Brahms and Mozart had done: continue the tradition by carrying it further in ways it seemed to demand.

Even so, it is hard not to understand his works, and Debussy's, as signals from the rushing tempo of the times. The period around 1900 was one of unparalleled social and technological change. The slow move towards equality for women and for non-white people had some representation among composers, in the reputations acquired by, for example, Cécile Chaminade (1857–1944), Ethel Smyth (1858–1944) and Amy Beach (1867–1944), or in the great acclaim accorded the black British composer Samuel Coleridge-Taylor (1875–1912) for his oratorio *Scenes from 'The Song of Hiawatha'* (1898–1900).

As for technology, its immediate impact on music was also just beginning. Sound recording, introduced in time to catch a snatch of Brahms at the piano in 1889, was by the start of the new century providing a means of disseminating musical performances. The voice of Enrico Caruso

(1873–1921), who made his first recordings in 1902, was the herald of things to come. A more transitory phenomenon was the 'reproducing piano', a sophisticated kind of player piano, for which performances could be recorded on paper rolls that preserved nuances of touch and pedalling. Introduced in 1904, the instrument could soon offer performances by Debussy and Mahler.

Among composers none was listening for fore-echoes of the future more acutely than Busoni, who in 1905–9 conducted concerts of new music in Berlin, and in 1907 published *Entwurf einer neuen Ästhetik der Tonkunst* (Sketch for a New Aesthetic of Music). Sounding a call for freedom as resolute, optimistic and evocative as Debussy's, Busoni asked for forms let loose from the standard patterns, for new scales and for intervals smaller than the semitone – intervals he thought might be available on electrical instruments. Like Debussy, too, and like so many predecessors, he wanted a return to nature – or, rather, an advance into nature as infinite possibility. This was, he said, his dream. Soon it would be realized.

PART VII

Time tangled 1908–1975

Periods do not begin or end but phase into one another, and yet 1908 saw a special and determining moment in the history of music: the completion by Schoenberg of the first compositions to dispense with the harmonic system based on major and minor keys, a revolution in which he was rapidly followed by his pupil Anton Webern (1883–1945). Often described as 'atonal', this new music could include all kinds of note combinations in its chords, though any particular piece might be organized in quite exact ways, whether deliberately or intuitively. Also, there was no force impelling the music towards resolution in the home key, for there were no keys now and no homes.

Schoenberg's innovation provided in some sense the freedom that he, along with Debussy and Busoni, had been hoping for. It also, contrary to his wish, made innovation a way of life in music, opening a period, still uncompleted, during which further possibilities of radical change were explored: the period of what is commonly called modernism. In that respect, atonality's arrival may be compared with abstraction's in painting, which happened at almost the same time – in 1910, with Wassily Kandinsky's first such work. Like abstraction, atonality came as a radical break not only with the past but with cultures in other parts of the world: hitherto all music had been based on some central note or harmony. Also, all music had been grounded in longstanding traditions, whereas the great imperative of modernism was to make things new – and then to make them new again.

Some varieties of modernism, through a rooting in folk music, found ways to maintain or create a harmonic stability and a notion of tradition, while still breaking fundamentally with the harmony of the western classical tradition, as modernism by definition must. Here comparisons suggest themselves with, for example, Picasso's enthusiasm for African art. Thus not all modernist music is atonal, though perhaps all atonal music is in essence modernist. And, at least in its early decades, modernism defined itself as contrary not only to classical music's traditions but also to the majority of the audience for that music. Modernist music was made to be difficult and to encounter objection.

Even so, Schoenbergian atonality certainly had links with western culture's most recent history. Just as abstraction could be seen as extending from the work of many painters in the previous three or four decades, so atonality could be understood in logical succession to the extreme uses of dissonance in late Liszt, or in Mahler and Strauss as well as Schoenberg. Indeed, the justification for so extraordinary a step was found as much in this historical continuity as in the freedom brought to the art.

A historical placing of atonality, as of abstraction, would also have to take into account the role of popular art as negative paradigm. Where the modernist impulse exists, it exists in reaction not only to the traditions of classical music but also to those of the popular styles that became so powerful through the twentieth century, largely because of the machinery that, in 1902, was projecting Caruso.

Modernism is and was determinedly not made for the market-place. And the marketplace has shown little inclination to embrace modernism.

Modernism, again like abstraction, shifted attention from the product to the process, to the how and why of composition. Most importantly, in reducing or removing the direction-forcing tendency of tonal harmony, modernist techniques allowed composers to create music in which time can be perceived in many different ways, often in several simultaneously: the stationary time of immobile harmony, the repeating time of ostinato, the confused rush of chord progressions that do not quite make sense in traditional terms, the reversing time of events being repeated backwards, the double time of old forms and genres unexpectedly reinterpreted. In this respect modernism fits not only with abstraction but with another development of the period: the revelation, by Einstein in 1905, that time is not a universal constant but can vary with the position and movement of the point of view – that time is not one but many.

This multiplicity of time is perhaps what makes modernist music difficult, for it involves an avoidance, rejection or complication of the continuous, goal-directed unfolding that is so strongly projected by almost all western music from the sixteenth century to the early twentieth and that, by giving the flow of time orderly shape, has such power to move and to console. The jagged, irregular, multifarious or dissolved temporal contours of modernist music provide harder lessons.

They are the lessons, though, of the culture in which modernist music has been made. Unity – as it was, say, in the 1880s, when Brahms, Bruckner, Franck, Grieg and Tchaikovsky were all speaking the same language, as were

Johann Strauss II in his waltzes or the US bandmaster John Philip Sousa (1854–1932) in his marches, and when there was general agreement about the nature and history of the western tradition – took a hard knock in 1908. Since then western musical languages have become as various as those spoken on the planet – or more various, given the lack of agreement about music's subject matter or mode of comprehension.

At the same time, recording has given music a history not only of compositions and traditions but of performances, keeping these available for decades. Recording has also brought about a world in which musical experience is no longer special, requiring an outing or expertise, and no longer personal, happening only when listener and musician are in the same space. Music is everywhere. Music can also come to us from innumerable sources: from the court traditions of Burma or Burgundy, from singers to the lute or electric guitar, from Ligeti, Liszt, Lassus or Landini. The relativity of time is all around.

CHAPTER 18

To begin again

Modernism started with songs, songs Schoenberg made to recent poems by Stefan George, who wrote, in visionary but quiet language, of journeys of the soul. Two works came out of this encounter between Austrian musician and German poet: the composer's Second Quartet (1907–8), with a soprano singing George's words in the last two of the four movements, and his song cycle *Das Buch der hängenden Gärten* (The Book of the Hanging Gardens, 1908–9) for soprano and piano. The quartet enacts the historical process by which atonality had arrived, almost as if Schoenberg had wanted to provide a justification. The first movement is in F sharp minor, an extreme and awkward key, appropriate to music that sounds straitened. Then comes a set of variations on a popular song, intensifying the tune's melancholy in a somewhat Mahlerian way, after which the soprano enters with the first George poem, again in an unusual key: E flat minor. In the finale such precarious holds on tonality are let loose. The strings float in boundless space, and the soprano sings George's words: 'I feel air from other planets'. Coming immediately afterwards, the song cycle is entirely atonal.

Schoenberg might have stopped there, reserved this special language of atonality for the special occasion of

George's ungrounded poetry, which Webern was setting atonally at the same time. But both composers regarded their departure as a historical breakthrough, not a provisional experiment, and for the moment there was no going back. By the end of 1909 Schoenberg had added to his atonal output a one-act, one-woman opera (*Erwartung*, Awaiting) as well as sets of Five Pieces for orchestra (not a symphony, for the old forms had gone with the old harmonies that had supported them) and Three Pieces for piano. He had also written to Busoni, explaining that his motivation was not just to extend musical possibilities but, even primarily, to provide a more truthful kind of musical expression. 'It is *impossible*', he insisted, 'for a person to have only *one* sensation at a time. One has thousands simultaneously . . . And this variegation, this multifariousness, this *illogicality* which our senses demonstrate, the illogicality presented by their interactions, set forth by some mounting rush of blood, by some reaction of the senses or the nerves, this I should like to have in my music.'

As he put it in the same letter, echoing Busoni and Debussy: 'Harmony is *expression* and nothing else.' In order to express the complexity of experience, harmony would have to be complex, and musical form would have to be constant evolution, with no repeating themes or consistent metres. And if Schoenberg had asked himself why human experience was particularly complex right now, he might have pointed to the variety of pace in cities that were beginning to fill with motor vehicles, or the variety of stimuli from traffic noises, electric light and the growth of advertising. He might also have mentioned the ideas raised in his own city of Vienna by Sigmund Freud, for in this letter to Busoni he refers finally to the 'subconscious'. Just as, for Freud, a subconscious desire could give rise to feelings and actions seemingly unrelated to it or to each other, so in Schoenberg's atonal harmony connections and relationships lack the evident logic that the traditional major-minor system had sustained. This is harmony proceeding, as it were, in the dark.

It may also have come out of the dark, in the sense that Schoenberg was working intuitively. Indeed, the speed at which he composed suggests this: *Erwartung* – a half hour of very colourful orchestral music, where abundant harmonic variety is mirrored in the constantly changing instrumentation and texture – was drafted from beginning to end in seventeen days. The libretto, written by a Vienna-trained physician, Marie Pappenheim, is the monologue of a woman searching a forest at night for the man who has left her, a text that provides for such mixed emotions as Schoenberg wanted to express: love and fear (and the fear of love), anger and sorrow, all interwoven with uncertainty and self-deception. The score testifies to Schoenberg's success in making music more real, having it follow the speed and complexity with which feelings are felt. But the atonal language of emotional representation was an extension of the tonal language: it worked only with reference to what it was negating, and could not therefore claim to be freer or more immediate.

Other music of 1908–9, whether atonal or not (and most of it was not), belongs in this same area of emotional complexity. Schoenberg's correspondent Busoni found harmonies on the fringes of atonality for his delicate and moving *Berceuse élégiaque* (Elegiac Lullaby, 1909) for orchestra. Strauss's *Elektra* (1906–8) – like *Erwartung* a one-act opera, but lasting two hours, and similarly focussed on a single character in a state of awaiting, Electra, expecting the return of her brother Orestes to avenge the murder of their father Agamemnon – wields dissonant harmonies that, savage or seductive, only just maintain a sense of key. The title character, on stage almost throughout, sings from within a turmoil of rage, grief, love and longing, and those around her are drawn with Strauss's customary exactness, of both vocal and orchestral writing: the younger sister Chrysothemis, whose comfort Electra cannot accept; the mother Clytemnestra, rattling with guilt. For Strauss extreme harmony was indeed an expressive device, not a historical necessity, and having approached atonality in *Elektra* he moved on to a fully tonal world of sumptuous waltzes and luscious, winging soprano voices, the world of *Der Rosenkavalier* (The Rose Chevalier, 1909–10).

Mahler's works of this period were the last he completed: *Das Lied von der Erde* (The Song of the Earth) and his Ninth Symphony. The former is a symphony in six orchestral songs, for tenor and mezzo-soprano (or baritone), and the choice of Chinese poems, in German translation, opens the door to an occasional pentatonic touch. However, the long, slow finale is thoroughly western and Romantic in expression: entitled *Der Abschied* (The Farewell), it is an adieu couched within a language that is itself on the point of expiring. Without voices, the Ninth Symphony ends similarly. Then in the first movement of the unfinished Tenth (1910) alarm – alarm conveyed by the music about itself, as well as about the world or the persona whose feelings are being expressed – sounds out in a chord of violent dissonance. It is as if the fabric of tonal harmony, wearing thin in the last movements of *Das Lied von der Erde* and the Ninth Symphony, were now starting to tear.

In Mahler and Strauss, as in Schoenberg, dissonance speaks of personal feeling, in line with the Austro-German Romantic tradition. It was also in music from this tradition, the tradition having the most all-embracing harmonic logic, that dissonance was most powerfully felt. Elsewhere the expansion of harmony could proceed with less ado — as it did, for instance, in Debussy's music — and carry messages of a less subjective nature.

Schoenberg's move into atonality was probably made easier by the presence around him of close, gifted and admiring pupils, including, besides Webern, Alban Berg (1885–1935). But though Schoenberg's works were widely known (there was a performance, for instance, of the Five Pieces for orchestra in London in 1912), they were not so widely understood and had little influence for the moment outside his own circle. In the United States, however, Ives had arrived at atonality independently and for quite different purposes, nearly always within a context that embraced tonality as well. His *Unanswered Question* (1908) is a sound drama for instrumentalists in three different positions, such multi-locality being another of his innovations. A solo trumpet keeps placing the barely tonal question, to which woodwinds respond with atonal scurryings that suggest evasions, while strings, like seers, guard their own answer in slow descents of dense concords. The glowing consonance here is remarkably close to that of Vaughan Williams's Fantasia on a Theme by Thomas Tallis for string orchestra (1910). Neither composer could have known of the other at this point, but they lived in the same world, where major-minor chords guided by modal scales could produce effects that were fresh but spoke of timelessness, in implicit or explicit contrast with the timefulness of Schoenbergian atonality.

For Schoenberg himself, though, atonality could address transcendence, as it had when it first appeared, in the finale of his Second Quartet. In Russia, too, such ideas were current, largely through the work of Aleksandr Scriabin (1872–1915); abstract art and atonal music were both burgeoning in these two regions centred on Moscow and on the Munich–Vienna axis. Around 1905 Scriabin's music began to hover around static harmonies formed on the same principles that had produced stasis in Debussy and Liszt, including the whole-tone scale. His orchestral piece *Le Poème de l'extase* (The Poem of Ecstasy, 1905–8) combines such harmonies with urgent propulsions that come from a trumpet melody, resulting in a series of waves that mount with unabashed sexual connotations. Here the ultimate goal, long in sight but repeatedly delayed, is consonant resolution, but in Scriabin's next phase, when his works were exclusively for solo piano, dissonances take on radiant auras of stability. Among these unmoving discords is what the composer called his 'mystic chord', having six different notes and not easily understandable within the logic of tonality.

Reactions to the harmonic crisis could be very different. Hans Pfitzner (1869–1949), in his effulgent and richly characterful opera *Palestrina* (1912–15), created both an argument for and an example of older values. Strauss remained on course. So did Sibelius, even if his Fourth Symphony (1911) is his most starkly dissonant. And Scriabin's former classmate Rachmaninoff continued as if nothing had changed, into his Third Piano Concerto (1909). Not so another, younger Russian, Igor Stravinsky (1882–1971). He arrived in Paris in 1910 from St Petersburg with the Ballets Russes, a company the impresario-connoisseur Sergey Diaghilev (1872–1929) had formed to bring Russian music, choreographers and dancers to western Europe. *The Firebird*, Diaghilev's first commission, was given that year and proved a sensation, thanks in large part to Stravinsky's luxurious post-Rimsky-Korsakov music, in which there were touches also of Scriabin and of his own taste for music as mechanism.

Once in the west, though, Stravinsky recognized fast that times were changing, and that he could help change them. His second score for Diaghilev was the wholly original *Petrushka* (1910–11), which established him among music's radicals, but as one whose radicalism was very different from Schoenberg's. Largely dispensing with the Romantic harmony of *The Firebird*, Stravinsky kept his music lean, and created complex textures by overlaying different streams of music, each with its own rhythm and direction. Form is built in the same way: the music can jump from one idea to another provided the pulse remains identical or closely related. Pulse operates almost as key had done in the past, to unify – and it is pulse that drives the music, through shifting patterns of metre. So relatively unimportant is the melody that it can be fairground music or elementary folksong. The piece is governed, as in the new art of film, by pace and editing. There are also parallels with the collages put together from everyday materials by Pablo Picasso and other artists.

The attention given to pulse was, of course, rightful in a ballet score, but *Petrushka* showed how resourcefully this purely functional matter could be addressed by the imaginative composer. One result, thanks to Diaghilev's encouragement and flair, was to place ballet music on the agenda of almost every composer in Paris and beyond: among those who wrote for the Ballets Russes during ensuing years were Ravel (*Daphnis et Chloé*, 1912), Debussy (*Jeux*, 1913), Strauss (*Josephs-Legende*, 1914) and Satie (*Parade*, 1917). Another effect of *Petrushka* was to demonstrate that folk music could be used in ways very different from those of

Dvořákian symphonism, though in ways that had been partly prepared by Lalo, Chabrier and Grieg. No longer blended into traditional harmony, folk ideas could keep their freshness and vitality, which they did in the string of folklore-based works Stravinsky himself produced during the next few years, as well as in those of colleagues as diverse as Ravel, Falla and Bartók.

Petrushka is the story of a Russian puppet character related to the melancholy loner of Italian-French traditional theatre, Pierrot, who was the subject of a work by Schoenberg that followed soon after: *Pierrot lunaire* (Moonstruck Pierrot, 1912) for reciter with a mixed instrumental quintet. The coincidence is not so surprising, for puppets and masks had become pertinent figures at a time when the arts were helping to revise notions of human volition, consciousness and independence. Schoenberg's *Pierrot*, however, is as different from Stravinsky's *Petrushka* as could be: a song cycle in which the songs are half-spoken, rather in the manner of cabaret performance, with music that underlines the range from monstrous violence to playfulness. The central persona here is split into fragments, held together partly by the tightness, intensity and fascination of the instrumental score. Among those who attended early performances were Stravinsky and Ravel, who both, in works written soon after, expressed a fascination with the score's harmonic and instrumental resources – though not with its speech-song, which remained a Schoenberg-school speciality.

On 31 March 1913, in Vienna, Schoenberg conducted an orchestral programme including, besides his own First Chamber Symphony, atonal works by his pupils Berg and Webern: the former's Altenberg Songs, setting brief poems by a Viennese contemporary, and a group of six orchestral pieces by the latter. These two works are highly characteristic of their composers, and could therefore prove, at an early date, the range of atonality on Schoenberg's model. Webern's pieces are mostly very short, lasting a minute or two; the fourth of them, a funeral march of four minutes, seems in context immense. Berg's songs are quite short, too, but their breath is much larger, and their sensuous orchestration is at some remove from Schoenberg's or Webern's. Not all of them, though, were heard, for this 'Skandalkonzert' (scandal concert), as it came to be known, was disrupted by the noisy audience in the middle of the Berg performance and had to be abandoned.

Two months later in Paris, on 29 May, another wild evening took place when Stravinsky's next ballet, *The Rite of Spring*, had its first performance. As much as *Petrushka*, *The Rite* was a celebration of pulse, but now propounded with far greater force by a larger orchestra through more insistent rhythms of repetition, ostinato and syncopation. The music is at once an evocation of ancient ritual and a depiction of modern machinery, with cogwheels of music in slow or furious circulation, working towards the implacable pulsed finales of the ballet's two parts, the second finale – the 'Sacrificial Dance' with which the ritual completes itself – being precisely one and a third times as fast as the first. The noise of the score, which evokes a primitive ensemble of pipes and drums, and its rhythmic energy brought protests from the first audience; but unlike Schoenberg, who had no Diaghilev to take care of his promotion, Stravinsky swiftly emerged the victor. Public fury was evidence of artistic triumph. *The Rite* was soon repeated as a concert piece throughout the western world, whereas Berg's Altenberg Songs were not attempted again until 1952 (and then successfully, the age of scandal being over).

Given by Diaghilev just two weeks before *The Rite*, Debussy's *Jeux* (Games) caused far less commotion, though it is quite as radical a score. The constant renewal of *Jeux de vagues* is here maintained through a duration of twenty minutes, and through music containing many different varieties of texture, tempo (sometimes two at once) and harmony. The games of the title are erotic, involving tennis players in the ballet, and the music extends from the *Prélude à 'L'Après-midi d'un faune'* in evoking rushes of intense feeling that may end in nothing. Often there is intensity and puzzlement at the same time – a complexity such as Schoenberg would have wished, but created by exquisite chords that, just, keep contact with tonality.

Also that year came music that sought, more radically than anything in Debussy, Stravinsky, Schoenberg or Ives, a new start: the music for noise-making machines created by Luigi Russolo (1885–1947), who belonged to the Italian group known as futurists. The future, as these artists saw it, would be the age of the machine, celebrated far more overtly than in Stravinsky's *Rite*. Most of the futurists were painters or poets, and it was as a painter that Russolo had begun. But his lack of a musical grounding was not a problem, for what he demanded – in *The Art of Noises*, one of the manifestos typical of the group – was a wholly new art, in tune with the modern world: 'The machine today has created so many varieties and combinations of noise that pure musical sound – with its poverty and its monotony – no longer awakens any emotion in the hearer.' Russolo's own machines were destroyed during World War II, but the ideas he voiced were not uncommon. Musicians were as conscious as anyone else of living in a new age, the age of the motor car, aeroplane, gramophone and wireless telegraphy. But it was not to be through ominous boxed-in *intonarumori* (noise-intoners) on a concert platform that this new age was to express itself.

In any event, lyrical vauntings of modernity petered out after August 1914. Berg's reaction to the war was a set of Three Pieces for orchestra (1914–15), of which the last is a huge march in an atmosphere of catastrophe. An era seems to be ending in this music, and so it proved. Soon Berg, among many musicians of his generation, was wearing an army uniform. Some promising composers died in action, among them George Butterworth (1885–1916) and Rudi Stephan (1887–1915). Concerts became less frequent, and, with so many men involved in the combat, some orchestras admitted women players for the first time. Here and there a big new piece was presented, including Sibelius's mighty Fifth Symphony in Helsinki in 1915, but many composers chose to concentrate on more economical forms.

Schoenberg had done so already. So had Strauss, in writing for a chamber orchestra in his next opera after *Der Rosenkavalier*, *Ariadne auf Naxos* (Ariadne on Naxos, 1911–12). Indeed, reduction in scale was motivated just as much by artistic decisions as by practical necessity. Stravinsky in Paris discovered an instrument in accord with his mechanical rhythm, the player piano, and began making arrangements of his music for that domestic medium, besides giving it an original piece (Etude, 1917). Debussy, suspicious of Schoenberg before the war and now feeling himself never more French, looked for some connection with national traditions, and found it by writing sonatas (for cello and piano, for flute, viola and harp, and for violin and piano) that slyly sneak glances at Rameau and Couperin. These works are, though, still as free-flowing and harmonically venturesome as *Jeux*, and as emotionally multivalent. Of the second, Debussy wrote to a friend: 'It's terribly sad and I don't know whether one ought to laugh at it or cry? Perhaps both?'

Bartók's nationalism was of a different sort. The lessons he learned from folk music were those of sharing between peoples, and during the war he made arrangements of Romanian and Slovak as well as Hungarian songs; he also used all these sources in his original music. His ballet *The Wooden Prince* (1914–17) is a contribution to the debate in which Stravinsky, Schoenberg and Russolo had also engaged, concerning nature and artifice, and though the former wins through, with a final return to the idyllic music of the opening, the score's biggest moment is the dance for the puppet of the title. A work Bartók wrote in the same period, his Second Quartet, is concerned with subjectivity and objectivity. Like Schoenberg's Second Quartet, the work begins with music of exacerbated personal feeling, but its ending is quite otherwise, in an exuberant medley of village dances.

For Bartók the village provided an antidote to the city's problems of mechanization and disinterest, and a frame within which he could still embrace the modern urban sounds of dissonance and pulse-driven rhythm. Stravinsky's works of this time show similar ideas at work. But there were also composers dreaming of more distant utopias: Karol Szymanowski (1882–1937) using the heady harmonies and colours of Scriabin and Debussy to evoke a spangled east in his Third Symphony (1914–16) and other works of the war years, or Sergey Prokofiev (1891–1953) imagining in his 'Classical' Symphony (1916–17) how Haydn might now have been writing. With Russia in the throes of revolution, this could have seemed a peculiarly airy fantasy, but the music has its feet on the ground, and its light, retrospective, ironic spirit was to be as important to the future as the modernist initiatives that, on the outbreak of war, had been left unfinished.

Also waiting, not quite in earshot, was the new popular music of the United States. Stravinsky first encountered ragtime through sheet music, and responded with his own *Rag-time* for eleven players (1918). At that time it must have seemed that here was another kind of folk music, to be imitated, transformed and incorporated, just like the Russian songs and dances that Stravinsky similarly discovered on paper – not, like Bartók, out in the field. The great symbiosis of popular music and recording was not yet under way.

CHAPTER 19

Forwards and backwards, and sideways

World War I changed the western landscape. Germany was weakened by demands from the victor nations for reparations; the vast Austrian empire disintegrated; Russia became a communist state; and the United States emerged as a world force. Throughout the western world women were starting to gain equal rights, and workers were acquiring some measure of economic control. In Russia after 1917, as in France after 1789, culture was expected to keep pace with politics in revolutionary change. Change, however, did not have to be imposed, for it was everywhere, stimulated by the widening audience, new technology and shifting economic power. Privileges previously reserved for the bourgeoisie, of leisure and money, were becoming more generally available, and public radio, introduced in Europe and the United States in the early 1920s, conveyed music almost everywhere, virtually free.

In one area, though, very little altered. What was broadcast by radio stations in Moscow, Berlin and Chicago in the 1920s was, to a very large degree, what had been played in the concert halls of those cities in the 1890s. Programming had become fixed around a repertory running from Bach to Strauss and Debussy, and from here on most people's musical experience – including, of course, the experience of composers – was centred there, in a receding past.

Realizations of that past were being given permanent form in increasing numbers, as recordings. Soon after the war flat shellac discs ousted both cylinders and the player piano's paper rolls, and though those discs could accommodate only four minutes or so of music on each side, large orchestral works and operas were recorded entire in numerous slices, especially after the introduction of the microphone in 1925. (Previously musicians had been obliged to crowd in front of a horn, which would capture their sound for direct, mechanical recording.) Henceforth the primary sources for music's history include performances as well as compositions, and this must be counted the period not only of Stravinsky and Schoenberg, Bartók and Berg, Ives and Janáček, but also of – to name only a few performers from among many whose recordings continue to be valued – the conductors Felix Weingartner (1863–1942) and Willem Mengelberg (1871–1951), the sopranos Amelita Galli-Curci (1882–1963) and Elisabeth Schumann (1888–1952), and the pianists Josef Hofmann (1876–1957) and Alfred Cortot (1877–1962). Cortot was close to Ravel, Schumann was one of Strauss's favoured singers and Mengelberg conducted Bartók, but recording companies reflected – if they did not yet influence – concert life in giving relatively little attention to new music. Bartók, himself a pianist, was able to record only a small proportion of his music for commercial release. Stravinsky, as a conductor of his own music, only began recording in 1928. The gap was opening between the commercial-institutional world, which could happily survive on music already available, and the contemporary composer.

An early reaction to this was the Society for Private Musical Performances founded by Schoenberg in Vienna within months of the end of the war, in November 1918. The society's concerts featured only music from Mahler onwards, and only music for small forces (orchestral scores being played in arrangements for piano or chamber group), cultivating an atmosphere of appreciation and debate. Applause was not required. Nor were critics. Doors were shut against the world of publicity and careers. The society disbanded after four years, but by then its place as a forum for new music had been taken by a much larger institution, the International Society for Contemporary Music (ISCM). Such quiet places for music, removed from commercial musical life, have continued to draw together creative musicians and sympathetic audiences.

More radically, some composers after World War I concluded that there was no need for them any more, or that the conditions under which they had worked – conditions of widespread agreement about harmonic language and musical expression – no longer obtained. Hence the great silences of the 1920s, from among those who had been leading composers of the decades before. Elgar completed only minor works after his Cello Concerto (1918–19), an elegy for the age. Dukas produced just two tiny pieces after 1912. Rachmaninoff gave up in 1917, returned to composition in 1926, but only got going again solidly in the 1930s. Strauss and Vaughan Williams both stayed productive through the 1920s, but their best works were all earlier or later. Ives, who had never looked for recognition, found his creativity diminishing, still unnoticed. Sibelius, most powerfully silent of them all, wrote his compact and muscular single-movement Seventh Symphony (1924), gave it a postscript in his symphonic poem *Tapiola* (1926), and then lived on through more than three decades of being celebrated as a master of an art he had abandoned, or had it abandon him.

To the extent that the art depended on a nineteenth-century inheritance of symphonic form (or at least symphonic amplitude), tonal harmony and unified expressive voice, it had indeed abandoned everybody. The evident public taste for just those features, a taste encouraged by radio networks, was not enough. Something had died in World War I, along with the millions of servicemen, and it was confidence in subjectivity – in that consistent voice and consistent temporal flow that gave nineteenth-century music its continuing appeal, intensified now by loss.

Ravel's works offer a measure of this, and of the consequences. One of the great masters of instrumentation, he had produced a large quantity of orchestral works before the war, these and piano pieces forming the bulk of his output. Creative abundance went with exuberance, with a supremely colourful language of harmony and instrumental colour inherited from Liszt, Rimsky-Korsakov and Debussy. After the war that changed. In the orchestral *La Valse* (1919–20), which Diaghilev declined to use for a ballet, he composed a dance of death placed at the centre of European musical culture, in nineteenth-century waltzing Vienna. At once hedonistic and disturbing, the piece was his last major concert piece for orchestra until the two piano concertos he wrote simultaneously a decade later. Meanwhile he kept himself in practice by orchestrating other music, notably Musorgsky's *Pictures at an Exhibition* in 1922. He also composed a one-act opera, *L'Enfant et les sortilèges* (The Child and the Spells, 1920–5), where the orchestra is continuously important in helping delineate singing characters that range from a tree to a teapot. Otherwise his principal works of the 1920s were for chamber resources, and notably sparer. Two sonatas, for violin with cello (1920–2) and with piano (1923–7), are abstract music, lacking the evocativeness of *La Valse* and most of the pre-war works, though the later sonata includes a blues slow movement, complementing the jazzy dance number for teapot and cup in *L'Enfant*. In *Chansons madécasses* (Madagascar Songs, 1925–6), for soprano with flute, cello and piano, Ravel returned to the exotic-erotic sultriness of *Shéhérazade*, but now with the music's gestures clearly articulated and delineated. Schoenberg's atonal *Pierrot lunaire* is in the neighbourhood; so are Stravinsky's recent essays in folk style. Debussy and Rimsky-Korsakov are beyond the horizon. The rhapsody of the ego is held in check.

One route to a new objectivity was through old music, and here Ravel had been a retrogressive pioneer along with Prokofiev, writing his piano work *Le Tombeau de Couperin* (Memorial to Couperin, 1914–17) in the form of a Baroque suite. Music of the eighteenth century gave both composers models of clear form and contrapuntal texture, and their works convey their pleasure and relief in discovering old manners. There is a similar feeling to the compositions of Busoni and Reger engaging with Bach: old mixes easily with new, and the increasing presence of Baroque music in the concert hall may have helped. It is otherwise with Stravinsky's *Pulcinella* (1919–20), a ballet score for Diaghilev based on pieces ascribed to Pergolesi (many of which turned out to be eighteenth-century fakes stealing a popular name). Here old and new are as oil and water. The source material is given a harmonic-orchestral dress that does not fit; the experience is bifocal.

Stravinsky was delighted by this: the work gave him, he said, his 'passport' to his future. With his Symphonies of

Wind Instruments (1920), a ceremony of chants and chorales for orchestral woodwind and brass, he wrote the funeral service for his period of involvement with Russian folklore — and with Russia, to which he had not returned since before the war, and to which he had not wanted to return since the 1917 revolution. One task remained to be accomplished: the orchestration of the choral ballet *Les Noces* (The Wedding). This, another ceremony, was the final glory of his music of pulse; he had drafted it in 1914–17, but not until 1923 did he find its ideal accompaniment, mechanical yet supple, in an orchestra of four pianos and percussion. After this his works would be thoroughly western, thoroughly modern. Bach would be his folklore, but treated so as to again produce a split experience of involvement and observation, fascination and parody. In his Concerto for piano and wind (1923–4), for example, Bachian gestures are constantly subverted by 'wrong' notes in the harmony, by jump cuts, by jazzed rhythms and by the instrumental sounds. In *Oedipus Rex* (1926–7), a one-act opera designed to work in the concert hall as an oratorio, the models include Handel and, for the character of Jocasta, a Verdi-style mezzo-soprano. In *Apollo* (1927–8), a ballet score for strings, Lully is placed in company with café music of the 1920s, and, as in all these examples, the mixture holds and the incongruities are all deliberate. This was what came to be known as neoclassicism, which owed its cool and its strict rhythm not so much to the eighteenth century as to how the eighteenth century was being presented to the modern age by such performers as Landowska.

It was enormously influential. Stravinsky's presence — admixed with the stimulating effect he and Diaghilev had on patrons — helped make Paris in the 1920s as musically lively as it had been in the 1830s. Prokofiev, there through most of the decade, kept Stravinsky at arm's length but could not avoid his influence. Older French composers, such as Ravel and Albert Roussel (1869–1937), adapted themselves to the acerbic spirit of neoclassicism, which those now emerging, such as Arthur Honegger (1892–1955), Darius Milhaud (1892–1974) and Francis Poulenc (1899–1963), took as their native style. As in Stravinsky's music and Ravel's, elements of form, gesture and counterpoint from older music could be combined with touches of the latest jazz or dance music, all given a twist by spiky harmony and orchestration. The neoclassical cocktail also reached Germany, to give the energetic Paul Hindemith (1895–1963) his new start, and nips were taken by established composers, like Janáček, Bartók and Szymanowski, all of whom had been keeping an ear on Stravinsky since *Petrushka*. No less remarkably, the Danish composer Carl Nielsen (1865–1931) showed in his later symphonies and concertos that neoclassicism and Romanticism did not have to be alternatives but could coexist, producing a language of spruce, driving force.

The use of models and distancing effects, comparable with that of figurative elements reappearing in the painting of the time, made neoclassical music distinctly contemporary, but often the message would be reinforced by references to jazz or to machine imagery that had long survived the brief pre-war heyday of the Italian futurists. An example of the latter is Honegger's symphonic movement *Pacific 231* (1923), portraying a steam locomotive as it pulls out of a station. Jazz, which spread to Europe as it spread around the United States in the immediate post-war years, was absorbed with enthusiastic rapidity. Milhaud heard jazz groups in London in 1920 and New York in 1922, and incorporated their sounds in his ballet *La Création du monde* (The Creation of the World, 1923), which was exactly contemporary with the first recordings by 'King' Oliver (1885–1938) and Louis Armstrong (1901–71). Allied to jazz, the new dance styles were also assimilated: Hindemith's Piano Suite '1922', so titled to indicate its up-to-date character, includes a shimmy, a Boston and a ragtime. Soon there were jazz or blues pieces not only by these composers, Stravinsky and Ravel, but also by the Czechs Bohuslav Martinů (1890–1959) and Erwin Schulhoff (1894–1942), and even by Schoenberg. More than that, there seemed the possibility of a fusion from the 'other' side. In 1924 George Gershwin (1898–1937), hitherto known only for popular songs and Broadway shows, created *Rhapsody in Blue* for piano and jazz band; the next year he wrote a piano concerto.

Jazz offered not only contemporaneity and rhythmic life, valuable as those were, but also the possibility of addressing the recently widened audience, which was finding its music in the new songs and dances. Many composers, having left-wing sympathies, felt some alliance with jazz necessary for them to have a role in social and political change. In the view of Kurt Weill (1900–50), objectivity, which music had regained after Romanticism by re-establishing counterpoint, pulse and clear design, gave composers the means to address, now, not their own concerns but those of society, and success in that enterprise would mean a dialogue with popular culture. He found a ready colleague in Berlin in Bertolt Brecht, and together they produced two full-length stage works: *Die Dreigroschenoper* (The Threepenny Opera, 1928), based on *The Beggar's Opera* of eighteenth-century London, and *Aufstieg und Fall der Stadt Mahagonny* (Rise and Fall of Mahagonny City, 1927–9), set in a dark-fantasy United States. By bringing together aspects of Bach, popular music and dissonant harmony, Weill's music defamiliarizes the familiar and gains qualities of acid irony with which it can underscore the social criticism in the text. The worlds of the two operas are dystopias, in which most people are doing the best they can under adverse circumstances, and the music expresses both corruption and hope. But, in a further irony, several of the numbers, such as *Morität von Mackie Messer* (Mack the Knife) from *Die Dreigroschenoper*, were soon repossessed by popular culture, with their sting removed.

Commerce had less luck with the music of another Berlin composer, Hanns Eisler (1898–1962), who joined the communist party in 1926 and became critical of much that he had learned as a pupil in Vienna of Schoenberg. For him at this point, as for some composers in the Soviet Union, music was socially useful if it could be sung – if it could carry a progressive message within a popular style drawing not on the jazz of the United States (suspect as capitalist entertainment) but from the home store of folksong.

There was, however, an alternative view in the Soviet Union, coupling social revolution with revolution in the arts. For this wing of opinion, Stravinsky and Prokofiev, although in self-imposed exile, opened the new age, not so much because their music was objective and could therefore act on society, but rather because it carried a revolutionary impulse, and just needed a text or scenario for that impulse to be revealed. Dmitry Shostakovich (1906–76), whose First Symphony (1923–5) had its première when he was still in his teens, rapidly emerged as the leading composer of the first Soviet-trained generation and did just what was required. Nor is there any reason to suppose he did so, in his early twenties, with anything other than enthusiasm for a revolution that was promising so much. He set revolutionary texts in the choral finales of his next two symphonies

(1927 and 1929), scored two revolutionary ballets (*The Golden Age* and *The Bolt*), and gave the revolution a comic opera after Gogol (*The Nose*, 1927–8), full of sardonic humour and fantasy, and carrying musical revolution so far as to include an interlude for percussion alone.

By now neoclassicism had been espoused in some form by a great variety of composers, who probably agreed only in what they – and neoclassicism – refused: the Romanticism too much associated with the pre-war world and thereby with the war itself. The silence of so many erstwhile Romantic composers was further concurrence, as was the decline of others, such as Pfitzner.

Schoenberg, however, forbore to be silent or to decline. Seeing his work within a historical continuum, rather than as enabled by a recent change in mentality, he could not deny his Romantic origins. At the same time he found it difficult to persevere in a musical realm, that of atonality, where intuition was the only guide. Words could provide a frame, as they had in *Pierrot lunaire* and in an oratorio of the soul's struggle in heaven, *Die Jakobsleiter* (Jacob's Ladder, 1916–17), which he began to his own text but abandoned. Yet there was still the deeper need for an armature such as tonality had been, and this he found, possibly with some input from the self-taught Viennese composer Josef Matthias Hauer (1883–1959), in his 'method' of twelve-note composition, or serialism.

The method is quite straightforward. Atonal music, in order not to come near any perceptible mode or key, had to maintain a constant circulation of all or most of the twelve notes in the scale. Serialism simply organized this. The twelve notes would be set out in a succession: the series. And this succession would be repeated throughout the piece in multitudinous different forms, however the composer might wish. All that the method required was that the series be respected. It would then guarantee some consistency in melodic contours and the make-up of chords, and Schoenberg soon found how one chosen form of a series could work rather like a home key in tonal music. That was what he was after: a principle that would secure instrumental forms, as they had been secured by tonal harmony in the past. Accordingly, the first serial works he completed, all in 1923, included movements of conventional types: a waltz, a march, a minuet and an entire Baroque-style suite. Soon after came a set of choral 'satires' in which he poked fun at 'little Modernsky' for writing wrong-note Bach. Yet his own serial works were marked just as much as Stravinsky's by the spirit of neoclassicism.

Of his leading pupils, Berg was just tasting success with the première in Berlin in 1925 of his *Wozzeck*, the first full-length atonal opera. Here the language of free, non-serial atonality perfectly reflects the hostile and incomprehensible world in which the central character, a simple soldier, finds himself, and suits, too, the violent illogicality with which he reacts, while shafts of tonality enter the score for purposes of irony or consolation. The work was repeated around the German-speaking world as well as in Leningrad (1927) and Philadelphia (1931). Meanwhile, Berg had begun using serialism tentatively in his Lyric Suite for string quartet (1925–6).

By contrast, Webern took to serialism immediately and with a will, and used it to create highly abstract forms, persistently transforming a small number of motifs. Where Schoenberg's hope was to establish a new basis for composition – 'One has to follow the basic series; but, nevertheless, one composes as freely as before' – Webern disagreed. Though, as much as Schoenberg, he felt himself to belong to the great Austro-German tradition, whose forms and genres he reintroduced in his serial music, his works are unlike anything else in their self-similarity and their brevity. His Symphony (1927–8) has no neoclassical bifurcation; there is no precedent for its weave of exquisitely expressive melody tracing patterns as perfect as those of a flower or a crystal.

Webern's model for his imitative polyphony was that of the Renaissance: as a doctoral student he had edited mass settings by Isaac. In a similar way Bartók learned from studying folk music how short melodic elements can be put together in different ways, and how a tune can vary from village to village, singer to singer. Using this experience creatively, he came up with music that, like Webern's, is tightly constructed from small motifs, and that attains objectivity not so much by referring to the past as through its own qualities of clarity and symmetry: an example is his Fourth Quartet (1928). As before, he by no means confined himself to Hungarian sources, conjoining in his orchestral *Dance Suite* (1923) several traditions he had encountered in central Europe and north Africa.

Also learning from folk music, and from the example of Stravinsky's folk pieces, Janáček produced most of his great works in the 1920s, past the age of sixty-five. In his operas, beginning with *Katya Kabanova* (1920–1) and *The Cunning Little Vixen* (1922–3), he heightened the melodies of spoken Czech except for occasional passages of vocal soaring, and kept up in the orchestra an almost speech-like pace, with ideas that are compact, highly coloured and immediately expressive. These operas, like those of Berg, Hindemith and Weill, were enthusiastically received by the many German opera companies, now municipally funded and more eager to participate in living culture than were orchestras and concert halls of the time. Where the latter were concerned, a composer's best hope was to write a concerto, which would offer something of a known quantity (virtuosity), together with, very often, the prestige and publicity value of the composer as performer. Bartók, Stravinsky and Rachmaninoff, depending on performing fees at a time when commissions were scarce and remunerative orchestral performances infrequent, all wrote piano concertos for themselves, and though Ravel's were written for others, he began them after witnessing a new potential for concert music on his tour of the United States.

From the perspective of a Europe whose musical culture was becoming increasingly conservative, the United States seemed to offer bright prospects. The appeal of jazz came partly from its status as the new music of the new world, and response to US culture in the Brecht–Weill *Mahagonny* is as much eager as wary. Prokofiev, Bartók and Stravinsky all preceded or followed Ravel on the concert trail; Rachmaninoff from 1918 was a resident. As for US-born composers, post-war wealth and confidence provided many more opportunities. Even Ives came out from obscurity. In the early 1920s he published, at his own expense, a book of songs and his Second Piano Sonata. At the same time he completed several orchestral scores, including *Three Places in New England* and the symphony *New England Holidays*. These works, like the sonata and many of the songs, look back to the time of the composer's boyhood, and create their atmospheres of recollection by means of misty harmonies in contrast with a boy's fully remembered athletic vigour. Both the distance and the presence of times past are evoked, with the help of a free musical imagination running to atonality, highly irregular rhythm and complex textures. Often, too, musical memory is recreated in a welter of hymns, marches, popular songs and ragtime. The imaginary past becomes the musical future: Ives's overlayings of diverse musical streams and of quotations, as yet unheard, did not begin to be played regularly or appreciated fully until the 1950s, when time had caught up with them.

Other US composers wanted the future now. Among them, Henry Cowell (1897–1965) began experimenting with piano sound as a teenager in San Francisco, working with 'clusters' of adjacent notes performed with the palm or forearm (*The Tides of Manaunaun*), to which he later added operations inside the piano, plucking or brushing the strings (*The Banshee*, 1925), along with other new techniques. He toured Europe, including the Soviet Union, and with support from Ives founded the New Music Edition (1927) to publish adventurous works by both US and European composers. Among the beneficiaries was Edgard Varèse (1883–1965), who had left his native France in 1915 for New York, specifically to discover a new musical world. This he found in such works as *Hyperprism* (1922–3), for an ensemble of wind players and percussionists – music made of abutting blocks, like the recent works of Stravinsky, but with a high level of dissonance and of rhythmic complexity. There are no harmonies here but rather sounds, combining wind sonorities into gleaming and brazen wholes, against a patter of rhythms. Certainly there is no neoclassical modelling on the past. Already imagining how electronic means could give sound an energy and freedom only sketched in such works as *Hyperprism*, he was looking only ahead. But he was looking almost alone.

CHAPTER 20

The people's needs

Around 1930 the stand-off between creative musicians and concert institutions began abating. Many of the leading composers had been born in the extraordinary decade or so from the mid-1870s to the mid-1880s – they included Schoenberg, Stravinsky, Bartók, Webern, Varèse and Berg – and now, entering middle age, they may have wanted to find places for themselves in the mainstream of concert life. Where Stravinsky, for instance, had written nothing for symphony concerts since his *Pulcinella* suite (1920), a steady succession of such works started with his *Madrid* (1928), Capriccio for piano and orchestra (1928–9), *Symphony of Psalms* (1930) and Violin Concerto (1931). He also began spending more of his time conducting, and making records. Schoenberg's Variations (1926–8), his first new orchestral score since the war, was introduced by the Berlin Philharmonic under their conductor Wilhelm Furtwängler (1886–1954), while Leopold Stokowski (1882–1977), at the head of the Philadelphia Orchestra, gave the first performance of Varèse's *Arcana* (1925–7) – a work, however, making few concessions to symphonic proprieties.

Concessions were not immediately inevitable, because radical new music – 'modern music', or even 'ultramodern music' – was starting to be accepted on its own terms, for what it was, rather than being rejected for what it was not (symphonic Romanticism). Brahms did not have to be protected from the likes of Webern and Bartók. Brahms, it was by now clear, would survive, and Webern and Bartók could be appreciated alongside him. Radio had done something to encourage this change of attitude. For example, the BBC Concerts of Contemporary Music (1926–39), run by Edward Clark, brought many outstanding composers to London to conduct, play or supervise their works, including Schoenberg, Stravinsky, Bartók and Webern.

Perhaps the cinema also helped familiarize people with the work of living composers. In some theatres silent films had been accompanied by a live orchestra; Strauss had made a version of *Der Rosenkavalier* for that purpose in 1924. The introduction of the soundtrack, in 1927, then made it possible for orchestral music – and most film scores, since these earliest times, have been orchestral – to be heard wherever films were shown. Among composers involved in the earliest years of sound film were Shostakovich, Honegger and Eisler, while Schoenberg wrote a concert piece to show how serial music might contribute to cinematic atmosphere: *Begleitmusik zu einer Lichtspielszene* (Accompaniment to a Film Scene, 1929–30).

But however much radio and films had readied the audience, composers were soon making their own gestures towards rapprochement. To counter Romanticism was no longer as necessary as it had been in the directly post-war years; besides, one cannot go on saying no without feeling the urge some time to say yes. Many of the erstwhile most vociferous gainsayers were indeed now saying yes, as Stravinsky and Schoenberg were in the greater breadth of their new orchestral works. There was more to this than a new artistic tack. Just as incorporating aspects of jazz, a few years before, had appeared to offer the route to a larger audience, so success now seemed more likely to come from adjusting to the familiar language of the concert hall. At a time of danger, with unemployment and inflation flowing internationally from the Wall Street crash of 1929, the Beethovenian urge to speak to all was being felt again. Hence the reascendence of the symphony, in the hands of, among others, Honegger (No. 1, 1929–30) and Stravinsky.

Stravinsky's psalm symphony – three movements for choir and orchestra in which, as he put it, the singing of psalms is symphonized – testifies also to a religious revival among some composers (not Bartók and Varèse, who remained unyieldingly atheist). A member of the younger generation in Paris, Olivier Messiaen (1908–92), was beginning his creative life with sacred works, whether for the organ, his own instrument, or for the orchestral concert hall: he made versions of *L'Ascension* (The Ascension, 1932–4) for both. Disliking the duplicity and the potential flippancy of neoclassicism, he had his music move with singleness of purpose, even while it drew on a range of sources (chant and late Romantic orchestral sound, birdsongs and irregular rhythmic patterns) with no attempt at synthesis. Indeed, his mosaic forms, coupled with static harmonies derived from his personal system of modes, give even his earliest pieces an original sense of time not as flow but as pre-existing, revealing itself to human temporality in sequences of brilliant unalike instants.

His precedent on a formal level was Stravinsky, but the Stravinsky of *Petrushka* and *The Rite* rather than of such recent works as the *Symphony of Psalms*. That piece was, as Stravinsky inscribed the score, 'composed to the greater glory of God', and its movements create a sequence from prayer through promise to praise song. In the composer's view, however, what makes it religious is not its subject matter but its form, and in this respect he made no regression from neoclassicism. Sacred art, he averred, must be 'canonical' not only in what it says but in how it is made; it must abide by such ancient principles as those of fugue, in the particular case of the symphony's middle movement. From how Stravinsky handled those principles, however, it is clear that strict adherence was by no means a requisite. The music had only to sound strict, in its melodic imitations, to place a severe mask over whatever inner turmoil.

Canons of a very different sort were being imposed in Stravinsky's native country, where composers were expected to address not just people but 'the people'. In 1931 the Association for Contemporary Music, which had stood for revolutionary innovation and had invited Bartók and Cowell, was dismantled, and the following year the Union of Soviet Composers was set up as the single national body. That same year the official cultural programme was promulgated: socialist realism, which meant the representation of things as they are, directed not by an artist's personal vision but only by a social perspective which, in a revolutionary nation, would have to be optimistic. How this could apply to music was to cause much difficulty. In the immediate instance, the philosophy did not prevent Shostakovich's second opera, *The Lady Macbeth of Mtsensk* (1930–2), from becoming a great success, even though the work presents a tale of crime and degradation in terms of grotesque caricature, with rampant musical lampooning of the police force.

By this time the major cities of Russia and Germany were rivalling Paris as musical hubs. Berlin was home for Weill, Eisler, Hindemith and, from 1925, Schoenberg, and its Kroll Opera had been founded in 1927 to concentrate on new works and innovatory productions. Just four years later, though, the company folded in the face of worsening economic and political conditions, and the appointment of Adolf Hitler as German chancellor, on 30 January 1933, brought this period in the capital to an end. Berg – at work on his second opera, *Lulu* (1929–35), a rich mix of serialism with Romantic tonality, of social criticism with sensuality, of modernism with modernity (a vibraphone, a film episode) – found himself writing for a culture that had disappeared, which may be partly why he left off work on the last act to write his Violin Concerto (1935).

Weill left Berlin in March 1933 for Paris; Schoenberg went a few months later, also to Paris. Stefan Wolpe (1902–72), a Berlin composer who had associated himself with opposition to the Nazis' rise, went first to Vienna, where he studied with Webern, then to Palestine. Hindemith stayed a while, but it soon became clear that the Nazis' 'cultivation of the true artistic strengths of our German music', to quote from a speech given in 1938 by the minister for enlightenment and propaganda, Joseph Goebbels, had no room for him or anyone like him. In Nazi Germany, as in the Soviet Union, music was being judged by the presumed needs of 'the people', needs politicians felt that they themselves, not composers, were best equipped to divine.

Hindemith's principal concern at this period was *Mathis der Maler* (Mathis the Painter), an opera considering the artist's responsibilities in troubled times (its central character is Matthias Grünewald, caught in the Reformation wars of religion), but though a symphony drawn from the score was played in Berlin in 1934, again with Furtwängler conducting, the staging of the opera, in 1938, had to be in neutral Switzerland. Like almost every other composer of the time, Hindemith had found his music becoming in the

1930s more consonant, more symphonic, and *Mathis* is a glowing score. But its glow did not warm Goebbels. The minister gave his speech at a music festival in Düsseldorf, where an exhibition of 'Entartete Musik' (Degenerate Music) showed what was not wanted. Even the catalogue's cover accomplished that, displaying a black saxophonist wearing a star of David. Jewish music and jazz were alike anathema. Hindemith had gained from both. In 1940 he left.

Apart from Weill, Eisler, Schoenberg and, eventually, Hindemith, music in Germany lost much else. Bartók, who had given the first performance of his exuberant Second Piano Concerto in Frankfurt just a week before Hitler entered the chancellery, determined he would not return to Germany under the Nazis. Stravinsky did go back, in 1938, but his music was soon proscribed. Other composers later paid the ultimate price in the concentration camps, Schulhoff among them, in a massacre that enduringly scarred western culture.

That culture was also challenged by experience during roughly the same period in the Soviet Union, where Joseph Stalin had gained supreme power by the end of the 1920s. Stalin shared Hitler's belief that the health of a nation depended on the health of its music, the two dictators being in that respect distant disciples of Plato and Confucius. In January 1936 Stalin paid a visit to Shostakovich's *Lady Macbeth*, then playing in three Moscow theatres, and did not see the joke. At once the official newspaper *Pravda* printed a report, 'Chaos instead of Music', which quite accurately describes the opera, if in loaded terms: 'Snatches of melody, the beginnings of a musical phrase, are drowned, emerge again, and disappear in a grinding and squealing roar.' According to this article, the work was a contradiction of what ordinary people understood by opera – or,

rather, of what the writer believed they should so understand, for there had been ninety-seven performances in
Moscow, presumably well attended. The work was a pro-
vocation, and as such a product of formalism, or the belief
that new forms could be progressive. That was an idea
characteristic of bourgeois leftists, and the success of the
piece abroad should be a warning, not a commendation.

Promptly the piece was withdrawn from the Soviet
stage, and its composer censured by his colleagues in
the Leningrad Composers' Union, with the valiant exception of Vladimir Shcherbachev (1889–1952). Shostakovich
decided to put aside his new symphony (No. 4, 1935–6)
and write another (No. 5, 1937), to provide, as the *Pravda*
correspondent had wanted, not 'leftist distortion' but 'what
the Soviet audience expects and looks for in music'. It was
clear what this meant: strong tunes, consistency of voice,
music that sounds like music. Accordingly Shostakovich's
Fifth frankly adjusts itself to Tchaikovsky and Borodin,
and was duly acclaimed in *Pravda* as a 'Soviet artist's
creative reply to just criticism'. So far from being viewed
ever after as a forced compromise, however, the piece has
been widely regarded as among its composer's finest and
most personal achievements. If it is, that can only be
because Shostakovich was so fissured and ambiguous an
artist that his intentions are endlessly disputable. The
ironies inherent in neoclassicism, where mistakes of style
can be right and correctness meaningless, become in his
music knots that can never be untied.

The case is complicated further by how developments
in Soviet music were mirrored in the United States,
where there was no *Pravda*, and where Franklin Delano
Roosevelt offered scant resemblance to Stalin. Even so,
Ruth Crawford Seeger (1901–53), whose String Quartet of

1931 is dazzling in its interplay of original processes applied to pitch, rhythm and texture, was led by her left-wing principles to concentrate on folk music, and Aaron Copland (1900–90), who had drawn towards Schoenberg in his Piano Variations (1930), turned to a vivacity that brought the Hispanic style of Chabrier, Lalo and Bizet into the jazz age with his orchestral picture of a Mexico City bar, *El Salón Mexico* (1933–6). That was his point of entry to a homegrown style, rooted in folksongs and hymns as much as Ives's music had been, but harmonically straightforward and speaking with a unified voice – the style of his ballets *Billy the Kid* (1938), *Rodeo* (1942) and *Appalachian Spring* (1943–4). These, in suites and arrangements, were performed on concert programmes across the country, their success rivalled only by that of the Third Symphony (1938) of Roy Harris (1898–1979), which similarly provided a strong, immediate and heroic image of the pioneer spirit. Meanwhile, Varèse fell silent and Cowell was in prison on a homosexual charge.

Everywhere in the later 1930s music was becoming simpler and modernism was in retreat. In Britain the earlier part of the decade had seen the darkest, most complex symphonies of Vaughan Williams and Arnold Bax (1883–1953): the former's F minor (1931–4) and the latter's Sixth (1934). Both composers then came more towards the light. So did Stravinsky in such works as his 'Dumbarton Oaks' Concerto for chamber orchestra (1937–8), a sprightly and luminous homage to Bach's Brandenburg Concertos, named after the residence of the composer's US patrons. So did Bartók, who created progressions from harmonic sombreness to liveliness and clarity in his Music for Strings, Percussion and Celesta (1936) and Sonata for Two Pianos and Percussion (1937).

The questions composers faced, more acutely than at any other time, were as much moral as musical. Whether working under a commercial system or a communist one, many saw themselves as creating from within society, and yet the music most valued, in societies across the world from Russia to California, was the intensely individual music of Romanticism, and of jazz and popular song. Bartók, by finding his basic material in music that came from societies rather than individuals, provided himself with the means for a more generalized expression, which he intensified by the objective construction he maintained even as his harmony grew milder, and also by so often making the aim of his music a communal dance.

Bartók and Stravinsky were among the many musicians in the exodus to the United States that had begun in 1934 with the arrival in Los Angeles of two Austrians: Schoenberg and Erich Wolfgang Korngold (1897–1957). Schoenberg, whose creative life had been disrupted when he broke off work on his opera *Moses und Aron* while still in Berlin, settled into writing a violin concerto and a string quartet, followed by an affirmation of his Jewishness in *Kol Nidre* for rabbi, choir and orchestra (1938). Korngold's reaction to his new environment was different. In Europe he had made his name principally as an opera composer; in the United States he quickly became the most prominent composer of film music, and in such scores as that for *The Adventures of Robin Hood* (1938), created a Hollywood sound deriving in opulence and versatility from the decades-old symphonic poems of Strauss. Here again was a musical development of the later 1930s that, in terms of language, was a step back.

Schoenberg in Los Angeles continued his work as a teacher, his early pupils there including John Cage (1912–92), who found ways far more radical than Bartók's to place socially generated materials in objective forms. Having also studied with Cowell, he had his ears open, and in 1935 began working with amateur percussion ensembles whose instruments included tin cans, electric buzzers and items of hardware. Since there was no question of pitch or therefore of harmony, he made rhythm the determining element, organized according to the incontrovertible facts of pulse and numerical proportion. The resulting music is strikingly close to that of non-western traditions, especially Balinese; all the period's anxieties with regard to the great western tradition are let slip, for it is as if that tradition had never been. Harry Partch (1901–74), another Californian, was also happy to stride off by himself, in his case towards pure, untempered intervals, for which he had to reconstruct traditional instruments or design new ones. Yet, loners as they were, both these composers were expressing social concerns typical of the time. Partch, leading a hobo existence himself, set words by drifters; his music and Cage's alike cherished sounds that the mainstream had excluded.

Meanwhile, the transatlantic liners were bringing more musicians into exile. In 1935 Weill travelled to New York, where he stayed as a composer for Broadway shows. For him this was a natural development. In a modern democratic society popular culture was not an alternative to high art but the very embodiment of it, and it was as appropriate now for a composer to write musical comedies as it had been for Beethoven to write quartets and symphonies. The abrasiveness of Weill's German scores disappeared as he quickly adapted himself to the styles and standards of Broadway composers such as Jerome Kern (1885–1945) and Richard Rodgers (1902–79), to achieve hit numbers like 'September Song' (from *Knickerbocker Holiday*, 1938). Even the more politically active Eisler, shaken by the pact

Stalin signed with Hitler in 1939, felt that social equality might be coming to pass in the United States, whose popular arts the composer could nobly serve, in his case by writing film music.

Eisler had arrived in New York in 1938 (as had Wolpe), and settled in Los Angeles in 1942, alongside Schoenberg. Stravinsky followed in 1939, halfway through writing his Symphony in C for Chicago, and he too found a home in Los Angeles – though, despite repeated efforts, he had no luck with the film companies. Bartók went the next year and stayed in New York, while Hindemith's destination was Yale. There were also conductor refugees, among them Otto Klemperer (1885–1973) and Bruno Walter (1876–1962). Arturo Toscanini (1867–1957), whose dynamism and intensity offered a contrast with the grand continuity advanced by his contemporary Furtwängler, like Bartók absented himself from Nazi domains and spent more and more time in New York.

Those who remained in Germany may have done so because, as Furtwängler seems to have felt, the country could not just be abandoned to the barbarians. Strauss, after accepting appointments and commissions in the early Nazi years, withdrew into privacy and produced in his final opera a work above anything he had written in thirty years: *Capriccio* (1940–1), an opera about opera, in which the old debate about the primacy of words or music is played out seductively in the vying of a poet and a composer for the affections of the countess who is their patron. The period's social questions are nowhere. Romanticism extends itself without embarrassment, for in the work of this composer it had never been rescinded.

With the world now at war again, Strauss's opera received far less international attention than Shostakovich's

Seventh Symphony (1941), subtitled 'Leningrad' and giving expression, at least on its magniloquent surface, to the resilience of those who had withstood the German siege of the city. Even Stravinsky, normally scornful of anything coming out of the Soviet Union, or of any Romantic-style notion of expression, was impressed enough to write his own topical symphony, the Symphony in Three Movements (1942–5), which he said in his programme note reflected 'this our arduous time of sharp and shifting events, of despair and hope, of continual torments, of tension, and at last cessation and relief'. Bartók could have said the same of the work he wrote during the same period, his Concerto for Orchestra, in which, however, he parodied the 'Leningrad' Symphony's grandiosity and ended, as usual, with relief in dance. In 1944–6 the air was full of victory symphonies: Prokofiev's Fifth, Copland's Third, Shostakovich's curiously skittish Ninth. Experience of war had created a social cohesion unknown for decades; as it ended composers found their personal heartbeats in synchrony with the pulse of the age. Time was untangled, at least for the moment.

CHAPTER 21

To begin again again

Stravinsky was surprised when, more than thirty years after the première of *The Rite of Spring*, and in the same Paris theatre, music of his once more caused a commotion. This time the noise came not from a society crowd shocked or bemused to be witnessing an artistic revolution, but from a group of recent students outraged that the revolutionary had turned so genial. In 1913 the earth had split. Now, in 1945, the mildest Grieg was being invoked, in one of the scores Stravinsky had salvaged from failed film projects: *Four Norwegian Moods*. He made some enquiries, and discovered that the leader of the protesters was Pierre Boulez (b. 1925), who had studied with Messiaen and also with René Leibowitz (1913–72), the Schoenberg group's standard-bearer in Paris.

Boulez had been a student in a city under Nazi occupation, and had gained from that experience the intensity of a resistance patriot. Music, he felt, had been held in check not only by the Nazis' proscriptions, especially of Schoenberg, but also by a general lack of stamina among those who had carried forward the adventure of progress in the years before the previous war. For him, that adventure was not over. Neoclassicism had been a distraction, the new symphonism of the last fifteen years an unworthy capitulation to public laziness. The principles of Schoenberg's and Webern's early atonal works – total harmonic freedom, unpredictable rhythm, no themes, each piece creating its own form – were valid still. Serialism, with which its inventor had instilled order, could and must be used in a totally different way, critically, to disrupt music's inclination to settle into familiar patterns. On the rhythmic level, the intemperateness and irregularity of *The Rite* must be followed through, as Messiaen had partly suggested in his piano cycle *Vingt Regards sur l'Enfant-Jésus* (Twenty Views of the Child Jesus, 1944).

That work does indeed have its bizarre moments, though there are others that are sweet, calm, magnificent or overwhelming: the twenty pieces make up an entire recital, and they draw on moods and manners from throughout the piano literature, spiked with elements from the composer's favourite ancient (chant), exotic (Indian) and avian sources. Boulez, however, was seized by what was most hectic in his teacher's music, which in his own earliest compositions he made collide with Schoenberg's, to their mutual annihilation. It was his Second Piano Sonata (1947–8) that had most exposure, a four-movement torrent in which all music's easy consolations are obviated or disrupted. Like composers of three and four decades before, Boulez wanted a fresh start, though for the moment what his music conveyed most forcibly was his anger.

In having no truck with neoclassicism – and certainly none with the popular music of the time, whether such songs as Frank Sinatra (1915–98) recorded or the new bebop of Charlie Parker (1920–55) – Boulez expressed some agreement with the German philosopher Theodor Wiesengrund Adorno (1903–69), a writer closer to the practice of composition, and more influential, than any since E. T. A. Hoffmann. Adorno, like Hoffmann, believed in music's progress. In his view, composers, as members of society, could not avoid dealing in their music with society's tensions, and inevitably, in increasingly complex and divided societies, increasingly complex music would arise. Neoclassicism and restored Romanticism, in looking back to previous states of music and therefore of society, were efforts to disguise current tensions, and therefore betokened a failing of moral will. Serialism represented music at its most advanced, and alone offered possibilities for authentic expression. The fact that this language had gained little support from performing institutions, radio and recording authorities or the public was not a condemnation but a proof of its validity, for the commercial business of music was utterly unconcerned with composition and had seriously injured the public's capacity for musical experience. Radio and records had devalued music. A Beethoven symphony thus heard was loaded with the mollifying messages of those in control of society, insinuating that culture was available to all with no effort, that the great works all came from long in the past and had been duly sorted out, that music could be a home comfort. The difficulty communicated in true modern music was its pride, in making it resistant to such appropriation.

The dramatis personae of Adorno's study *The Philosophy of Modern Music* (1949) offered no surprise: the hero was Schoenberg and the villain Stravinsky. Recent works by both might have been made to illustrate the case. Schoenberg's String Trio (1946) brought extremities of tension into a coherent form, while his *A Survivor from Warsaw* (1947), for orchestra and choir with spoken narration, insisted on music's social agency, even if Adorno might have been troubled by the work's direct reportage:

based on a newspaper article, it depicts the oppressed Jews of the war-time Warsaw ghetto rising up in a protestation of faith. Stravinsky, meanwhile, was writing a Bach-tea-shop concerto for jazz band (*Ebony Concerto*, 1945), another for strings (Concerto in D, 1946) and *Orpheus* (1947), a coolly luminous ballet score playing gently with many classical tropes.

Adorno's challenge set out a lonely path for the composer, away from the security of the known and acceptable, and many were to follow. But many were not. A lot of composers would have agreed with Boulez that some compound of the early twentieth-century masters was required, but without endorsing the explosive mixture the young Frenchman proposed. In Germany the thirst for what the Nazis had banned led to the founding in 1946 of a summer school at Darmstadt, where Leibowitz and Messiaen taught in the early years, and where one of the first students was Hans Werner Henze (b. 1926). He absorbed Schoenberg, Stravinsky and jazz in a prolific output of orchestral and theatre music that by 1951 included three symphonies, several concertos and a full-length opera. In England, Benjamin Britten (1913–76) showed in his opera *Peter Grimes* (1944–5) how lessons from Berg and Stravinsky could be subsumed within a style of dramatic naturalism and clear tonality, while the music of Michael Tippett (1905–98) created a harmony from Bartók, Hindemith and English folksong. For these composers, as also for Vaughan Williams, being active in society meant working within existing institutions – including the BBC, which in 1946 launched the Third Programme to disseminate serious culture – and creating new ones, such as the festival which Britten established in his home town of Aldeburgh in 1948, and to which he devoted much of his creative work thereafter.

With his prestige making Aldeburgh a national and even an international phenomenon, Britten countered the still decreasing interest in living composers on the part of mainstream concert organizations. Leading conductors of the late 1940s and 1950s in western Europe and the United States – many of them ageing figures, such as Furtwängler (following a two-year ban on him enforced by the allies), Toscanini, Klemperer, Walter, Pierre Monteux (1875–1964) and Thomas Beecham (1879–1961) – gave very few new works. Nor was much new music recorded. Instead the arrival in 1948 of long-playing (LP) records, accommodating up to an hour of music, was the occasion for re-recording the standard repertory, whose latest components – Debussy, the earlier Strauss and earliest Stravinsky – had been fixed in place a generation ago.

The place for new music was diminishing also in the Soviet Union, for different reasons. In 1948 Shostakovich, Prokofiev and other Soviet composers were officially accused, as Shostakovich had been twelve years before, of pursuing formal notions at the expense of socialist realism. Once again Shostakovich decided he had best put a new work (his Violin Concerto No. 1) aside, and this time his 'reply to just criticism' was a bland oratorio in praise of Stalin's afforestation.

Adorno had already expressed his suspicion of society's controllers dictating how social forces and directions should be musically construed, but he had not predicted that radio, which for him was part of the problem, would provide composers with their greatest champions and support, especially where the most radical new music was concerned. The radio in Munich sponsored the annual Musica Viva festival founded in 1946; the Freiburg station was behind the Donaueschingen Festival, a pre-war venture which was refounded in 1950 to become one of the principal showcases for new music. In 1948, at the studios of French radio in Paris, Pierre Schaeffer (1910–95) opened the door to electronic composition by creating the first examples of what he called 'musique concrète' (concrete music), music made with actual sounds, recorded on disc and transformed by re-recording – at different speeds, backwards or in combination with other sounds. Three years later the Cologne radio station set up a permanent studio for electronic music. Tape recorders were now available, facilitating electronic composition, and the Cologne studio distinguished itself from the group around Schaeffer by preferring sounds synthesized by electronic means, not recorded.

There was a rationale for this. In 1949 Cage, who had himself done creative work in US radio stations, went to Paris for some months and struck up a close collegial friendship with Boulez. Out of their discussions, it seems, came the notion of sound as having four dimensions, or parameters – pitch, duration, loudness and timbre – and so the idea that the basic principles of serialism could be applied to all of these. Milton Babbitt (b. 1916), who was teaching at Princeton, had created a system of duration serialism in his Three Compositions for piano (1947). So had Messiaen in parts of his *Turangalîla* Symphony (1946–8), another of his works in which highly abstract and venturesome thinking is combined with rapturous, almost abandoned enjoyment of sensuous triadic harmony and modal melody, to create in this instance a great love song in ten movements. It was Messiaen who wrote the first piece based on a series of loudness levels as well as on separate series of pitches and durations in his piano piece *Mode de valeurs et d'intensités* (1949–50). Adorno had complained that radio 'atomized' musical experience, encouraged the listener to hear a sequence of tunes and snatches, not the whole work. Now composers were deliberately creating atomized music. And the advantage of this in electronic composition was that the aesthetic of creating element by element was in accord with the practicalities of a medium in which sounds had to be composed one by one before assembly.

Boulez, in Schaeffer's studio, produced two serial-electronic studies in 1952. Karlheinz Stockhausen (1928–2007), who had been bowled over by hearing Messiaen's recording of the *Mode de valeurs* at Darmstadt in 1951, went to study with Messiaen the next year and returned to create his two serial-electronic studies in Cologne in 1953–4. Both these composers also worked with the new ideas in the instrumental domain, as did another Messiaen pupil, Jean Barraqué (1928–73). There was now no question of serial composition going, as Schoenberg had put it, 'as freely as before'. Every instant involved a dialogue between determination (following the highly elaborated serial plan) and choice. The constraints could be such that a piece, or many of the elements in it, would unfold automatically, like a machine that the composer had merely set in motion: the severe opening section of Boulez's *Structures I* for two pianos (1951–2) is like that, as is Stockhausen's contrarily jazz-inflected *Kreuzspiel* (Crossplay, 1951) for oboe, bass clarinet, piano and percussion. But the work that most thoroughly conveys the desperation of a locked but feeling consciousness is Barraqué's forty-minute, single-movement Piano Sonata (1950–2).

Even Barraqué, though, said little in his public writings about expression. The rhetoric was all of creating new languages and new techniques: indeed, had the Soviet authorities been aware of Boulez and Babbitt, they could hardly have censured Shostakovich and Prokofiev as form-alists. Particularly for composers in western Europe, the experience of 1933–45 had left a heavy suspicion around human ideas of naturalness; organization, based on objec-tive truths (numbers, the fundamentals of sound), would provide the way forward, into a future that was vaunted as much as the need for premeditation. 'Structure' Boulez declared to be the 'keyword of our epoch'.

Such thinking was by no means felt only by the circle around Messiaen: there were expressions of it also in archi-tecture and jazz, in painting and in literature. Elliott Carter (b. 1908), a close contemporary of Messiaen's but musically quite unalike, left New York for Arizona for a year in order to leave behind also the neoclassical style he had, like Copland, learned in Paris. What he came up with was his First Quartet (1950–1), music standing alone in its drive through wide-ranging harmony, textural density and chan-ging metres. The ample characterfulness of Ives's music was reapproached by abstract means, without quotations. In France, Henri Dutilleux (b. 1916) similarly moved towards a style more complex harmonically and formally, and, like Carter, began to produce his elaborate works at a slower pace.

Cage, in New York, remained in touch with Boulez by correspondence, but communicating from a distance that was artistic as much as geographical. For him, as for his European colleagues, the application of strict serial controls brought the possibility of music that could proceed by itself, the composer's intention limited to setting it going. But the conclusions to be drawn were different in every case. Boulez had thought of giving his *Structures I* the title of a painting by Paul Klee: *Monument at the End of Fertile Land*. The work was an exercise in style – or in stylelessness, a

trip to the edge of the abyss of total creative automation —
from which the composer could return clarified. This was a
testing of the difference being considered also by computer
scientists, that between mind and machine. Barraqué, by
creating a largely mechanical composition that spoke with
the intimacy of a mind, went further, his sonata conveying
frustration and despair with its own voice. Stockhausen, like
Messiaen deeply Catholic, saw in the most abstract and will-
free processes an image of divine purity. For Cage, different
again, the point of removing creative will was to 'let the
sounds be themselves', introduce the possibility of music
that said nothing but just happened. In his *Music of Changes*
for piano (1951) he used coin tosses to answer all questions
about the choice, placing, length and loudness of events — a
procedure as time-consuming as that of following a complex
serial system. The next year he took the further, drastically
simple step of eliminating composition altogether. In his
4'33" he asked his closest musical associate, the pianist
David Tudor, to sit at the keyboard for that length of time
and play nothing. The piece was of course provocative, an
indication of Cage's closeness not only to east Asian (especially zen) ideals of non-intention but also to the 'anti-art'
of Europe in the 1920s. But it was also an invitation to listen
to whatever sounds were being produced in the room or
outside. Music was liberated from composers, performers,
instruments and occasions. It was everywhere.

All these developments of 1950–2 took music a further
bound away from the art's conventions than had been
achieved in 1908–13, and away from most people's expectations of what music must be. At least Carter's quartet and
Barraqué's sonata accorded, in scale, genre and seriousness,
with the traditional concept of a work of art. But the
compositions of Boulez and Stockhausen offered no rational

continuity, and 4'33" was empty of all content. Such music was not meant for normal concert life. Its composers found their performers among a few dedicated adepts and their audiences under radio auspices or at educational institutions. Babbitt, who spent his working career at Princeton, decided there could be no safe contact with the orchestra, which could not afford to rehearse a modern score, or with the normal concertgoer, who wanted what contemporary music could not give. In society as it was, composers could not expect to communicate generally, any more than could specialists in any other branch of learning – though Babbitt's works of the later 1950s, such as his Second Quartet (1954) and *All Set* for modern jazz combo (1957), seem geared in their spirit and humour to more than academic approbation. Meanwhile, Cage and Wolpe found a haven within the adventurous, cross-disciplinary courses run by Black Mountain College in North Carolina. 4'33" was first presented there, and the atmosphere encouraged Wolpe to a free-wheeling synthesis of serialism and jazz in such works as his quartets for tenor saxophone, trumpet, piano and percussion (1950) and for oboe, cello, piano and percussion (1955).

Wolpe was also among the teachers at Darmstadt, along with Boulez, Stockhausen and Luigi Nono (1924–90), who had been a classmate there of Stockhausen's in 1951. Darmstadt offered students from all over Europe the chance to learn from composers at the forefront of innovation, and to witness challenging differences of opinion. Where Boulez was moving towards a consummate mastery of style and technique in works such as *Le Marteau sans maître* (The Hammer with no Master, 1952–4), for voice with instrumental ensemble, and abandoning more experimental projects (his Third Piano Sonata of 1955–7, in which the player was offered multitudinous pathways through the written material), Stockhausen was sketching whole new concepts in each piece. Three orchestras overlaid different tempos as an image of tangled time in *Gruppen* (Groups, 1955–7); an electronic drama, *Gesang der Jünglinge* (Song of the Youths, 1955–6), involved a boy's recorded voice interacting with flames and flurries of synthesized sound; another, *Kontakte* (Contacts, 1959–60), had two live musicians, on piano and percussion, capture, elicit and converse with the features of an evolving sonic landscape on tape. Nono's was yet another approach. Persuaded neither by Boulez's sophistication nor by Stockhausen's excitable pursuit of new means, he used the transgressiveness of new musical possibilities boldly to register a fiercely expressive protest against what had happened under Nazism and during the Spanish Civil War – dangers, which for him, as a communist, had not been permanently surmounted by the western victory. A continuing tension sings out passionately in his *Il canto sospeso* (The Suspended Song, 1956), a setting for soloists, choir and orchestra of excerpts from letters by prisoners of the Nazis.

Despite their differences these three composers felt themselves to be participating in a joint endeavour, and all remained committed to the idea, at least, of serialism. The first challenge to that idea, from within the ranks of rising composers, came from Iannis Xenakis (1922–2001), who brought to his music a sense of volume and shape derived from his training as an architect. In his first important work, *Metastasis* for orchestra, he wrote for all the string instruments independently in great storms of glissandos (pitch slides), vastly amplifying a kind of sound production, the slide through a large interval, that had been almost eradicated from orchestral practice as a symptom of nineteenth-century sentimentality. Xenakis made it boldly new, in music of an unabashed sound drama recalling only Varèse among the early modernists, and the work's first performance at Donaueschingen in 1955, coupled with its author's criticism of serialism in an article, caused consternation. For Boulez, Xenakis's music was crude, betraying his lack of musical training and experience. Rough as it was, though, it could not be ignored.

By this time Boulez, Stockhausen and Nono, still young men, were being taken seriously by others besides students at Darmstadt. Adorno, who was also there regularly in the 1950s, was dismayed by music that concentrated on issues of compositional technique and that found a refuge in specialist courses, radio programmes and festivals, but still, by his presence and his engagement, he lent these composers intellectual weight. They were simultaneously gaining official promotion, partly because culture was one of the battlefields of the Cold War and their music – together with that of their older US contemporaries Carter, Cage and Babbitt – could be shown as exemplifying a creative freedom in contrast with the Soviet state control that had survived Stalin's death in 1953. This would have been another reason for Adorno's disappointment, that music of questioning and resistance was being endorsed by the status quo, whose power thus to neutralize dissent came to seem limitless.

Soviet authorities were slow to learn this lesson. Composers there could now write a little less circumspectly, as witness the dark power of Shostakovich's Tenth Symphony (1953), apparently a posthumous portrait of the great leader. But an opening towards new western ideas came only gradually, and at first only in outlying parts of the communist bloc. The Warsaw Autumn festival, founded in 1956, brought those ideas to Witold Lutosławski (1913–94) and other Polish composers, while the Hungarian György Kurtág (b. 1928) had the rare opportunity to study in Paris and visit Cologne, where he heard *Gruppen*. But differences of culture persisted, in that composers in eastern Europe were unable or unwilling to abandon traditional kinds of musical communication. Where Webern in the west was a pioneer of rotating intervals within chords (Boulez) or of form as the product of serial process (Stockhausen), in the east, for Kurtág, the pathos mattered as much as the tight construction.

The young western European composers were also having an effect on their seniors. Observing their wariness of imagination unguided by system, Messiaen in the 1950s retracted the opulence of his *Turangalîla* and looked to nature for his material. The songs, calls and shrieks of birds, many of them notated in the field, he amplified and dazzlingly coloured through his choices of harmony and sonority in his compact piano concerto *Oiseaux exotiques* (Exotic Birds, 1955–6) and other works. Carter and Wolpe both noted the paradox, in the new European music, of system guaranteeing constant unpredictability. In other cases there may have been no direct influence but rather a movement in parallel, as in the featuring of tuned percussion not only in Boulez's *Marteau* but also in Britten's ballet score *The Prince of the Pagodas* (1956) and Vaughan Williams's Eighth Symphony (1953–5). Another example would be the preordained processes, usually involving canons with parts in different speeds or metres, that Conlon Nancarrow (1912–97) set up in studies for an instrument that could easily provide rhythmic complexity: the player piano. Like Ives before, he sought no recognition, just storing up his punched paper rolls at his home in Mexico City.

At the opposite extreme of public prominence, Stravinsky certainly learned from the younger generation. While working on *The Rake's Progress* (1947–51), a full-length opera looking back to Mozart (plus Verdi, Donizetti, Monteverdi, etc.), he took into his household in Los Angeles a young conductor whose interests embraced not only his host's music but that of the Schoenberg school: Robert Craft (b. 1923). In 1951 Schoenberg died; the two composers had been near neighbours for more than a decade and had encountered each other only at the funeral of the writer Franz Werfel, in 1945. A few months after Schoenberg's death Craft made a recording of one of his serial pieces, the Suite for septet of 1925, and Stravinsky attended the rehearsals. Within a few months more this careful listener was at work on a septet of his own, and beginning to try a more chromatic style, with some elements of serialism. Thus, past seventy, he started to learn a new creative language. The early results were pieces in which a music-history echo chamber could still be constructed: *Canticum sacrum* (Sacred Song, 1955), for soloists, choir and a dark, brassy orchestra, made for Venice and resounding with Gabrieli, or the ballet *Agon* (Contest, 1954–7), whose references range from Renaissance dances to Webern. Then in 1957–8 he heard Boulez's *Le Marteau* (conducted by the composer in Los Angeles) and Stockhausen's *Gruppen* (in Donaueschingen), and the course of his music took another turn, towards the airiness and rarefaction of *Movements* for piano and chamber orchestra (1958–9). Here he brightly reflected the athematic abstraction, rhythmic flexibility and instability of the younger composers' works, with no loss to his old virtues of precision, lightness and vim.

By this time the new music was finding a larger public base. In 1954 Boulez founded a concert series in Paris, eventually known as the Domaine Musical, to present new works in a context of twentieth-century classics and of old music that displayed a comparable concern with questions of construction (Bach, Gabrieli). Later in the 1950s he began conducting the German radio orchestras in similar repertory. Many of the early Domaine performances were recorded for release on disc, including the première of Barraqué's *Séquence* (1950–5), which, like *Le Marteau*, is scored for a female singer with a percussion-heavy ensemble, but which differs in its continuity, its drama and its sense that the voice is that of the work itself, expressing its determined but precarious hold on existence. Boulez had spoken of *Le Marteau* as 'seizing delirium and, yes, organizing it', in line with his continuing enthusiasm for the convulsive, shamanistic view of art espoused by Antonin Artaud; and yet what he produced, with its prepared exoticism and its polish, suggests a new Ravel. *Séquence*, setting poems by Friedrich Nietzsche, is radiant but raw, and looks only within.

The correspondence between Bach and new music was further demonstrated in a 1955 recording of the Goldberg Variations having somewhat Boulezian qualities of structural clarity, independent thought and indeed atomized sound: the debut on an international label (Columbia) of Glenn Gould (1932–82). The record market, though, was being dominated increasingly by music of another kind. Barraqué's second work for the Domaine Musical – . . .*au delà du hasard* (1959), for voices and instrumental groups, with the voices again singing of the anguish, agony and fulfilment of self-definition – obliquely reflected his appreciation of modern jazz, especially of Thelonious Monk (1917–82) and the Modern Jazz Quartet. But in the seven years since his sonata popular music had changed.

Stravinsky's absorption of serialism coincided with the emergence of rock and roll; Barraqué's *Séquence* and Messiaen's *Oiseaux exotiques* were introduced at a Domaine Musical concert on 10 March 1956, just six weeks after the release of a song, *Heartbreak Hotel*, that rapidly normalized the name of Elvis Presley (1935–77).

CHAPTER 22

Whirlwind

In 1962 György Ligeti (1923–2006) – who joined the young composers of western Europe late, having arrived from Budapest after the Soviet invasion of 1956, and who remained something of an outsider – imagined a piece that would provide a clear image of time as a knotted web, and yet would do so with materials of elementary simplicity. Just a hundred mechanical metronomes are required for this *Poème symphonique* (Symphonic Poem), clicking at different speeds and running down at different rates, and thereby producing a thicket of noises that thins to various interweavings of pulses and so to eventual silence. An instrument that measures time like a clock thus becomes, through multiplication, the generator of a cloud of sound, to borrow terms the composer himself borrowed from the philosopher Karl Popper, who used them to distinguish between phenomena that are rationally predictable (clocks) and those that are in some measure chaotic (clouds).

The belief widely promulgated in the early 1950s saw western music altogether as a clock, a system moving forward in a determined direction either gradually or, as at that time, through periods of revolution. Support for that belief came from the whole history of music in the west: the modes had given way to keys; the possibilities of the keys

had been extended; then had come atonality. But very soon –
partly because of internal disagreements, partly, paradoxi-
cally, because the plausibility and success of the new way
forward drew so many adherents – the clock was coming to
seem more like a cloud.

Boulez had insisted on the necessity of serialism, but by
the end of the 1950s the term had been expanded so far as to
be virtually meaningless. Certainly there was little that
united the professedly serial composers, from Nono to
Stravinsky, or divided them from those who made no such
claim. Even so there was general agreement on the importance of system, with even Cage participating, for he had
persistently used systematic procedures, less laborious than
those of *Music of Changes*, to determine the will of chance.
Thus composers as widely separated, in location and aesthetic, as Nancarrow and Xenakis, or Babbitt and Ligeti,
were using creative routines to limit, direct or stimulate the
imagination. And they all did so from a mistrust of the old
codes of expression, as well as from a confidence that they
were working towards music's future, even at a time when
the whole future of humanity had been thrown in doubt by
the threat of nuclear war. The cloud was, to that degree,
bounded.

Ligeti's arrival was followed the next year by that of
Mauricio Kagel (1931–2008), coming from Buenos Aires, while
Luciano Berio (1925–2003) also became part of the network.
All these composers, who had not experienced the rage of
almost total determination in 1950–2, took a more relaxed
approach to the notion of constant innovation. For Berio,
musical languages were not to be constructed but rather
absorbed, developed and set in critical commentary on one
another. Kagel was always the joker in the pack, fastening
on ideas his colleagues had rejected or using their notational

precision ironically. Ligeti could be humorous, too, but he also set about his own creation of a new musical language, starting not from small units, as in serial composition, but from undefined sound, out of which he could draw swathes of different textures. His orchestral piece *Atmosphères*, introduced at the 1961 festival in Donaueschingen, provoked the biggest shock since Xenakis's *Metastasis* in the same place six years before, for here was a musician who had published an analysis of Boulez's baldest essay in pre-programmed composition (the first section of *Structures I*) but who, in his own work, was sidestepping serialism to work with slowly changing clusters. The effect – of colours emerging, altering, disappearing – was awe-inspiring.

So was the impression the previous year in Cologne of Kagel's *Anagrama* for four singers, speaking choir and instrumental ensemble. The speaking choir linked the work not with the official modernist forefathers (Schoenberg, Webern, Stravinsky, Debussy) but with Milhaud and the Russian-Swiss composer Wladimir Vogel (1896–1984), while the use of non-standard vocal techniques made connection with the *Ursonate* (1932) of the artist Kurt Schwitters (1877–1948), a poem suggesting such sounds through its typography of nonsense syllables. Kagel was to continue to insist that music has not one history but many, especially since the early twentieth century, and that the norms of musical life are only social conventions. In the particular case of *Anagrama* he also unloosed sonic possibilities that stimulated many of his contemporaries.

That those possibilities came from an unprecedented line-up made *Anagrama* typical of the period from the mid-1950s to the early 1970s, when the emphasis was on difference from tradition. However, since the traditional appurtenances of concert life have gone on into the twenty-first century with little change, such works, lacking the frisson of a first performance, have not become familiar through a history of performance. They remain, like comets, in outer darkness, swirling towards the light for occasional festival or anniversary revivals. Yet this is almost as true of works for standard formations, even including Stravinsky's *Movements* and orchestral Variations (1963–4). The period's radical departures may have been tolerated by the general culture, but the toleration had a time limit. Quantities of music – Stravinsky's serial works, some of the finest pieces by Stockhausen and Kagel, the entire output of Barraqué – were wastefully abandoned.

At the time, though, there was optimism. Several composers around 1960 were writing big works with a solo voice. Nono produced an opera, *Intolleranʒa 1960* (Intolerance 1960), to his own libretto about the inhumanity meted out to a migrant worker. Boulez, moving ever further from Artaudesque frenzy and the total musical revolution he went on propounding in essays and interviews, found his creative ideals of purity, linguistic innovation and evident form reflected in the poetry of Mallarmé, which he set in *Pli selon pli* (1957–60), for soprano and an orchestra rich in tuned percussion. Berio wove together a sequence of different styles of vocal communication, from the alleluiatic to the spoken, in *Epifanie* (1959–61), which he wrote for his wife, Cathy Berberian (1925–83), with orchestra. Stockhausen's piece was *Momente* (1961–4), again for a solo female vocalist, this time with a small choir and an instrumental group including two electric organs, all used to explore new sounds as in the Kagel prototype, but without irony. Ligeti's Requiem (1963–5), for two women soloists, choir and orchestra, decidedly does have irony among its means, in the black-comedy Dies Irae that fits among movements where the *Atmosphères* style becomes sombre, threatening and, finally, luminous.

By now some aspects of the music of the post-war generation – non-tonal harmony, discontinuous forms, complex textures, unusual ensembles – were almost omnipresent among composers. Shostakovich made his Thirteenth Symphony (1962) a compact and combative cantata, in which, at a time of relaxed state controls, he could abhor not only a Nazi atrocity of the war but careerists nearer home. Lutosławski, without losing his Polish neoclassical roots, took into his music lessons from Cage (in matters of freedom in ensemble playing) and Boulez (in terms of sonic finesse). Britten wrote for a mixed instrumental group in *Curlew River* (1964), in which he even anticipated the vogue among his junior colleagues for small-scale theatre works with music. Tippett left the exuberance and enchantment of his first opera, *The Midsummer Marriage* (1946–52), for a multi-coloured music of resonant shards in his second, *King Priam* (1958–61).

Being accepted, the younger composers were faced ever more acutely with questions of how to relate to the mainstream of musical life. Boulez was a regular guest with the Concertgebouw Orchestra in Amsterdam from 1960 and with the Berlin Philharmonic from 1961; in 1963 he conducted *Wozzeck* at the Paris Opera, and in 1965 he made his US debut as an orchestral conductor with the Cleveland Orchestra. Composition he virtually forsook, apart from revising *Pli selon pli* and other scores. Stockhausen successfully built a performing career on his own terms, touring from 1964 with an ensemble of musicians on standard instruments and electronics. Nono abandoned traditional concert venues to give concerts in workplaces, for which he created a new repertory that similarly emphasized electronic sound, but in his case in order to bring the noises of factories and streets into the music, as in his *La fabbrica illuminata* (The Factory Lit Up, 1964) for mezzo-soprano and tape. Babbitt, in the years 1961–4, worked only with an electronic synthesizer, which allowed him to realize his compositions without performers and without concerts.

While Babbitt was in his studio the world outside was noticing the first recordings of the Beatles, Bob Dylan, the Beach Boys and the Rolling Stones – musicians whose work brought benefits to the record industry that spilled over into classical music. With the completion in 1966 of the first commercial recording of Wagner's *Ring*, under Georg Solti (1912–97), the entire core repertory was available on LP, and companies looked to other fields. One was 'early music', which initially meant music from before Bach, now being unearthed with mounting enthusiasm and public success: landmarks of the time included the foundation of the Early Music Consort (1967) by the English musician David Munrow (1942–76) and the performance at the London Proms the next year of Monteverdi's Vespers under John Eliot Gardiner (b. 1943). The other fresh area for recording was that of new music, which had hitherto been neglected, except for Columbia's attention to Stravinsky and Decca's to Britten. Deutsche Grammophon's annual multi-record 'Avant Garde' volumes, initiated in 1968, were only the plushest of such ventures.

As the costs of records fell in relative terms, so the LP became the dominant form for popular music as well as classical. Popular musicians naturally began to think in terms not of the song but of the album, which might even be conceived as a whole (the Beatles' *Sergeant Pepper's Lonely Hearts Club Band*, 1967). For the audience, records became as important as the radio, and then more important.

Sleeve design helped make them objects of desire. The cover of *Sergeant Pepper*, designed by Peter Blake, incorporated a crowd of heroes, among them Stockhausen, whose work in electronic sound transformation the Beatles had noted. Nor was this an esoteric choice. In the collections of many students of the time, this album could have been brushing against some Stockhausen on disc, with perhaps on the other side one of the latest Nonesuch records, issued from 1965 under the artistic direction of Teresa Sterne (1927–2000) as forays into music old, new and unusual.

Even if the distinction between pop and classical held, overlaps were inevitable. The joyful simplicity of early 1960s pop came just when some classically trained musicians were reconsidering fundamentals. In 1963 La Monte Young (b. 1935), who had written a serial string trio in 1958 with very long notes, began giving performances in New York based on drones and repeating figures, with some influence from Indian music. Here was the origin of what was soon known as minimalism, marked by tonal harmonies that change very slowly, being perpetuated by repetition and, very often, a strong pulse, paralleling popular music's beat. An early classic was *In C* (1964), by Young's Californian classmate Terry Riley (b. 1935), who invited his musicians to work independently through fifty-three figures to produce glowing static harmonies of togetherness. Among those involved in the first performance, in San Francisco, was Steve Reich (b. 1936), who applied principles of staggered repetition to a fragment of taped speech in *Come out* (1966).

Minimalism has been interpreted retrospectively as a challenge to the recognized modernist tradition. Yet that tradition was far from monolithic. Babbitt and others in the United States, bringing the utmost rationality to their procedures, were scornful of what they saw as scientific-mathematical window-dressing in the theories of Stockhausen. Boulez, by no means hostile only to Xenakis, lost interest in Stockhausen after *Gruppen* and conducted nothing by Ligeti until the 1970s. At the time, minimalism appeared as just another strand in the rich fabric of contemporary music, along with the diverse enterprises of these more senior composers and with other new departures. In England alone, Harrison Birtwistle (b. 1934) was giving modernism the resonance of antiquity and the immediacy of drama in such works as *Ring a Dumb Carillon* (1965), for soprano, clarinet and percussion, while Cornelius Cardew (b. 1936), having studied with Stockhausen, was playing in the improvisation group AMM. At the same time, as Ives's music became better known, many composers were working with quotations, notably Bernd Alois Zimmermann (1918–70) in such works as his *Monologe* for two pianos (1964, in fact a 'polylogue' in which the voices include those of Bach and Messiaen) and his post-Berg opera *Die Soldaten* (1958–64). Differences – and agreement that questions of artistic philosophy mattered, and were vital to music's future – helped give the period its energy.

That energy became most intense, and multifarious, as the 1960s came to an end, and as composers reacted to – or participated in – the period's disruptions: many young people were taking part in street protests which, originally aimed against US involvement in Vietnam, took on a more general programme of change; but radicalism also became rejection, and a search for inner truth in eastern spirituality. Even among composers committed to the political left wing, expressions were various. Nono worked on big electronic frescos that could be presented in diverse public places, while Henze carried the message of revolution into the concert hall with such works as his oratorio in memory of

Che Guevara *Das Floss der Medusa* (The Raft of the Medusa, 1968). The première, in Hamburg, was cancelled when the soloists (or, by some accounts, the orchestra) refused to perform with a red flag draped over the podium, and Henze spent long periods in 1969–70 teaching and learning in Cuba. Cardew at the same time wanted music not just to express engagement but to model an egalitarian society, and in 1969 he set up in London the Scratch Orchestra, whose admission criterion was interest, not musical ability, and whose programmes included popular classics, new compositions chosen by vote, and 'scratch music' in which performers played their own music independently but with regard for others.

The inclusiveness, but not the political aspiration, came from Cage, who since the early 1960s had been producing not works but recipes for musical action. His *HPSCHD*, for up to seven harpsichordists and up to fifty-one tapes, was first presented at the University of Illinois in 1969 with slides and films added to the mix; the Nonesuch recording, to do justice to the essential variability, came with a computer printout suggesting a schedule of volume changes, different for each copy. *HPSCHD* was Cage's first venture in using a computer to come up with the random data he was seeking, but computers were also being used musically in other ways. If rules of composition could be described, then a computer could compose according to a given program: Lejaren Hiller (1924–94), who worked with Cage on *HPSCHD*, had been responsible for the first computer composition in 1957 (*ILLIAC Suite* for string quartet). Xenakis, too, had designed computer programs to work out the details of musical textures he wanted to define only globally, textures that would be like clouds, containing many elements whose precise qualities were unimportant.

Other composer-technicians, notably Max Mathews (b. 1926) in Boston and John Chowning (b. 1934) at Stanford University, were developing software for sound synthesis. So again, within the relatively confined field of computer music, assorted kinds of activity were going on.

Where the work was with traditional media, the range was no less vast. To mention only works first performed in 1969, Messiaen's oratorio *La Transfiguration de Notre Seigneur Jésus-Christ* (The Transfiguration of Our Lord Jesus Christ) united his brightly fashioned birdsong style with the modal melody and glorious concords of his earlier music in a succession of gospel narratives and meditations on his favourite themes of mountains, light and divine presence. Carter moved into a new ebullience with his Concerto for Orchestra, commissioned for the New York Philharmonic and Leonard Bernstein (1918–90), who, while studying the score with the composer, was taking calls from the Black Panthers, a revolutionary offshoot from the civil rights movement. Birtwistle made instrumental theatre of alarm calls and disputes in *Verses for Ensembles*, for groups of wind and percussion, while for his compatriot Peter Maxwell Davies (b. 1934) the year included a theatre piece for a wildly vocalizing male singer with ensemble (*Eight Songs for a Mad King*) and an enormous orchestral threnody (*Worldes Blis*). Shostakovich created his Fourteenth Symphony as a sequence of songs on death, alternately bleak and sardonic, with an orchestra of strings and percussion. Kagel wrote a solo scene for one of the new virtuosos of contemporary music, the Slovenian trombonist Vinko Globokar (b. 1934): *Atem* (Breath) was a portrait of an exhausted musician, close in style and feeling to recent pieces by Samuel Beckett. For another of the same breed of new-music exponents, Heinz Holliger (b. 1939), Berio wrote

Sequenza VII, in a series of studies in solo performance. Within the minimalist tradition Philip Glass (b. 1937) produced *Music in Fifths* for an amplified ensemble, music like rapidly rotating twelfth-century discant. Outside of it Babbitt, by now drawn back to writing for performers, offered complexity within serenity in his Third Quartet.

After all this, music, like Kagel's dilapidated wind player, drew breath. Several composers, having made their music increasingly free in the late 1960s, pulled back. One such was Stockhausen, whose work with his own ensemble had advanced so far that in 1968–9 he felt he could offer them a score consisting only of a verbal message, to which they would respond intuitively. Then came *Mantra* for two pianists (1969–70), a fully notated set of imbricated variations on a melodic 'formula', to use his term for what is something between a series and a theme, and after that the spellbinding *Trans* (1971), in which not only the music but its staging is laid down: the orchestra is seen behind a gauze curtain in violet light, and the sound of sustained string chords is shaken every so often by the recorded noise of a spinning shuttle. Cage, even more surprisingly, returned to normal notation with *Cheap Imitation* (1969), written to follow the phrasing of a Satie work that his personal ally and frequent collaborator Merce Cunningham had choreographed, only to find the rights unobtainable. Having made that break, after more than a decade away from staves, Cage found other possibilities opening, such as that of the virtuoso *Etudes australes* for piano (1974–5).

For younger composers, the many born in the 1930s, the retrenchment was a maturing. It was time for a big work, such as Birtwistle created in his orchestral piece *The Triumph of Time* (1972), where the instruments seem to be processing past the listener in an immense funeral march, some slowing or staying for solos. Or it was time for experiment and underground reputations to give way to a public statement, such as Reich made in his concert-length *Drumming* (1970–1), for his own percussion-based ensemble. Another example here would be the string quartet *Gran torso* (Large Torso, 1971–2) by the German composer Helmut Lachenmann (b. 1935), who had studied with Nono and accepted his teacher's zeal for musical advance. The task, as Lachenmann saw it, was to cultivate worlds which electronic experience had opened up beyond pitched tones, the worlds of what he called 'instrumental musique concrète', of noises and flutterings such as had previously been avoided in instrumental performance. *Gran torso* established such sounds as material for a work that answered the demands of music's most prestigious medium.

Meanwhile, Nono, too, was reconsidering. At the invitation of the conductor Claudio Abbado (b. 1933) and pianist Maurizio Pollini (b. 1942), he went back to writing for the concert hall with *Como una ola de fuerza y luz* (Like a Wave of Force and Light, 1971–2), a piano concerto with soprano and tape, as powerful as his music of the 1950s and still reacting to political actuality in its response to the death of a Chilean revolutionary. And from Ligeti there was *Melodien* (1971) for orchestra, the work in which his progressive recuperation of musical resources, from the amorphous sounds of *Atmosphères* through the harmonies and late Romantic auras of *Lontano*, had reached a bubbling liveliness of inventive and expressive melody – melody which, however, only glancingly or dimly recalled music of the past.

It was otherwise with works that came soon afterwards. The US composer George Rochberg (b. 1918), who had in his late thirties adopted serialism and soon afterwards begun including quotations in his music, moved beyond that to a full-scale revival of the styles of Mahler and late Beethoven in his Third Quartet (1972). In Germany, Manfred Trojahn (b. 1949) made a stir with the restored Romantic rhetoric of his First Symphony (1973–4). Suddenly the Soviet Union, where, to western observers, musical progress had been frozen in a Mahler–Tchaikovsky stone age since 1936, became relevant. Stylistic advance had now been stalled in the west since the late 1960s; it was as if every possible change or liberation had been tried. What remained was a change of sensibility, a willingness to revisit the past, with whatever degree of irony. And – as it turned out, once Soviet music was better known in the west – composers in Moscow and Leningrad had been at the forefront. Alfred Schnittke (b. 1934) produced in his First Symphony (1969–72) what he called a 'polystylistic' mixture that, while rooted in Shostakovich, included aspects of western modernism, vulgar music and jazz, and Shostakovich himself, in his Fifteenth Symphony (1972), had his music move unsettlingly into quotations from Wagner and Rossini.

There was, though, an earlier example from the west, in another piece commissioned by Bernstein: Berio's *Sinfonia* (1968–9), for orchestra with eight vocalists. As an essay in the structure of languages, this work starts with instrumental and vocal sounds as if in a state of nature, calling from some primeval jungle. As a testament to the times, it includes a moving elegy to the US black leader Martin Luther King. But at its centre is a replay of a Mahler movement, the Second Symphony's scherzo, onto which are grafted quotations that create a swirling history of twentieth-century music, from Debussy and Strauss to Boulez and Stockhausen. Here was time flowing ever on, in the Mahler, but, like a river, bearing innumerable whorls, eddies and slipstreams. Progress? That was yesterday.

PART VIII

Time lost 1975–

Linear narrative has its limits. Even the increasingly entangled lines of music in the first three decades after World War II have escaped it, for the preceding two chapters not only omitted or elided much in the compositional energies of the period but said almost nothing about the great continuing flow of musical life, against which, as judged by brute quantities of performances or recordings, all new music was mere skittering on the surface. And that mass of the surviving past is still with us, now doubly in the past, for a huge number of commercial recordings have gone on being re-released, and joined by releases of broadcast performances.

Anyone interested in, say, how John Barbirolli (1899–1970) conducted Mahler's First Symphony can compare his 1957 Manchester recording for Pye with a performance two years later in New York. Moreover, the same work can be heard in other recordings of that time, similarly brought out from radio or orchestral archives, by such varied and valued conductors as Rudolf Kempe (1910–76), Igor Markevitch (1912–83), Dimitri Mitropoulos (1896–1960) and Bruno Walter – not to mention the versions made specifically for records by Walter and others. The same goes, of course, for innumerable other pieces, and for the careers of countless performers, all thoroughly documented. In terms of the aural evidence available to any particular listener, therefore, the musical past of half a century ago is far denser now than it was when it was happening.

Even within the area of new music, not only do some — but only a very few — works of 1945–75 go on being performed and recorded, and thereby enriched (the outstanding example is *Le Marteau sans maître*, recorded five times by Boulez alone), but new broadcast performances from those decades continue to appear on compact disc.

The arrival of that medium, in 1983, and the assiduity of record companies in trawling their back catalogues, prompted a widespread interest in historical performances that, fifteen years before, had been the province of aficionados. This resurrection of the past is, though, more than a phenomenon of the record business. By end of the 1980s the early music movement, basing its authority not on living tradition but on a reinvestigation of the sources, was laying claim to a repertory up to and including Brahms. Here again, history was being worked over. The familiar was being defamiliarized (for Beethoven sounded new), and the unfamiliar brought into view (in that long-lost fourteenth-century Florentine songwriters, or seventeenth-century Italian violin virtuosos, or nineteenth-century Scandinavian symphonists were restored to life). In that respect early music and new were as one. Both were about change and new possibility. Boulez, too, distrusted tradition.

To return to Mahler, his music reinforced the lesson of history's mutability, in that its revival in the 1950s thoroughly and seemingly permanently established it in the central repertory, thereby changing existing notions of the period around 1900. If history could change once, why not again? And if history could change at all, what could history be? It could only be a story about the past, a story which, though told with care for the facts, would gradually lose its relevance as time passed and history altered. The past is not a path we and our predecessors have travelled but a labyrinth, and a labyrinth forever in flux.

It was the path metaphor that made possible the whole development of western music we have witnessed. Tinctoris in the fifteenth century, Mozart in the eighteenth and Schoenberg in the early twentieth all made the same point, about music moving on, whether towards greater comprehensibility, power to move, or richness within itself. Nothing moves on, however, within a shape-shifting labyrinth. Our clocks measure only the labyrinth's steady expansion. There is no stable axis for development, no reason for one thing to follow from another, no reason not to make immediate connections through centuries, as Stravinsky did, for instance, in aligning Bach and jazz in his Concerto for piano and wind, or as Reich has done in conjoining Perotin with Balinese percussion orchestras.

In the confusion that has certainly not abated since 1975, composition has seen no startling innovation other than the absence of innovation. Many composers have ably and imaginatively continued with the language of modernism as it existed in the works Stravinsky, Messiaen, Carter, Babbitt, Nono, Boulez, Barraqué and Stockhausen produced in the 1950s and 1960s. Others, however, have revived earlier languages, such as those of English music in the early twentieth century or Russian in the late nineteenth. Still others have crisscrossed through the labyrinthine past. All that must be asked, wherever they go, is that they find something hitherto unheard.

Such a criterion may be enough for any individual listener, but not for a whole listening culture, since the judgement of originality can only be a personal one in the absence of norms. Not surprisingly, western culture has had great difficulty in deciding what to value from music since 1975 – or even since 1945. All these many yesterdays remain as yet unassimilated.

This is a rich period for music. It is also a melancholy one. Lost in the labyrinth, music seems unable now to call out to the unknown future – as Beethoven did, or as Debussy, Schoenberg and Stravinsky did in their several ways, or, more quietly, as Chopin and Du Fay did. Those times are gone – or they are here, and we cannot shake them off.

CHAPTER 23

Echoes in the labyrinth

In entering the treacherous territory of the postmodern, the temptation is to proceed as if things were normal — as if there were important composers, great works, historically important works (not necessarily the same ones), lines of connection, trends and directions of development. Given the quantity of extraordinary music that continues to appear, that temptation becomes compelling. And yet the conditions for certainty have gone.

At the beginning of the period in question Ligeti wrote a pertinent opera, *Le Grand Macabre* (The Great Macabre, 1974–7). A self-styled bringer of doom, Nekrotzar, arrives in a Renaissance fantasy land to announce the end of the world. This duly comes (or possibly it does not). But then everything goes on exactly as before.

The end of the world for music came in 1950–2, when Cage finally dared to offer complete emptiness in 4′33″, when Boulez created the total eclipse of the first part of his *Structures I*, and when Barraqué made annihilation speak for itself in his Sonata. Everything after that, wonderful as so much of it is, was made in the attempt to stave off awareness — or else to rejoice (Cage) or despair (Barraqué).

But this is perhaps to see time in linear terms. There are histories in which the musical events of 1950–2 were an aberration, just as there are histories in which atonality was a terrible mistake (indeed, many composers since the mid-1970s have depended on them). All histories have to be acknowledged now as partial views, and there are myriads on offer. Perhaps every composer – perhaps every composition – since the time of Ligeti's opera has proposed a different way of understanding the past; no doubt the act of listening, too, is partly a placing in context, and there may be congruence or not between the music's sense of its past and the listener's. This is the relativist nightmare, where communication is all internal.

If there is, still, music that conveys the unexpected, and if there are modes of listening open to it, then they probably require some recognition that postmodernism is not an alternative to modernism but the consequence.

Yet if a postmodernism without modernism is impossible, so is a modernism without postmodernism. In 1977 Boulez gained his longstanding wish for a forum for musical adventure when the Institut de Recherche et Coordination Acoustique/Musique (IRCAM) opened under his direction in Paris. The rhetoric of his pronouncements was unchanged from the early 1950s, or, indeed, from what Varèse had said three decades before that: music was to be carried into the future on a wave of investigation into sound, temporal structure, instruments and performance, investigation that would unite the efforts of theorists and performers, technicians and composers. But, quite apart from returning that year to conduct the centenary *Ring* at Bayreuth, Boulez in his concerts was including music from far off the modernist high road: more Berg, more Ravel, even Richard Strauss, not to mention the wider nineteenth-century and contemporary repertories he had taken on as chief conductor of the BBC Symphony Orchestra (1971–5) and music director of the New York Philharmonic (1971–7). His latest work was a solemn ceremonial having some kinship with Messiaen (*Rituel* for orchestra, 1974–5), and the big piece that came out of his first years at IRCAM, *Répons* (1980–4), had the quality more of a celebration than an advance. It addresses its audience with imposing confidence: six soloists on tuned percussion instruments (including two pianos) surround both the small orchestra and the listening public, and their sounds are spectacularly amplified and transformed by machinery developed at the institute. But if the result is not a breakthrough (its basic principle of dialogue between percussive and sustained sounds had appeared in *Eclat*, a 1965 fragment for fifteen-piece ensemble), it is a wonder of iridescent sound and infectious rhythmic life.

The carnival mood, reflected with black comedy in Ligeti's opera, appeared elsewhere, too. Reich, having worked with increasingly rich ensembles in the early 1970s, produced Music for Eighteen Musicians (1974–6), where changes of pulse and harmony drive through a grand progression lasting an hour. The work's public success, in concert and on record, helped motivate the composer to begin publishing his music, which hitherto he had reserved for his own performing ensemble. So just when Boulez, in *Répons*, was creating a composition that could not be realized without his own team of IRCAM technicians (a sign of the work's relatively limited ambitions), Reich was moving his music out into the wider world. Glass's similar move came with *Einstein on the Beach* (1975–6), a largely narrative-free chain of chants and dances on which he collaborated with the US theatre director Robert Wilson.

This was also the period of two of Xenakis's finest pieces: *Jonchaies* for large orchestra (1977), his answer to

The Rite of Spring, and *Akanthos* for soprano and octet (also 1977), which looks more to Ravel. In these works and others Xenakis was taking a renewed interest in folk music, which Berio drew into his *Coro* for forty singers and forty instrumentalists (1975–7). Here immense tuttis, suggestive of oratorio, set words of implacable protest by Pablo Neruda, while more lightly scored elements make wreaths combining traits out of musical traditions from around the world. Again, as in *Répons*, *Jonchaies*, *Einstein* and Music for Eighteen Musicians, there is the character of festival, except that in *Coro* the jubilation is more varied in tone. The work asks questions that western societies were keenly reconsidering, about how diverse cultures might coexist and communicate, about conceptions of the natural in human behaviour (once, for example, women had rejected old expectations, and homosexuals had asserted their normality), and about the individual's responsibilities to the whole. It offers both a model of harmonious integration and a warning that struggle will be endless.

Folk music was for other composers, too, a talisman of nature, to be grasped when music's evolution had halted. The English composer Brian Ferneyhough (b. 1943) was, with Lachenmann, among the few who refused to believe that advance could not go on. And in their music it did go on. However, Ferneyhough's *Unity Capsule* for solo flute (1975–6), a virtuoso piece in both composition and performance, bringing into one rush of time a host of motivic venturings and different voices, also belongs in the culture of the most ancient and widespread of instruments, the culture going back to Jiahu and beyond.

If not folk music, the touchstone might be found in western musical history. The Estonian composer Arvo Pärt (b. 1935) in the 1960s had been among the many young

Soviet composers – Schnittke was another – to interest themselves eagerly in serialism and other western innovations. But for him these had palled, and in the early 1970s he abandoned composition for study and readaptation. Then in 1976–7 came his first pieces in a new style he called 'tintinnabulation', after the effect of listening to a single harmony, as if from a bell. In these pieces – among them *Tabula rasa* (Blank Canvas) for string orchestra and *Fratres* (Brothers), which the composer has published in several arrangements – the notes of a triad (usually that of A minor) are sustained or rotated to accompany slow, calm melodies in the relevant scale. Music so pure slides through historical periods: it can sit beside Vivaldi or twelfth-century organum. In its ubiquity, though, it belongs entirely to its own era.

For many who had come of age musically in the 1950s, or before, the return to tonality on the part of many younger composers – whether minimalists following Reich, latterday Romantics in the wake of Trojahn or puritans on the Pärt model – was depressing. Ligeti, after five years of virtual stalemate following the completion of his opera, answered his students with his Horn Trio (1982), from a world where Brahms is a species of folk music along with others from the Caribbean, and where natural tuning on the horn (i.e. playing pure overtones rather than tempered notes) produces delicately distressed harmony; but he came to regret the work's formal consent to old patterns.

Stockhausen wrote cadenzas for eighteenth-century concertos in 1978 and 1983–5, but only for members of the family circle that was his new performing ensemble: the clarinettist Suzanne Stephens and his trumpeter son Markus. From 1977 he was essentially off by himself as a composer, extending his technique of composition with melodic formulae to cover the immense span of seven operas for the evenings of a week. This project, under the collective title *Licht* (Light), engaged him until 2003 and produced a vast number of separately performable scenes, particles and offshoots, for diverse combinations that most often include solo instrumentalists as musician-actors in the operas' principal roles. By becoming his own publisher (from 1969, ending a relationship with the Viennese house of Universal Edition, home to composers from Mahler to Birtwistle) and record issuer (from the mid-1980s, after nearly two decades of consistent support from Deutsche Grammophon) he further distanced himself from the musical world. And though the first three *Licht* operas were presented in turn through the 1980s by La Scala, the last two experienced long delay.

Nono's move inwards was of a different kind, prompted by consternation at the decline of radicalism after the early 1970s not only within music but in the political sphere. Feeling that the failure in both areas was a failure to listen, he set himself to writing music that would not so much project, which his earlier works had done, as draw in. Asked by Pollini for a solo piece he composed . . . *sofferte onde serene.* . . (. . .serene waves endured. . . , 1976), in which the piano itself seems to be listening, to sounds of itself on tape. Repeated resonant chords, from different parts of the instrument, suggest bells echoing across the lagoon of the composer's home city of Venice: 'calls to work and to meditation,' as he put it. There may be reverberations, too, within this hard-edged, open-eyed nocturne, of the sound dramas of Gabrieli, recalled also in the play of timbre and space that was Nono's big work of the next few years: *Prometeo* (Prometheus, 1978–84), a kind of concert opera, or 'tragedy of listening'.

This was an extraordinary period for such large under-takings. Largest of all, Messiaen's opera *Saint François d'Assise* (St Francis of Assisi, 1975–83) is a glorious summation of all his styles: the luscious harmonies and driving rhythms of his earliest orchestral pieces, the other-worldly melody of the ondes martenot (an electronic instrument he had used in *Turangalîla* and other pieces of the 1930s–1940s), abstract serialism, grounded modal chanting for the principals and chorus, and, almost everywhere, the sounds of birds, realized by the instruments of an enormous orchestra. Birtwistle also completed a longstanding project, his opera *The Mask of Orpheus* (1973–83), the myth retold as a shattered monument, with a modern-ancient orchestra of wind and percussion. Berio produced *Un re in ascolto* (A King Listening, 1979–84), an opera in which the enacted events – preparations for a production of *The Tempest* – are entrammelled in the central character's dreams and memories, and a work which again is a call to listen.

For many composers at this time, listening to the physical nature of sound was more essential than paying heed to folk music or to the cultivated music of the past. Stockhausen had tried in the 1950s to create artifical timbres by assembling electronic tones or instrumental sounds, but such efforts had little success until the late 1970s, when computers of increased power could be used to analyse sound spectra. Horatiu Radulescu (1942–2008), a Romanian who moved to Paris in 1969 and became something of a wild card in French music, worked with grand pianos that he had retuned to pure frequency ratios and turned on their sides so that their strings could be bowed; he also used whole orchestras of flutes, or other instruments, to create new timbres. Further stimulus came from IRCAM, which soon became more closely defined as a computer music studio, dropping its concern with new acoustic instruments. Several younger French composers who spent time at IRCAM in the early years, notably Gérard Grisey (1946–98) and Hugues Dufourt (b. 1943), took timbre composition as a principal challenge, and for their work Dufourt coined the term 'spectral music'.

They had some influence on the early music of the English prodigy George Benjamin (b. 1960), one of Messiaen's last and favourite pupils, who was making fresh, sure and poetic use of the orchestra while still a student (*Ringed by the Flat Horizon*, 1979–80). They may also have had an effect on the Montreal composer Claude Vivier (1948–83), who in the last years of his life created music where simple but original melody is offset by dense yet luminescent chords composed as artificial spectra (*Lonely Child* for soprano and chamber orchestra, 1980). Two young Finnish composers who worked at IRCAM around this time, Kaija Saariaho (b. 1952) and Magnus Lindberg (b. 1958), certainly gained much from the spectral movement. But the biggest achievement of early spectralism was Grisey's *Les Espaces acoustiques* (The Acoustic Spaces, 1974–85), a concert-length sequence of six works of growing size, from a viola solo to a score for large orchestra and an epilogue, all based on the overtone spectrum of a low E. From simple elements – the spectrum, regular rhythm, short melodic motifs – a vivid drama of orchestrally synthesized sounds is generated. Ferneyhough similarly, though untouched by spectralism, composed a concert of separable works at this time, his *Carceri d'invenzione* (Dungeons of Invention, 1981–6), where a flautist sets out the path, like Ariadne's thread, from an opening piccolo solo through scenes mostly of frenzied exaltation for diverse sub-orchestral groupings, though the ending is in a mirror cabinet as the soloist, on bass flute, plays among recorded self-images. Unalike as these two sequences are – dissimilar on the broadest scale in their trajectories: the one a great crescendo, the other a descent – they are testimonies to imaginative fortitude and power unassisted by any straightforward recourse to the tonal past.

These compendia by Grisey and Ferneyhough, coupled with Birtwistle's *Earth Dances* (1985–6) – an orchestral score of gigantic crunching strata but also of lament singing out from woodwind instruments – marked a highwater point of aim and achievement. The music of the later 1980s would often be smaller in scale, and marked by tones of fragility, defiance or regret, in response perhaps to the continuing lack of an evident way forward (even from IRCAM, where hopes had been so high), or to larger dangers, which included a harsher economic climate for the performing arts and the spread of AIDS. Contrasting optimism about détente between the west and the communist bloc, following the arrival of Mikhail Gorbachev as Soviet leader in 1985, had its musical climax on Christmas Day 1989, when Bernstein conducted Beethoven's Ninth Symphony in the formerly communist sector of Berlin to celebrate the opening of the Berlin Wall the month before. This optimism was muted, however, by the nature of the recent Soviet music that was now, thanks to Gorbachev's policy of glasnost (openness), being freely exported.

Oppression, it seemed, had only intensified expression. Soviet composers – most notably Schnittke – had learned from Shostakovich how to maintain a sense of the personal expressive voice, depending, as in the nineteenth century, on the major-minor system and on flowing continuity. They had learned, too, how to speak with more than one voice at a time. Schnittke's Second Symphony (1979) and his Fourth (1984) are religious works in which the subject matter can only be mimed, the former a mass without words, the latter a coalescence of Orthodox, Catholic and Jewish chants. Other works of his, especially concertos and chamber pieces, continued directly in the Mahler–Shostakovich line of extreme emotion, exhausted sensibility and self-mockery. His contemporary Sofia Gubaidulina (b. 1931) came clearly from the same world, but with her the most disparate contrasts would be justified by a steady vision, a juggling act of sustained improvisational sureness. Among the works that made her reputation in the west, *Perception* (1983), for soprano, baritone and string septet, is a dialogue of female and male, spiritual and earthly, while *Offertorium* (1980) is a violin concerto in which the six-part ricercare from Bach's *Musical Offering*, as orchestrated by Webern, becomes an offering that is broken up and reassembled into something new. With Galina Ustvolskaya (b. 1919), a rugged elementariness, often with bald repetition, might produce a fearless intensity, presence and necessity, as in her Fifth Symphony (1989–90), subtitled 'Amen', for a male speaker with a disparate instrumental ensemble (violin, oboe, trumpet, tuba and a large wooden cube played with a hammer). For a more restrained kind of spirituality there was Pärt. For a more serene, nostalgic and grandly beautiful view of music in a state of collapse there was Valentyn Silvestrov (b. 1937), especially his Fifth Symphony (1980–2), which seems to begin where a slow movement by Bruckner, Tchaikovsky or Mahler might have ended, and then to go on ending.

The inwardness and resilient independence of these Soviet composers' works struck a chord at a time when many composers elsewhere were making an interior withdrawal and seeking a musical homeland. Ligeti set Hungarian texts for the first time since leaving the country (*Hungarian Studies* for choir, 1983), but found his true territory in an imaginary domain where central European melody, Latin American rhythm and east Asian timbres could all intersect, the domain of his Piano Concerto (1985–8). Also in 1985 he began a series of piano études, in which elaborate mechanisms, somewhat in the manner of Nancarrow, bring proximities to Debussy, Bartók and others, besides allowing passion to be felt through multicoloured screens of virtuosity. His compatriot Kurtág, prone to long periods of doubt and silence, was composing much more freely in an atmosphere conducive to the intimate, producing at this time an hour-long sequence of forty settings, all sharply expressive, for soprano and violin of aphorisms and anecdotes from Kafka's diaries and letters, *Kafka-Fragmente* (Kafka Fragments, 1985–7), and a string quartet, *Officium breve* (Short Service, 1988–9), whose movements, again short, constitute an instrumental Requiem.

With the inner life so much coming to the fore, the first opera of John Adams (b. 1947), the tragicomedy *Nixon in China* (1985–7), makes a point of its characters' vacuity, as also of their lostness within the world of high politics and the world, too, of a pounding, exuberant score deriving from Reich–Glass minimalism and Broadway. Cage's late music, from 1987 onwards, provides notes to be played within marked periods, colouring drifts of time. Carter, in the same period, turned towards short pieces of spirited, conversational chamber music, interleaved with brief orchestral commemorations and concertos. Reich wrote *Different Trains* (1988), for string quartet and recordings, whose musical lines spring from fragments of speech in a darkening reminiscence of rail travel in the 1940s. Music, where it might be found, was coming from private experience and memory.

CHAPTER 24

Interlude

The deaths of Messiaen and Cage, in the spring and summer of 1992, robbed music of its best known composers. Many of those who remained were in their fifties or sixties, or even their eighties in the case of Carter. In such a context the appearance of bright, new creative talents, such as that of Thomas Adès (b. 1971), was greeted with as much relief as enthusiasm. Here was a composer of striking imaginative precision and wide range, able to draw from many different kinds of music – popular, classical, ethnic – and to do so decisively and distinctively.

Not only the young, though, have been refreshing the art of composition by – from their own ground – looking and listening elsewhere. Such works of Ligeti's as his lively and humorous set of songs for mezzo-soprano and percussion quartet, *With Pipes, Drums, Fiddles* (2000), fuse traditions from three or four continents into a folk music of the world.

The classical tradition always had fuzzy edges, places where it intersected with commercial music (Brahms with Johann Strauss II, Ives with David T. Shaw, author of 'Columbia, the Gem of the Ocean'), folk music (virtually everyone back to, in all probability, the troubadours) or sacred music. What is different today is the variety of such sources to which composers can open their ears, through radio, recordings and, since the mid-1990s, the internet.

In the new century, as standards of sound fidelity improved, the internet became a medium through which composers could transmit their works. Given that most people in western societies have access, through computers, to sound samples (including music of so many kinds), and to routines for synthesizing and transforming sounds, composition may soon become as widespread as the writing of poetry.

Yet there will still be composers, as there are still poets. Electronic music, despite some stirring successes, has become ever more marginal since the 1960s – not because classical music is inherently conservative, or because it has become so (though with the ageing of the composing population it may have done somewhat, for the moment), but because this music is essentially a ménage à trois, involving composer, performer and listener. All have their parts to play.

Electronic music's decline has been balanced by the rise of the performing group whose line-up gives it a particular character. One of the earliest was the Fires of London (1970–87), consisting of the musicians required for Schoenberg's *Pierrot lunaire* plus a percussionist, and led by Davies, who wrote numerous original works and arrangements for them. More recent examples include Elision (formed in 1986), an Australian group whose plucked strings and electronics lend it a special flavour, and the Ensemble Recherche of Freiburg (founded in 1985), a mixed nonet. Such formations contribute to the spangling of colours across the map of new music, but without so far endangering the supremacy of the score. Ferneyhough's works, for example, are strongly promoted by both Elision and the Ensemble Recherche, whose identities are sustained partly by their (however much overlapping) repertories.

Being performable, and reperformable, classical music can keep its past alive – and at no time in that past has it done so more comprehensively than today. From new music this presence of the past cannot be disguised. Birtwistle's *Pulse Shadows* (1989–96), for soprano and ensemble with string quartet interludes, traces a path from the poetry of Paul Celan back to ancient traditions of lamentation, while his orchestral piece *The Shadow of Night* (2001) is a meditation on a Dowland song. The dark room of Gesualdo's creative mind is reentered in some of the whispering, rustling, exquisitely sensitive music of Salvatore Sciarrino (b. 1947). Berio's ultimate work, *Stanze* (Stanzas, or Rooms, 2003), for baritone, men's choir and orchestra, is a Mahlerian song cycle. Carter's *Symphonia* (1993–7) takes all other symphonies as read. The string quartet lives on for new adventures, such as the motile filigrees of the work produced in 2004 by the Swiss composer Hanspeter Kyburz (b. 1960). Lachenmann's opera *Das Mädchen mit den Schwefelhölzern* (The Little Match Girl, 1990–6) – while denying itself all the comforts of the genre, remaining out in the cold with its Hans Christian Andersen heroine, the cold of sonorities like scratched frost – upholds the tradition going back to Confucius and Plato, of music as a moral force.

The past nourishes us, and we nourish it, exactly by maintaining it, and retraining it, as part of our present. It can also, by what it lacks, show us the future.

Glossary

aria	Solo vocal piece, normally in an OPERA, ORATORIO or CANTATA.
atonal	Having no TONIC, the opposite of TONAL. Hence also 'atonality'.
augmentation	In a FUGUE, doubling the note values of the theme so that it is decelerated.
bar	Unit, generally repeating, made up of BEATS.
baritone	Medium-range man's voice.
Baroque	Style period running from the early seventeenth century to the mid-eighteenth, the period of Purcell, Bach, Handel, Scarlatti and Rameau.
bass	(1) Lower register, as distinct from TREBLE. (2) Music's bottom line, often directing the HARMONY. (3) Low man's voice.
beat	Fundamental unit of RHYTHM. Most often there are two, three or four beats to the BAR, of which the first – the downbeat – will be strongest.
brass	Robust blown instruments, including most commonly horn, trumpet, trombone and tuba.

317

cadence	Closing gesture. The most emphatic example in TONAL music is the perfect cadence, from DOMINANT to TONIC.
cantata	Work for voices (or just one voice) and instruments.
cantus firmus	*See* TENOR (1).
chamber music	Music for a small group of perfomers, normally between three and six.
chapel	Besides meaning a building or part of a building, the term can signify the body of clerics and musicians attached to a monarchical or noble court.
chorale	Lutheran hymn, usually in four-part HARMONY.
chord	Group of three or more notes performed together.
chromaticism	Use in tonal music of notes foreign to the scale.
Classical	Term used, with an initial capital, for the style associated with Haydn, Mozart and the younger Beethoven.
clef	Symbol indicating note positions on the STAFF. Commonest are the TREBLE and BASS clefs, which are used, for example, for the right and left hands in piano music.
cluster	Group of adjacent notes.
coda	Final section of a MOVEMENT.
concerto	Normally a work for one or more soloists and ORCHESTRA.
conductus	Twelfth-century compositional style.
conservatory	College for musicians.
consonance	Sense of euphony or blending in the sound of two or more NOTES at the same time.

consort	Group of voices or instruments, especially viols, the term being generally confined to music of the sixteenth and seventeenth centuries.
continuo	Harmonic foundation, often notated as a BASS line with numerals to indicate other notes in the CHORD. Continuo parts are almost omnipresent in music of the period 1600–1750 and afterwards in RECITATIVE. They may be realized by a keyboard soloist, lute player or small group.
counterpoint	POLYPHONY obeying clear rules about the harmonic relationships of notes. Hence 'contrapuntal'.
countertenor	Very high man's voice (with FALSETTO), in the same register as a MEZZO-SOPRANO.
da capo	Instruction to start again from the top. A da capo ARIA has its opening section repeated after a contrasting interlude.
discant	POLYPHONIC style having all VOICES in the same plain style, as distinct from ORGANUM.
dissonance	Sense of disunity or harshness in the sound of two or more notes at the same time.
dominant	Note or key a fifth above the TONIC.
drone	Sustained note.
ensemble	Group of performers or performing means. The term is most often used of operatic numbers for three or more singers, and of mixed instrumental

groups commonly deployed in music since 1950.

falsetto   Adjustment of the male vocal cords to sing an OCTAVE higher than normal.

fantasia   Instrumental composition emphasizing fantasy.

fifth   The fifth note of a scale (e.g. G in C major), or the INTERVAL between the first and that note (C–G).

final   Note on which a melody in a MODE will have to end (e.g. G for the Mixolydian mode).

fourth   The fourth note of a scale (e.g. F in C major), or the INTERVAL between the first and that note (C–F).

frequency   Speed of air vibrations constituting a sound, measured in Herz (Hz) units, which are cycles per second. Middle C, in standard modern tuning, has a frequency of 256 Hz.

fugue   Composition in which a principal theme is developed in imitative POLYPHONY.

glissando   Slide from one note to another.

harmony   (1) Everything in music that has to do with relationships among PITCHES. (2) Set of pitches sounding together.

homophonic   Having all the PARTS moving together in CHORDS.

imitation   Similarity between one melodic line and another at a moment before.

interval   Distance in pitch between two notes, or the corresponding harmonic quality – how two notes sound when heard together.

inversion	Turning a melody inside-out, i.e. replacing its rises with equivalent falls and vice versa.
key	Harmonic character, related to a key-note or TONIC and its MAJOR or MINOR scale.
major	Pertaining to one of the two kinds of scale or key common in music since the late seventeenth century, the C major scale being C–D–E–F–G–A–B–C. *See also* MINOR.
major sixth	The sixth note of a major scale (e.g. A in C major), or the INTERVAL between the first and that note (C–A).
major third	The third note of a major scale (e.g. E in C major), or the INTERVAL between the first and that note (C–E).
masque	Verse drama including song and dance, as cultivated especially at the French and English royal courts in the seventeenth century.
mass	Service commemorating Christ's Last Supper, as celebrated in the Catholic tradition.
mediant	Note or key a third above the TONIC.
melisma	Flow of short notes in place of a notional longer one.
mensuration	Medieval rhythmic system, whereby a notational sign would show whether a longer note was divided into two or three shorter ones.
metre	Repeating rhythmic unit, generally corresponding to the BAR.

mezzo-soprano	Medium-range woman's voice.
minor	Pertaining to one of the two scales common in music since the late seventeenth century, the other being MAJOR. The minor is distinguished particularly by its flattened or minor third (e.g. C–E$\flat$) and sixth (e.g. C–A$\flat$).
minor sixth	The sixth note of a minor scale (e.g. A$\flat$ in C minor), or the INTERVAL between the first and that note (C–A$\flat$).
minor third	The third note of a minor scale (e.g. E$\flat$ in C minor), or the interval between the first and that note (C–E$\flat$).
minuet	Courtly dance, often forming the third or second movement of a CLASSICAL SYMPHONY or QUARTET.
mode	Most commonly a scale of the kind inherited by medieval and RENAISSANCE musicians from the Greeks. There were eight such modes (e.g. the Mixolydian: G–A–B–C–D–E–F–G).
modulation	Change of key prepared by the HARMONY, e.g. in moving from TONIC to DOMINANT.
monody	Music on one line, with accompaniment, as distinct from POLYPHONY. The term is most often used for songs with CONTINUO from around 1600.
motet	(1) Polyphonic form, based on a CANTUS FIRMUS, in use from the twelfth century to the fifteenth. (2) Short sacred piece of the fifteenth century and later.

movement	Separate section of a longer work. SYMPHONIES customarily have four movements.
neume	Medieval notational sign for a note or group of notes, still used for chant.
notation	Representation of music in graphic signs.
note	Single sound, or notational sign for such a sound.
octave	The eighth note of a scale, or the INTERVAL between the first and that note. Two notes an octave apart have the same letter name and sound somewhat the same. The interval of an octave is therefore the frame for nearly all scales, not only in western music.
opera	Theatre work with more or less continuous music.
opera seria	Variety of opera in Italian with heroic, noble characters enacted largely by castratos and SOPRANOS, holding the stage from the late seventeenth century to the late eighteenth.
oratorio	Opera-style work designed for church or concert hall, normally on a sacred subject.
orchestra	Large group of instruments. The standard western orchestra has around sixty to eighty players, most of them on strings, with groups also of WOODWIND, BRASS and PERCUSSION.
orchestrate	Arrange a piece for large performing forces.

organum	Twelfth-century POLYPHONIC style having one or more ornamented VOICES.
ostinato	Regular repetition of a short figure.
overture	(1) Instrumental introduction to opera, oratorio or other large-scale work. (2) One-movement orchestral piece.
parody	Technique of sixteenth-century MASS composition, whereby an existing POLYPHONIC work — mass or MOTET — provides the musical material for the setting.
part	(1) Music for a member of an ENSEMBLE. (2) *See* VOICE (2).
percussion	Instruments that sound when struck, e.g. drums, cymbals, xylophone.
pitch	Basic quality of most musical sounds, dependent on frequency of vibration.
pizzicato	Plucked, on a string instrument which is normally bowed. In some twentieth-century music piano strings are played pizzicato.
polychoral	Laid out for two or more choirs separately positioned.
polyphony	Music having more than one melodic line. Hence 'polyphonic'.
pulse	Succession of strong BEATS.
quartet	Most often a STRING QUARTET, or an operatic number for four singers.
recitative	Narration or dialogue delivered in a speech-like manner. OPERA from the late seventeenth century to the early nineteenth was formally divided between RECITATIVE and ARIAS or ENSEMBLES, and

the distinction survives in much later works.

register PITCH level.

Renaissance Cultural period at its height in the fifteenth and sixteenth centuries, defined musically by the lucid POLYPHONY of Du Fay, Josquin, Palestrina and Byrd.

rhythm Aspect of time in music. The basic rhythmic values are subdivisions by a half: the semibreve (whole note), minim (half-note), crotchet (quarter-note), quaver (eighth-note), semiquaver (sixteenth-note) and demisemiquaver (thirty-second-note).

ricercare Composition in which a principal theme is developed in imitative POLYPHONY, often severe or restrained in mood.

Romantic Term used most often for music from Beethoven to Richard Strauss, implying frank expression and melodiousness within the system of major-minor HARMONY. It may alternatively be confined to the generation of composers born in or around the decade 1800–10 (Schubert, Bellini, Berlioz, Chopin, Schumann, etc.), many of whom had died or almost stopped composing by 1850.

scherzo Exuberant MOVEMENT replacing the MINUET in most nineteenth-century symphonies and QUARTETS.

score (1) Representation of a piece of music in NOTATION (*noun*). (2) ORCHESTRATE (*verb*).

second	The second note of a scale (e.g. D in C major), or the INTERVAL between the first and that note (C–D).
seventh	The seventh note of a scale (e.g. B in C major), or the INTERVAL between the first and that note (C–B).
sixth	*See* MAJOR SIXTH, MINOR SIXTH.
sonata	Instrumental composition, most often for one instrument (e.g. piano sonata) or two (e.g. violin sonata, for violin and piano). Sonatas often have three or four MOVEMENTS, of which the first may exemplify SONATA FORM.
sonata form	Form based on the exposition, development and recapitulation of contrasting themes. From the late eighteenth century to the early twentieth it was the standard form for first movements in SYMPHONIES, STRING QUARTETS and SONATAS.
soprano	High woman's voice.
sprechgesang	Kind of vocal delivery between speech and song, used by Schoenberg in *Pierrot lunaire*.
staff	Array of parallel lines (nearly always five) providing the frame for NOTATION.
string quartet	Work for two violins, viola and cello, most often in the form of a small-scale SYMPHONY.
strings	Instruments that sound when strings are bowed or plucked. Usually the term is reserved for bowed instruments, the standard modern kinds being the violin, viola, cello and double bass.

submediant	Note or key a third below the TONIC.
syllabic	Having one note per syllable.
symphonic poem	Orchestral piece with an explicit narrative or descriptive function.
symphony	Normally an orchestral work in four MOVEMENTS.
syncopation	Placing of strong accents on weak BEATS in the BAR.
tempo	Speed.
tenor	(1) Fixed melodic line forming the basis for a medieval or RENAISSANCE composition. (2) High man's voice (essentially without FALSETTO).
third	*See* MAJOR THIRD, MINOR THIRD.
toccata	Keyboard piece featuring rapid even movement.
tonal	Adhering to a major or minor key (most commonly) or other system having a TONIC. Hence also 'tonality'.
tonic	Fundamental note or key.
treble	Upper register, as distinct from BASS.
triad	Set of notes comprising the first (TONIC), third and fifth of a scale.
trill	Quick alternation between adjacent notes.
trio	(1) Piece for three performers. Piano trios, for example, are for piano, violin and cello. (2) Middle section of a MINUET or SCHERZO.
trio sonata	BAROQUE work for two instrumental soloists and CONTINUO.
virtuoso	Highly skilled performer. The term can also be used adjectivally of music requiring extreme skills.

voice	(1) Human sound-producing mechanism of the throat and mouth. (2) Line in a POLYPHONIC composition.
volume	Loudness.
woodwind	Slender blown instruments, including most commonly flute, oboe, clarinet and bassoon.

Further reading and listening

PART I   TIME WHOLE

I   FROM BABYLONIANS TO FRANKS

☐ Richard L. Crocker: *An Introduction to Gregorian Chant* (New
Haven, Conn., 2000)
David Hiley: *Western Plainchant: A Handbook* (Oxford, 1993)
Thomas J. Mathiesen, ed.: *Greek Views of Music* [*Source
Readings in Music History*, vol. 1] (New York, 1998)

◯ *Chant* – monks of Santo Domingo de Silos (EMI)
Chants de l'Eglise milanaise – Ensemble Organum (Harmonia
Mundi)
Edda – Sequentia (Deutsche Harmonia Mundi)

PART II   TIME MEASURED 1100–1400

☐ Richard H. Hoppin: *Medieval Music* (New York, 1978)
Tess Knighton and David Fallows, eds.: *Companion to Medieval
and Renaissance Music* (London, 1992)
Daniel Leech-Wilkinson: *The Modern Invention of Medieval
Music* (Cambridge, 2002)
James McKinnon, ed.: *The Early Christian Period and the Latin
Middle Ages* [*Source Readings in Music History*, vol. II]
(New York, 1998)
Gustave Reese: *Music in the Middle Ages* (New York, 1940)
Jeremy Yudkin: *Music in Medieval Europe* (Englewood Cliffs,
NJ, 1989)

2   TROUBADOURS AND ORGANISTS

☐ Elizabeth Aubrey: *The Music of the Troubadours* (Bloomington, Ind., 1996)

Christopher Page: *The Owl and the Nightingale* (London, 1989)

◯ *English Songs of the Middle Ages* – Sequentia (EMI Deutsche Harmonia Mundi)

A Feather on the Breath of God (chants by Hildegard) – Gothic Voices (Hyperion)

Perotin (organa and conductus) – Hilliard Ensemble (ECM)

Proensa (troubadour songs) – Paul Hillier with instrumentalists (ECM)

3   ARS NOVA AND NARCISSUS'S CLOCK

☐ Daniel Leech-Wilkinson: *Machaut's Mass: An Introduction* (Oxford, 1990)

Gilbert Reaney: *Machaut* (London, 1971)

◯ Machaut: *Messe de Nostre Dame* – Taverner Consort (EMI)

Machaut: motets – Hilliard Ensemble (ECM)

Lancaster and Valois (songs by Machaut and successors) – Gothic Voices (Hyperion)

The Medieval Romantics (songs by Machaut and successors) – Gothic Voices (Hyperion)

The Mirror of Narcissus (songs by Machaut) – Gothic Voices (Hyperion)

Narcisso speculando (songs by Paolo da Firenze) – Mala Punica (Harmonia Mundi)

PART III   TIME SENSED 1400–1630

☐ Allan W. Atlas: *Renaissance Music* (New York, 1998)

Howard Mayer Brown: *Music in the Renaissance* (Englewood Cliffs, NJ, 1976; [2]Upper Saddle River, NJ, 1999)

Claude V. Palisca: *Humanism in Italian Renaissance Musical Thought* (New Haven, 1985)

Leeman L. Perkins: *Music in the Age of the Renaissance* (New York, 1999)

Gustave Reese: *Music in the Renaissance* (New York, 1954, ²1959)

Gary Tomlinson, ed.: *The Renaissance [Source Readings in Music History*, vol. III] (New York, 1998)

4 HARMONY, THE LIGHT OF TIME

☐ David Fallows: *Dufay* (London, 1982, ²1987)

Reinhard Strohm: *The Rise of European Music, 1380–1500* (Cambridge, 1993)

◯ Du Fay: *L'homme armé* mass and motets – Hilliard Ensemble (EMI)

Du Fay: *Se la face ay pale* mass – Diabolus in Musica (Alpha)

Du Fay: *Ave regina celorum*, etc. – Binchois Consort (Hyperion)

Frye: *Flos regalis* mass, etc. – Hilliard Ensemble (ECM)

Ockeghem: *De plus en plus* mass and songs – Orlando Consort (DG)

5 THE RADIANCE OF THE HIGH RENAISSANCE

☐ Rob C. Wegman: *Born for the Muses: The Life and Masses of Jacob Obrecht* (Oxford, 1994)

◯ Browne, Carver and Taverner: motets – Taverner Choir (EMI)

Josquin: *Pange lingua* mass, etc. – Choir of St John's College, Cambridge (Meridian)

Josquin: motets – Choir of New College, Oxford (Meridian)

Music from the Eton Choirbook – The Sixteen (Meridian)

6 REFORMATION AND HEARTACHE

☐ Iain Fenlon: *Music and Culture in Late Renaissance Italy* (Oxford, 2002)

Peter le Huray: *Music and the Reformation in England, 1549–1660* (London, 1967; ¹Cambridge, 1978)

Joseph Kerman: *The Masses and Motets of William Byrd* (London, 1981)

Jerome Roche: *The Madrigal* (London, 1972; ²Oxford, 1990)

Glenn Watkins: *Gesualdo: The Man and his Music* (Chapel Hill, 1973; ²Oxford, 1991)

○ Dowland: *Treasures from my Minde* (songs, etc.) – Virelai (Virgin)

Gabrieli: *Music for San Rocco* – Gabrieli Consort and Players (DG)

Gesualdo: *Tenebrae* – Taverner Consort (Sony)

Palestrina: *Missa Papae Marcelli*, etc. – Choir of Westminster Cathedral (Hyperion)

Tallis: *Spem in alium*, etc. – Choir of King's College, Cambridge (Decca)

Victoria: *Requiem* – Choir of Westminster Cathedral (Hyperion)

7   TO SPEAK IN MUSIC

☐ Gary Tomlinson: *Monteverdi and the End of the Renaissance* (Oxford, 1987)

John Whenham, ed.: *Claudio Monteverdi: Orfeo* (Cambridge, 1986)

John Whenham: *Monteverdi: Vespers (1610)* (Cambridge, 1997)

○ Frescobaldi: *Fiori musicali* – Roberto Alessandrini (Naive)

Monteverdi: *Orfeo* – Concerto Vocale (Harmonia Mundi)

Monteverdi: *Vespro della Beata Vergine* – Monteverdi Choir (DG)

Monteverdi: *Ottavo libro dei madrigali*, vol. II – Concerto Italiano (Opus 111)

PART IV   TIME KNOWN 1630–1770

☐ Nicholas Anderson: *Baroque Music* (London, 1994)

James R. Anthony: *French Baroque Music* (London, 1973; [2]Portland, Ore., 1997)

Margaret Murata, ed.: *The Baroque Era* [*Source Readings in Music History*, vol. IV] (New York, 1998)

Claude V. Palisca: *Baroque Music* (Englewood Cliffs, NJ, 1968, [2]1981)

8   BAROQUE MORNINGS

☐ Peter Holman: *Henry Purcell* (Oxford, 1994)

○ Biber: *The Mystery of the Rosary* – Andrew Manze (Harmonia Mundi)

Corelli: *Sonate da chiesa* – London Baroque (Harmonia Mundi)
Lully: *Atys* – William Christie (Harmonia Mundi)
Purcell: *Dido and Aeneas* – Emmanuelle Haim (Virgin)
New World Symphonies – Jeffrey Skidmore (Hyperion)

9 FUGUE, CONCERTO AND OPERATIC PASSION

☐ Malcolm Boyd, ed.: *J. S. Bach* (Oxford, 1999)
Donald Burrows: *Handel* (Oxford, 1994)
Ralph Kirkpatrick: *Domenico Scarlatti* (Princeton, 1953, ʳ1983)
H. C. Robbins Landon: *Vivaldi* (London, 1993)
Michael Talbot: *Vivaldi* (London, 1978, ²1993)
Christoph Wolff: *Johann Sebastian Bach* (London, 2000)

◯ Bach: Brandenburg Concertos and Orchestral Suites – Trevor
Pinnock (DG)
Bach: *Das wohltemperierte Klavier* – Till Fellner (ECM)
Bach: St John Passion – Philippe Herreweghe (Harmonia
Mundi)
Handel: *Giulio Cesare* – René Jacobs (Harmonia Mundi)
Scarlatti: Sonatas – Ivo Pogorelich (DG)
Vivaldi: *The Four Seasons*, etc. – Trevor Pinnock (DG)

10 ROCOCO AND REFORM

☐ Cuthbert Girdlestone: *Jean-Philippe Rameau* (London, 1957;
ʳNew York, 1969)
Patricia Howard: *Gluck* (Oxford, 1995)

◯ Bach: *The Musical Offering* – Ensemble Sonnerie (Virgin)
Gluck: *Iphigénie en Tauride* – Ivor Bolton (Orfeo)
Handel: *Messiah* – Paul McCreesh (DG)
Rameau: *Castor et Pollux* – William Christie (Harmonia Mundi)
Arias for Farinelli – Vivica Genaux (Harmonia Mundi)

PART V TIME EMBRACED 1770–1815

☐ Wye Jamison Allanbrook, ed.: *The Late Eighteenth Century*
[*Source Readings in Music History*, vol. v] (New York, 1998)
Philip Downs: *Classical Music* (New York, 1992)
Charles Rosen: *The Classical Style* (London, 1971, ³1997)

11   SONATA AS COMEDY

☐ H. C. Robbins Landon: *Haydn: Chronicle and Works*, 5 vols.
(Bloomington/London, 1976–80)
H. C. Robbins Landon, ed.: *The Mozart Compendium* (London,
1990)
Robert Spaethling, ed.: *Mozart's Letters, Mozart's Life* (London,
2000)

◯ C. P. E. Bach: Sonatas and Rondos – Mikhail Pletnev (DG)
Haydn: Symphonies Nos. 31 and 45 – Charles Mackerras (Telarc)
Haydn: String Quartets Op. 33 – Quatuor Mosaïques (Astrée)
Mozart: Piano Sonatas – Mitsuko Uchida (Philips)
Mozart: Piano Concertos Nos. 19 and 23 – Murray Perahia
(Sony)
Mozart: *Le nozze di Figaro* – René Jacobs (Harmonia Mundi)

12   REVOLUTION'S MOMENTUM

☐ Malcolm Boyd, ed.: *Music and the French Revolution*
(Cambridge, 1992)
Maynard Solomon: *Beethoven* (New York, 1977, ²1998)
Glenn Stanley, ed.: *The Cambridge Companion to Beethoven*
(Cambridge, 1999)

◯ Beethoven: Symphonies Nos. 5 and 7 – Carlos Kleiber (DG)
Beethoven: Piano Sonatas, vol. VIII – Annie Fischer
(Hungaroton)
Beethoven: *Fidelio* – Otto Klemperer (EMI)
Cherubini: Symphony in D and overtures – Howard Griffiths
(cpo)
Haydn: Symphonies Nos. 101 and 104 – Charles Mackerras
(Telarc)
Haydn: 'Nelson' Mass and Te Deum – Trevor Pinnock (DG)

PART VI   TIME ESCAPING 1815–1907

☐ Leon Plantinga: *Romantic Music* (New York, 1984)
Jim Samson, ed.: *The Cambridge History of Nineteenth-Century
Music* (Cambridge, 2001)

Ruth A. Solie, ed.: *The Nineteenth Century* [*Source Readings in Music History*, vol. VI] (New York, 1998)

13   THE DEAF MAN AND THE SINGER

☐ Leo Black: *Franz Schubert: Music and Belief* (Woodbridge, 2003)
Christopher H. Gibbs: *The Life of Schubert* (Cambridge, 2000)
Richard Osborne: *Rossini* (London, 1986)
John Warrack: *Carl Maria von Weber* (London, 1968; ²Cambridge, 1976)

◯ Beethoven: Diabelli Variations – Piotr Anderszewski (Virgin)
Beethoven: Symphony No. 9 – Philippe Herreweghe (Harmonia Mundi)
Rossini: *Il barbiere di Siviglia* – Vittorio Gui (EMI)
Schubert: *Winterreise* – Matthias Goerne (Hyperion)
Schubert: Sonata in B flat – Leon Fleisher (Artemis)
Weber: *Der Freischütz* – Carlos Kleiber (DG)

14   ANGELS AND OTHER PRODIGIES

☐ David Cairns: *Berlioz*, 2 vols. (London, 1989, 1999)
Eric Frederick Jensen: *Schumann* (Oxford, 2001)
Peter Mercer-Taylor: *The Life of Mendelssohn* (Cambridge, 2000)
John Rosselli: *The Life of Bellini* (Cambridge, 1996)
Jim Samson: *Chopin* (Oxford, 1996)

◯ Bellini: *Norma* – Maria Callas (EMI)
Berlioz: *Symphonie fantastique* – Marc Minkowski (DG)
Berlioz: *La Damnation de Faust* – Colin Davis (Philips)
Chopin: Sonata in B minor, etc. – Martha Argerich (EMI)
Mendelssohn and Beethoven: Violin Concertos – Joshua Bell (Sony)
Schumann: *Carnaval*; and Chopin: Ballade in G minor, etc. – Youri Egorov (Royal)

15   NEW GERMANS AND OLD VIENNA

☐ Julian Budden: *Verdi* (London, 1985)
Winton Dean: *Bizet* (London, 1948, ³1975)

Joachim Köhler: *Richard Wagner* (New Haven, Conn., 2004)
Richard Taruskin: *Musorgsky* (Princeton, NJ, 1992)
Alan Walker: *Franz Liszt*, 3 vols. (London, 1983, 1989, 1997)

◯ Bizet: *Carmen* – Georg Solti (Decca)
Liszt: Sonata in B minor – Krystian Zimerman (DG)
Liszt: *Faust Symphony* – Jascha Horenstein (BBC)
Musorgsky: *Boris Godunov* – Claudio Abbado (Sony)
Verdi: *Don Carlos* – Antonio Pappano (EMI)
Wagner: *Tristan und Isolde* – Karl Böhm (DG)

16 ROMANTIC EVENINGS

☐ David Brown: *Tchaikovsky*, 4 vols. (London, 1978, 1982, 1986, 1991)
John Clapham: *Dvořák* (Newton Abbot, 1979)
Roger Nichols: *The Life of Debussy* (Cambridge, 1998)
Robert Pascall, ed.: *Brahms* (Cambridge, 1983)
Jan Swafford: *Johannes Brahms* (London, 1997)
Derek Watson: *Bruckner* (London, 1975; ²Oxford, 1996)

◯ Brahms: Symphonies Nos. 3–4 – Charles Mackerras (Telarc)
Bruckner: Symphony No. 8 – Carl Schuricht (EMI)
Debussy: Orchestral works – Pierre Boulez (Sony)
Dvořák: Symphony No. 9 – Leonard Bernstein (Sony)
Franck: Symphony in D minor – Leonard Bernstein (DG)
Tchaikovsky: Symphony No. 4 – Mariss Jansons (Chandos)

17 NIGHTFALL AND SUNRISE

☐ Peter Franklin: *The Life of Mahler* (Cambridge, 1997)
Michael Kennedy: *Richard Strauss* (London, 1976; ²Oxford, 1995)
Donald Mitchell and Andrew Nicholson, ed.: *The Mahler Companion* (Oxford, 1999)
Guy Rickards: *Sibelius* (London, 1997)
Allen Shawn: *Arnold Schoenberg's Journey* (New York, 2001)

◯ Debussy: *Pelléas et Mélisande* – Pierre Boulez (Sony)
Dukas: *L'Apprenti sorcier* – Leonard Bernstein (Sony)
Mahler: Symphony No. 4 – Leonard Bernstein (DG)
Schoenberg: Chamber Symphony No. 1 – Heinz Holliger (Apex)

Sibelius: Violin Concerto – Ida Haendel (EMI)
Strauss: *Ein Heldenleben* – Richard Strauss (Dutton)

PART VII TIME TANGLED 1908–1975

☐ Nicholas Cook and Anthony Pople, ed.: *The Cambridge History of Twentieth-Century Music* (Cambridge, 2004)
Paul Griffiths: *Modern Music and After* (Oxford, 1995)
Robert P. Morgan, ed.: *The Twentieth Century* [*Source Readings in Music History*, vol. VII] (New York, 1998)
Arnold Whittall: *Musical Composition in the Twentieth Century* (Oxford, 1999)
Arnold Whittall: *Exploring Twentieth-Century Music* (Cambridge, 2003)

18 TO BEGIN AGAIN

☐ Faubion Bowers: *Scriabin* (Tokyo, 1969; [2]Mineola, 1996)
Malcolm Gillies, ed.: *The Bartók Companion* (London, 1993)
David Nicholls: *American Experimental Music 1890–1940* (Cambridge, 1990)
Anthony Pople, ed.: *The Cambridge Companion to Berg* (Cambridge, 1997)
Jim Samson: *Music in Transition* (London, 1977)
Jan Swafford: *Charles Ives* (New York, 1996)
Stephen Walsh: *Igor Stravinsky*, 2 vols. (London, 1999, 2006)

◯ Bartók: String Quartets – Keller Quartet (Erato)
Berg: Altenberg Songs, etc. – Claudio Abbado (DG)
Ives: *Three Places in New England*, etc. – Orpheus (DG)
Schoenberg: *Pierrot lunaire* and *Das Buch* – Jan De Gaetani (Nonesuch)
Scriabin: *Vers la flamme* (piano anthology) – Christopher O'Riley (Image)
Stravinsky: *The Rite of Spring* – Igor Markevitch (BBC)

19 FORWARDS AND BACKWARDS, AND SIDEWAYS

☐ Kathryn Bailey: *The Life of Webern* (Cambridge, 2000)
Jonathan W. Bernard: *The Music of Edgard Varèse* (New Haven, Conn., 1987)

Laurel E. Fay: *Shostakovich: A Life* (Oxford, 2000)
Michael Kennedy: *Portrait of Elgar* (Oxford, 1968, [3]1987)
Arbie Orenstein: *Ravel: Man and Musician* (New York, 1975, [r]1991)

◯ Ravel: *Chansons madécasses*, etc. – Magdalena Kožená (DG)
Sibelius: Symphony No. 7, etc. – Osmo Vanska (BIS)
Stravinsky: *Oedipus Rex* – Claudio Abbado (Opera d'Oro)
Varèse: *Hyperprism*, etc. – Pierre Boulez (Sony)
Webern: Symphony, etc. – Christoph von Dohnányi (Decca)
Weill: *Aufstieg und Fall der Stadt Mahagonny* – Jan
Latham-König (Capriccio)

20   THE PEOPLE'S NEEDS

☐ Michael H. Kater: *The Twisted Muse: Musicians and their Music
in the Third Reich* (Oxford, 1997)
Boris Schwarz: *Music and Musical Life in Soviet Russia* (London,
1976)

◯ Bartók: Concerto for Orchestra and Music for Strings – Mariss
Jansons (EMI)
Copland: *Appalachian Spring*, etc. – Leonard Bernstein (Sony)
Prokofiev: Symphony No. 5 – Simon Rattle (EMI)
Shostakovich: Symphonies Nos. 5 and 9 – Yevgeny Mravinsky
(Chant du Monde)
Strauss: *Capriccio* – Wolfgang Sawallisch (EMI)
Stravinsky: *Symphony of Psalms, Canticum sacrum*, etc. – James
O'Donnell (Hyperion)

21   TO BEGIN AGAIN AGAIN

☐ Theodor W. Adorno: *Philosophy of Modern Music* (New York,
1973)
Milton Babbitt: *Words about Music* (Madison, Wis., 1987)
Pierre Boulez: *Stocktakings from an Apprenticeship* (Oxford, 1991)
John Cage: *Silence* (Middletown, Conn., 1961)
Allen Edwards: *Flawed Words and Stubborn Sounds:
A Conversation with Elliott Carter* (New York, 1971)
Paul Griffiths: *The Sea on Fire: Jean Barraqué* (Rochester, NY,
2003)
Robin Maconie, ed.: *Stockhausen on Music* (London, 1989)

Olivier Messiaen: *Music and Color: Conversations with Claude Samuel* (Portland, Ore., 1994)

Michael Nyman: *Experimental Music: Cage and Beyond* (London, 1974; ²Cambridge, 1999)

Bálint András Varga: *Conversations with Iannis Xenakis* (London, 1996)

☐ Babbitt: *All Set*; Wolpe: Quartet with saxophone, etc. – Arthur Weisberg (Nonesuch)

Barraqué: Sonata – Herbert Henck (ECM)

Boulez: *Le Marteau sans maître* – Pierre Boulez (DG)

Messiaen: *Turangalîla* Symphony – Esa-Pekka Salonen (CBS)

Stockhausen: *Gesang der Jünglinge*, etc. – (Stockhausen)

Xenakis: *Metastasis*, etc. – Hans Rosbaud (Col Legno)

22 WHIRLWIND

☐ Jonathan Cross: *Harrison Birtwistle: Man, Mind, Music* (London, 2000)

György Ligeti: *György Ligeti in Conversation* (London, 1983)

David Osmond-Smith, ed.: *Luciano Berio: Two Interviews* (London, 1985)

Steve Reich: *Writings on Music, 1965–2000* (Oxford, 2002)

Elliott Schwartz and Barney Childs, eds.: *Contemporary Composers on Contemporary Music* (New York, 1967, ʳ1998)

K. Robert Schwarz: *Minimalists* (London, 1996)

◯ Berio: *Sinfonia*, etc.— Peter Eötvös (DG)

Birtwistle: *Verses for Ensembles*, etc. – James Wood (Etcetera)

Ligeti: *Atmosphères*, etc. – Jonathan Nott (Teldec)

Nancarrow: Studies for Player Piano – (Wergo)

Nono: *Como una ola de fuerza y luz*, etc. – Herbert Kegel (Berlin Classics)

Reich: *Drumming*, etc. – Steve Reich and Musicians (DG)

PART VIII TIME LOST 1975–

☐ Richard Dufallo: *Trackings: Composers Speak* (Oxford, 1989)

Glenn Watkins: *Pyramids at the Louvre: Music, Culture, and Collage from Stravinsky to the Postmodernists* (Cambridge, Mass., 1994)

23 ECHOES IN THE LABYRINTH

☐ Brian Ferneyhough: *Collected Writings* (London, 1996)
Paul Hillier: *Arvo Pärt* (Oxford, 1997)

◯ Ferneyhough: *Unity Capsule*, etc. – Elision (Etcetera)
Grisey: *Les espaces acoustiques* – Pierre-André Valade and Sylvain Cambreling (Accord)
Lachenmann: *Schwankungen am Rand*, etc. – Eötvös (ECM)
Kurtág: *Kafka-Fragmente* – Adrienne Csengery (Hungaroton)
Messiaen: *Saint François d'Assise* – Kent Nagano (DG)
Pärt: *Tabula rasa*, etc. – Saulius Sondeckis (ECM)

24 INTERLUDE

◯ Adès: *Asyla*, etc. – Simon Rattle (EMI)
Birtwistle: *Pulse Shadows* – Reinbert de Leeuw (Teldec)
Carter: *Symphonia*, etc. – Oliver Knussen (DG)
Kyburz: *The Voynich Cipher Manuscript*, etc. – Rupert Huber (Kairos)
Ligeti: *With Pipes, Drums, Fiddles*, etc. – Amadinda (Teldec)
Sciarrino: *Infinito nero*, etc. – Ensemble Recherche (Kairos)

Index

Library
Medical School

WATERFORD CITY AND COUNTY

WITHDRAWN

LIBRARIES